NE OBLIVISCARIS

Campbell College
Preparatory School
Cabin Hill

Form 5 B   Prize

Awarded to

E.C. SALTHOUSE

P.W. V. Sutton

Head Master.

July, 19 48.

GREAT CONQUERORS

OF SOUTH AND CENTRAL AMERICA

GREAT
CONQUERORS

OF SOUTH
AND CENTRAL AMERICA

⟫⟫⟫⟫⟫⟫⟫⟫⟫⟫⟫⟫⟫⟫ • ⟪⟪⟪⟪⟪⟪⟪⟪⟪⟪⟪⟪⟪⟪

BY A. HYATT VERRILL

THE NEW HOME LIBRARY
New York

THE NEW HOME LIBRARY EDITION PUBLISHED FEBRUARY, 1943
REPRINTED DECEMBER, 1943

THE NEW HOME LIBRARY, 14 West Forty-ninth Street
New York, N. Y.

CL

CONTENTS

CONTENTS

GREAT CONQUERORS

OF SOUTH AND CENTRAL AMERICA

CHAPTER I

BEFORE THE CONQUERORS APPEARED

THE Spanish conquerors and the Spanish Conquest were the outcome of conditions and circumstances which have never been duplicated in the world's history. A New World had been discovered, and the tide of exploration, adventure and search for riches that, hitherto, had flowed to the east was immediately diverted to the west. Columbus' tales of marvelous lands where "in one day he had seen more gold than may be seen in Spain in one year"; his reports of precious stones, of spices, of strange beasts and birds; and the copper-skinned natives, fired the imaginations and excited the cupidity of his countrymen to an incredible degree. Here was a land where any one might become rich —a land whose streams ran over golden sands— where there were natives to be enslaved who would perform the strenuous work, where one might help oneself to whatever was desired—a veritable Paradise on earth according to the highly colored stories of Columbus and his men. Little thought was given to the other side of the picture—the hardships, the dangers, the tangled jungles or the thousand and one obstacles, including the hostility of the natives whose lands and property they dreamed of seizing. Only the glamour of the New World and its riches

1

filled the adventurers, and had enough vessels been available, much of Spain's population would undoubtedly have stampeded to America.

Ships and equipment were expensive, however; only the Crown or the very wealthy could dream of fitting out expeditions, and the only chance for which the ordinary man could hope was to ship as a sailor or enlist as a soldier. But the applications for such employment far exceeded the demand. It was natural that the men selected by the leaders of such expeditions as set sail for the New World were a far from desirable type as colonists or settlers. The hazards of the voyages and explorations called for men of a reckless, daring, unprincipled type. Later on, Spain sent some of her best citizens to guide the development of colonial life, but it must be admitted that in the first stages of the venture the participants, in considerable number, were actual or potential criminals, smugglers, pirates, and thugs. Among the early adventurers it was only by chance that now and then was found an out-at-elbows cavalier, a ne'er-do-well scion of nobility, or some restless, romantic soul of wealth and station.

With such a choice assortment of human flotsam and jetsam it is little wonder, then, that they should have committed every excess and atrocity conceivable, once they stepped ashore after weary weeks on a small vessel in a stormy sea. Nor is it any wonder that the natives, at first often friendly and hospitable, should have learned by bitter experience what they might expect from the strangers, and have changed their attitude to an implacably hostile one.

To be sure, few of the earliest visitors to the New World remained there. As a rule when the first towns were founded the settlers left there did not survive long. Their own debaucheries and outrageous treatment of the natives often sealed their doom. Most energies were devoted to extending the territory claimed for the King of Spain, seeking hopelessly for a passage to the Orient, accumulating gold, and spreading the Christian Faith. Indeed, it may be questioned if the last should not be placed first, for, from the beginning, the Church had seen in the New World a most marvelous field for its activities, and every expedition carried a horde of priests. The Church in those days was the Church Militant; every priest was—to a certain extent—a soldier, and every soldier a representative of the Church, and the banner of Spain and the Cross were invariably erected jointly.

With all the enthusiasm to secure the entire New World for the Spanish Crown and the Church, with all the expeditions that sailed westward, with all the explorers and adventurers that swarmed to America, the earliest of the Spanish voyagers seemed to restrict their interest to a rather limited sphere. To be sure, Columbus had cruised along the shores of Panama and what is now Colombia and Venezuela, and had discovered the Orinoco. Vespucci and others had established the fact that the shores were those of a continent and that there was no passage westward in that part of the world, and the more intelligent Spaniards realized that the New World was neither Japan nor India. But their ideas of the geography of the New World were very limited. Even as late as 1520 maps showed Cuba as an island of continental size extending north and south, Peru being situated on its southwestern portion, North America and Mexico nonexistent, and Florida an island. South America was bisected by the Rio de la Plata, the southern half of the continent being a purely imaginary territory called Lower Brazil, while Japan was placed nearer to Cuba on the west than was Santo Domingo to the east.

As Santo Domingo, or Hispaniola as the Spaniards called it, was the site of the first European settlement in America, it was quite to be expected that this immense island should have been the first to be conquered and occupied. It was rich in minerals, valuable woods, and natural resources, and it was thickly populated by Indians, who represented much prospective slave labor, and to the priests a wonderful field for spreading the Faith.

As a result, Hispaniola, which later declined rapidly, became the richest and most important of the Spanish colonies in the New World in the early years of the sixteenth century. It was the seat of government, the hub of the Caribbean. Its capital became a large, fortified city with a vast cathedral, imposing buildings, a university and palatial residences.

It became the See of the Church in America, and there is scarcely a figure of prominence in the history of the Spanish Conquest who did not, at one time or another, reside in Santo Domingo. Columbus' son, Diego, had his home there. Nicuesa, Balboa, Enciso, Pizarro, Cortes, Ponce de Leon, Hernando de Soto, Alvarado, Coronado, Valdivia, Almagro, Velasquez—every Don of fame trod the rough streets of Hispaniola's capital. And from Santo Domingo the Spanish adventurers set out on their innumerable expeditions to pillage and conquer.

While Spain was thus having it all her own way in the Caribbean, France, Holland and England were taking comparatively little interest in the New World. This was partly due to European wars that occupied the nations and drained their resources, but it was rather the lack of imagination, the absence of that romantic, temperamental, adventurous spirit of the Latins, that prevented the cooler-headed, more cautious Anglo-Saxons and Teutons from rushing headlong to the conquest of the New World. And, by the time they had waked up to the possibilities of America, the Spaniards had secured a firm foothold in the tropical areas and the Caribbean, and the other nations were forced to content themselves with other and less promising territory.

The Portuguese, following its chance discovery by Cabral, in 1500, settled Brazil where, as there were none but primitive savages, there was no outstanding conquest of another civilization, as in countries like Mexico and Peru.

The Dutch came into the picture a little later, but could not be counted among the *conquistadores*. So also the interests of the French in these early days were too small to be of any great importance. The British, finding the shores of North America too bleak and barren of riches to attract them, fell to preying upon the Spaniards, robbing the robbers so to say, and securing their gold, won at such terrible cost of human lives.

Of all the European powers, Spain was the only one that was in a position immediately following the discovery to enter into conquests of the New World on a large scale. Also it was only in the territory claimed by Spain that there were found civilized races under organized governments controlling millions of inhabitants and vast areas of land. And only in the territories claimed by Spain were there such stupendous, incredible stores of gold, silver, gems and other treasures to make conquests so attractive.

Spain, however, was lacking in funds to carry on costly civilizing processes, and her policy was to draw gold from the New World rather than expend it there. The Crown looked to the countries across the Atlantic as a source of revenue to refill its coffers, and at times it seemed to care little how this was accomplished or by whom, as long as the results were satisfactory. But the Sovereign and his advisers were no fools. They did not flatter themselves that any man—even an adventure-loving, romantic Don—would undergo hazards and hardships and risk his life from the purely patriotic incentive of gathering gold for the Crown. Neither did they delude themselves with the idea that any man employed at a fixed salary would resist temptation when surrounded by dazzling quantities of treasure won by his own efforts. So the King adopted the sensible if ancient idea of going shares with the adventurers, and of allowing them to keep all they secured after deducting for the Crown one-fifth of the treasure known as the *"King's Quinta."* Moreover, to further the interest in conquest, the Crown graciously agreed to issue royal warrants authorizing the exploration and conquest of definite areas, thus in a measure guaranteeing freedom from interference to the warrantee, upon whom were often bestowed high-sounding titles and orders.

There were few, however, who could afford, at their own expense, to fit out an expedition, which was after all something of a gamble. So, following the example of their Sovereign, those who desired to go a-conquesting—if we may use the term—joined forces and agreed on shares. To lessen expenses and to add incentive to the work, the same course was followed with the men who joined their forces. It was in fact precisely the same method that was adopted by the buccaneers in robbing the Spaniards a few years later. Each member had a definite proportion allotted to him, varying in amount according to his importance and station. As in those days few men could read or write, a notary was usually included in the company, to whom fell the task of keeping accounts, recording events and witnessing the marks that served as signatures of the participants. Even the priests who accompanied the expeditions usually received a share of the booty, which was, at least theoretically, used to defray the costs of erecting churches and spreading the Faith. But in many cases the padres' shares must have far exceeded their disbursements, since some accumulated large fortunes.

Often the backers of the ventures were merchants, officials or professional money lenders who did not accompany the expeditions, expecting to receive the lion's share of the results without endangering their own precious skins. Considering the type of men who set out on these perilous adventures and the type of most of their leaders, it is scarcely surprising that, very often, they figuratively snapped their fingers at these financiers, once they were out of reach, and pocketed their backers' shares with their own. Neither is it inconsistent with their characters that, with millions of gold before their avaricious eyes, they should have often begrudged the King's fifth and underrated the total so as to reduce the royal *Quinta* to the minimum. The earliest of the *conquistadores* were, as a rule, an utterly unprincipled lot—leaders and followers alike—brutal, callous, cruel, intensely avaricious, willing to murder, torture, enslave and rob for the sake of enriching themselves. Gratitude was a word that seldom seemed to exist in their vocabulary; they were faithful to one another only as long as it was to their own advantage; their word often meant little and, when opportunity offered, they seemed quite as ready to rob their countrymen or their King as to rob the hapless Indians.

Such was the stuff of which the conquerors were made, men of a type most admirably adapted to their undertakings, men who rose to fame through the peculiar conditions of their time and Spain's domi-

nance of America. Most of them under normal conditions would have remained obscure or ended their
lives on the block. Strangely enough, that was the
very fate that usually closed their careers.

Perhaps the greatest consolation we may have,
when we shudder at their cruelties and ruthlessness,
is the fact that they usually met with full retribution
in the end.

Immediately following the discovery of America,
the Spaniards, as I have already said, busied themselves with conquering the islands of the Caribbean.
It was not a very difficult nor dangerous undertaking. The Indians, whether friendly or hostile, were
primitive savages and considered merely as beasts
of burden. They were killed, tortured and enslaved
without mercy. Frequently the Spaniards would
make a holiday of a wholesale massacre, and after
herding the natives into some open space, would
amuse themselves by watching their savage dogs
fall upon the helpless people and tear them to pieces.
At other times the Indians were hunted down and
killed merely for sport, the carcasses of the human
"game" being used to feed the dogs and swine.

So rapid and effective was the enslaving and extermination of the Indians that, within twenty years
after the discovery of the Antilles, scarcely a single
living free Indian existed upon the larger islands.

Such atrocities could not be called conquests, however. The Spaniards soon sought treasure farther
afield and then the Spanish Conquest really began.
Various portions of Central America were explored
and the Indians subdued or destroyed; expeditions

penetrated certain sections of Venezuela and Colombia; and settlements were established upon the coast of the Castilla de Oro as Panama was then called. But it was not until after Balboa had made his epochal discovery of the Pacific and had heard tales of a great and incredibly rich empire to the south that the Spaniards began fully to realize the possibilities of conquest in New Spain.

It will be seen that we are here dealing with those to whom we may apply the term, conqueror, which for our purposes does not even include such an intrepid adventurer as Balboa, who, while he was of the type of which conquerors are made, did not find a strong body of aborigines to challenge his prowess, before he met his end at the hands of his own countrymen whom he had betrayed.

CHAPTER II

THE CONQUERORS AND THEIR WAYS

IN all the history of America there is no chapter more replete with adventure, romance, daring, and, unfortunately, ruthless cruelty and destruction, than the conquest of what is now known as Spanish America. And it is doubtful if the history of the entire world holds a parallel in respect to the incredible pecuniary rewards which fell to those who took prominent parts in this conquest. In some ways, too, the conquest of Spanish America differed from all others. In nearly all cases the conquest of vast territories teeming with valiant, civilized people possessing their own cherished ideals, their own customs and religion and their own well-established and powerful governments, has been a slow, gradual process extending over many years, often over centuries.

But the conquest of Spanish America—of the vast extent of territory including the West Indies, Mexico, Central America, the northern and western sections of South America, inhabited by a population estimated at fifty million, more than one-half of whom had attained to a civilized state with stable governments, well-trained armies and great cities—was largely accomplished within the space of a quarter of a century. Moreover, it was accomplished by a mere handful of men led by individuals who can be numbered on the fingers of two hands.

That less than two thousand men under a single leader could, within ten years, conquer and subdue a territory the size of Mexico seems little less than miraculous. And that less than half that number of men under the leadership of one man could do likewise in such a vast territory as Ecuador, Peru and Bolivia, whose inhabitants have been estimated at twenty millions, in a similar period of time, is even more amazing.

To be sure, the conquerors had the great advantage of firearms, horses, steel armor, and superior weapons. Probably most important of all, both the Aztec and Inca empires were at the time suffering from civil wars. But even so, it is nothing short of astounding that—as often happened—two or three hundred men, or even less, could not only defeat five or ten thousand natives, but could do so at times without the loss of a single life. Yet accounts of such battles are so numerous in the annals of the conquest that they become monotonous. Almost as numerous are the examples of individual valor: incidents wherein a single Spaniard battled hand to hand with a score or more of desperate Indians and came off victorious; cases where some Spaniard, cut off from his fellows, traveled hundreds of miles through hostile territory and surmounted the most terrible of natural obstacles in safety; accounts of deeds of daring, of hardihood, of endurance and of determination which would seem absolutely impossible were they not matter-of-fact records set down as incidents of little importance by the chroniclers of the times.

And the tales of the hardships, the sufferings, the tortures that these old conquerors and their men faced and withstood would cause us almost to believe that they were supermen or were—as they firmly believed themselves—under Divine protection.

No one, reading the unvarnished accounts of the lives of these men, can truthfully deny that they were brave beyond belief, valiant beyond words, romantic to a degree, fantastically religious and, very often, as gallant as the knights-errant of the days of chivalry. They were no weaklings, these old Dons. Any one who has traversed the burning deserts, the steaming tangled jungles, the precipitous mountains of South and Central America must do honor to the old Spaniards who did likewise, clad in full armor, carrying heavy cumbersome weapons, lacking every modern facility and comfort, beset at every turn by hostile Indians, possessing no knowledge of the countries, no maps, no charts, and not the remotest idea of the distances from one point to another.

That they performed deeds of heroism, of endurance, and over and over again accomplished the seemingly impossible, is undeniable, and that they could only have performed many of their feats when in an exalted state or inspired is evident. There is no doubt that they *were* exalted and inspired—inspired with a lust for gold that made every other consideration, even bodily suffering and death, seem trivial affairs by comparison; exalted with the idea of carrying the Christian Faith to the heathen.

Whether riches or religion was uppermost in their minds, which the greater incentive, it is hard to say. With the sword in one hand and the cross in the other, they sought with equal vigor, equal determination, equal perseverance and equal disregard of hardships and sufferings to divorce the natives from their possessions and to save their souls. They were as fanatically religious as they were ruthlessly avaricious, and they fought almost if not quite as desperately to convert the Indians to the Christian Faith as they did to separate them from their gold and gems. To their minds any means was justified by the end, whether the end were the sacking of a city or the baptizing of a pagan, and there can be no doubt that, in nearly every case, they were sincere in their belief that they were in the right, that they were emissaries of God, that they were in fact true crusaders.

No one can deny that they were ruthless, unprincipled, inhumane, pitiless and inexpressibly cruel. No one can deny that they committed indescribable atrocities, that they wantonly tortured, killed and destroyed; that they looted, raped and ravaged; that hundreds, thousands of peaceful, happy, innocent Indians were massacred in cold blood; that thousands more were put to death or enslaved merely because they attempted to defend their homes, their families and their lives from the invaders. But we must bear in mind that, in the days of the conquest, standards of morality and of humanity were not what they are to-day. The most fearful tortures were recognized as legal punishments for many offenses we would consider minor crimes, death was the penalty for trivial infringements of law or discipline; beheading, burning at the stake and similar disagreeable forms of execution were everyday matters, and mutilations, such as lopping off ears, noses, hands or burning out eyes, were considered much in the same category as we regard fines or a few days in jail. There is no evidence to show that the Dons were any more cruel towards the Indians they conquered or who resisted them than was customary when one European nation was fighting against another, or that the punishments they dealt out to the natives were any more severe than those they dealt their own countrymen for similar offenses—or alleged offenses. The cruelties, the inhumanities, the destruction and the enslavement of the Indians were not confined to the Spaniards. The Dutch, French, Portuguese, Italian and English of the times were just as cruel, as ruthless, and as utterly regardless of human rights, lives or agonies. In fact, the deeds of the English buccaneers in these same lands at times exceeded the cruelties of their Spanish predecessors.

Moreover, we must not forget that, under the code of laws in force in those days, and according to public opinion and practice, the pagan was not regarded as worthy of consideration, but was looked upon as little if any better than a beast, or was regarded as being possessed with Satan and hence to be destroyed. And if the unfortunate pagan refused to embrace the True Faith when he had the opportunity to do so, and thus proved that he preferred

the devil, he condemned himself to death or torture.
Under such conditions it is rather surprising than
otherwise that the conquerors did not treat the Indians far worse than they did. But they realized,
as did the Crown, that the natives of the New World
had never been given the opportunity of embracing
Christianity and hence could not be greatly blamed
for being pagans, and hence were to be treated considerately, at least until the principles of Christianity had been expounded to them.

In nearly every case, the royal warrants authorizing the exploration and conquest of new territories
included strict injunctions to the effect that the Indians should be treated with consideration and that
their rights should be respected. Also in practically
every case it was stated in the royal decrees that the
first and paramount purpose of conquest was to
spread the True Faith and convert the Indians to
Christianity. We may feel that the Spaniards'
ideas of the "rights" of the Indians, and their in-
terpretation of the word "consideration," were most
remarkable, for the taking of slaves and the customs of *repartimiento,* or allotting Indian slaves to
settlers, were accepted and legal. And assuredly, if
people possess any "rights" that should be "respected" they are those of protecting their own
homes from robbery, their own wives and daughters
from degradation and dishonor, their own freedom
and their own lives.

But once a conqueror was away from Spain and
the influence and control of the Crown he was a law
unto himself, and he cared very little for either

the letter or the spirit of the law. Regardless of
how lofty his own purpose might be, the desire for
riches was his prime motive, while the rough, illiter-
ate, unprincipled adventurers and soldiers who
formed his company, and upon whom his success or
failure depended, had only one thought—gold.

Any flimsy excuse that would warrant his exercis-
ing the severest measures was sufficient. Having,
as the law prescribed, read or recited the claim of
the Crown of Spain to the territory wherein he was,
and having called upon the natives to acknowledge
allegiance to the King of Spain, any resistance
thereafter made by the Indians, any effort to defend
their country or their homes, was, from the point of
view of the Spaniards, rebellion against the Spanish Crown, and as such was punishable by death or
torture. Likewise, once having erected a cross or
a figure of the Virgin, the priests decreed that any
violence or disrespect shown to those emblems of
the Faith was blasphemy and sacrilege, and as such
was punishable by the most terrible forms of death.
It made no difference whether the wondering natives understood what it was all about or not. The
formality having been gone through with—often in
Spanish which of course was incomprehensible to
the natives, in Latin which was no more intelligible,
or through an interpreter whose garbled version
made it no clearer—the consciences of the Dons were
fully satisfied. To them, as with our courts of
to-day, ignorance of the law was no excuse for violating that law. Of course, under such conditions,
the Spaniards could loot, burn, ravish and kill with

impunity, and rarely could be brought to book, even if the authorities disapproved, for there was always the word "rebellion" or "sacrilege" to bring forward in palliation of the offense. Very often this hollow form of establishing the sovereignty of the King and of the Church was used merely as a mask to cover premeditated destruction and wholesale massacres. But considering the conditions and the circumstances, it is remarkable that, as a rule, the conquerors were as considerate as they were.

Neither must we overlook the matter of the personal equation. With few exceptions the men who rose to the highest pinnacles of fame as conquerors were of the most humble and obscure origin, men who were by birth and early life unprincipled, brutal, ignorant and devoid of all sense of right, wrong or honor. Given sudden power, placed in command of the roughest, toughest of men; possessing the authority of generals, governors, judges and juries combined, and confronted with vast riches, it is little wonder that such men went to extremes and allowed their uncontrolled passions and desires to have full play.

Neither is it fair to judge all by the few. Men, whether Spaniards or others, varied as much in character and temperament in those days as at the present time. There are and always have been all sorts needed to make the world, and though we hear much of the leaders—the famed conquerors—and their misdeeds, we hear little of hundreds of others who were kindly, considerate, humane and honest; men of lofty principles, of high ideals, but who—

because of these very characteristics which, however admirable, had no place in the hard school of conquest—never rose to fame or fortune. The same was true of the priests who invariably were a most important part of the conquerors' forces. Many, in fact most, were fanatical, bigoted, cruel, narrow-minded and not animated entirely by spiritual motives. But others were gentle, patient, sympathetic, and did everything in their power to help the Indians, to mitigate their sufferings, to put a stop to cruelties and abuses. The former, playing into the hands of the militant avaricious leaders, rose to fame, fortune and high positions in the Church. The latter remained faithful, patient, long-suffering, true Sons of the Church; spreading the Gospel quietly and unobtrusively; healing the sick, comforting the oppressed, giving their sympathies, their services freely; sharing their last *centavo,* their last crust with the unfortunate. Many were martyrs, many were worthy of becoming saints, but few rose above their humble positions as sandaled friars or cowled monks.

Wherever there is conquest, whenever there is war, always when a stronger nation sees fit to expand and enrich itself at the expense of a weaker nation, there must inevitably be suffering, bloodshed, injustice, inhumanity, cruelty and oppression, and always the innocent must suffer with the guilty and lives be lost and home ties broken and destroyed. But never, probably, in the history of the world, was there a conquest that was won at a greater cost of injustices, and of cruelties. And certainly there has never been another that has been marked by a more ruthless and wanton destruction of entire civilizations.

Perhaps the most regrettable result of the conquest was the loss to the world of irreparable records, monuments, buildings, works of art, handiwork and innumerable other objects pertaining to the American civilizations destroyed by the Spanish conquerors. Very largely this wholesale destruction was due to the fanatical zeal of the servants of the Church who saw, in nearly everything, the symbols of Satan, and who thought it their duty to eliminate everything pertaining to paganism. But vast quantities of the most priceless works of art and handicraft were lost to the world by being melted down for the sake of their bullion by the conquerors who saw in them only their intrinsic value of precious metals.

Now and then, some priest, more intelligent and more broad-minded than his fellows, realized the historic and scientific value of codices, records and other objects, and either preserved them or described them. Occasionally, too, the Spanish adventurers, amazed at the wonderful skill of the native artisans, and forced to admire the beauty of their products, refrained from destroying some object and sent it in its original state to Spain. But for every such article saved or even described, ten thousand—yes, one hundred thousand—found their way to the melting pot or were broken into bits.

It is stated by the treasurer and the notary of Pizarro that it required sixty Incan goldsmiths working steadily day and night for one month to reduce the gold and silver objects accumulated at Cajamarca to bullion, and these were but a small portion of the whole obtained by the conquerors in Peru. At another place, an immense stone statue was found and broken up by order of the priests. So huge was this piece of sculpture that thirty men were employed for three days to destroy it. In Mexico, marvelous mosaics were ripped to pieces for the turquoise and semiprecious stones of which they were composed; woodwork was burned to recover the gold nails that were used, and wonderful mantles and costumes of feathers, and priceless textiles, were reduced to ashes in order to secure the golden threads of the fabrics.

Human sufferings may be forgotten in time, human lives are replaced by others; but the products of human minds and hands, the records of hundreds of generations, the histories of races, the monuments, the carvings, the architecture and the thousand and one things that tell the story of countless centuries of a race's development, can never be duplicated. Once destroyed, they are lost to the world forever.

We must admire the conquerors for their bravery, for their accomplishments, for their many admirable qualities. We may forgive them for much that we decry. We may excuse their cruelties, their inhumanity, their needless oppressions in view of their fanaticism and the customs of their day. But we can never forgive them for their wanton destructions of civilizations and all that went to the making of those civilizations. Yet, perhaps, we should be grateful for the fact that they left as much as they did, that some things were beyond their powers to destroy, that we may still obtain some idea of the art, the lives, the customs, the attainments and the culture of the immeasurably ancient civilizations wiped out by the conquerors in their lust for gold and their zeal for religion.

It must be remembered also that we are here dealing with the early conquerors, who were young adventurers of the low order, many with their characters scarcely formed when they set out from Spain, and that following this motley crowd, Spain began to send some of her best to organize and administer from the human standpoint the vast territory, which most naturally at the first blush of discovery, she had regarded as only a treasure house of gold. And during the terrible destruction wrought, even these early adventurers began a work of construction, founding cities, building churches, developing industries, and setting up Spanish political institutions.

CHAPTER III

A STOWAWAY DISCOVERS A NEW OCEAN

AN obscure, out-at-elbows adventurer, Vasco Nuñez de Balboa—whose name was far more imposing than his person—was one of the thousands of impecunious Spaniards whose imagination had been fired by the tales of gold and wonders in the New World, but who seemed doomed—through lack of means, friends and desirable qualities—to have his dreams forever unfulfilled. He was a resourceful and determined rascal, however, and, once he had made up his mind to seek fame and fortune— or either—in the New World, he was not easily to be prevented from doing so.

Secreting himself in an empty cask that was about to be loaded on a ship bound for the New World, he was not discovered until the vessel was well out to sea. Probably the captain was not sorry to find he had an extra hand aboard, for the little caravel was having a hard time of it in tempestuous weather, and the stowaway was a willing worker. But he was unprincipled, always ready to foment trouble when he could profit by it and, being a born leader, he became a great favorite with the rougher class of colonists and adventurers when he at last reached Santo Domingo. He was in fact a never-ending source of trouble and a thorn in the side of the officials, who were vastly relieved when they succeeded in getting him off their hands by sending him with Enciso to Darien. In all probability Enciso was anything but grateful for the ex-stowaway's presence, and he soon had every reason to wish that Balboa had been headed up in his cask and thrown overboard before he reached Hispaniola.

Hardly had the expedition established the settlement of Santa Maria del Darien when Balboa fomented an insurrection, refused to recognize the authority of Enciso, and declared himself Alcalde with the plan of allying himself with Nicuesa. But when the latter arrived and announced his intention of taking possession of the booty accumulated by Enciso, Balboa refused to allow him to land and forced him pitilessly to sea with only seventeen men in a leaky vessel that was lost off Yucatan.

Balboa's next step was to rid himself of Enciso, who was deported to Santo Domingo, after which he confiscated Enciso's property and started to explore and subdue the interior, slaughtering the Indians and looting their villages at every turn. He invaded the country of the caçique Careta, and forced that powerful chief to form an alliance with him by the simple if efficacious method of seizing and forcibly marrying the caçique's daughter. With his forces greatly augmented by Careta's warriors, and aided by his dogs that inspired the utmost terror in the Indians, Balboa had little difficulty in overpowering the few hostile tribes he met.

Most of the Indians were, however, friendly, and the chief Comagre received the adventurers in a most hospitable manner. It was while he was with these friendly natives that Balboa first heard of another ocean and of an empire where gold was—to use his own words—"as common as iron among the Spaniards."

The Dons were quarreling over the division of some gold while the chief's son, Panquiaco, was contemptuously watching them. Conceiving a brilliant idea of getting the far from welcome visitors off his father's hands, Panquiaco announced that if gold was what the Spaniards sought he could tell them of a land where the commonest people ate and drank from dishes of the precious metal. Towards the horizon, he declared, was a great sea and on the shores of that sea was a vast country ruled by a powerful king and wherein gold was as the sands on the shore. But, he added, to reach this El Dorado at least one thousand men would be needed in order to vanquish the many hostile tribes to be encountered on the way.

Fired by this tale, Balboa dispatched a messenger to Spain begging for more men and supplies to fit out an expedition. But being too impatient to await a reply—or perhaps fearing he might be summoned home to render an accounting of his high-handed methods—Balboa resolved to start at once; and on September 1, 1513, with only one hundred and ninety men and a number of bloodhounds, he set out on his historic journey across the Isthmus. He counted upon the aid of the friendly Comagre, and in this he was not disappointed. That caçique placed nearly one thousand of his men at Balboa's service, and it was largely due to these Indians that Balboa succeeded in crossing the Isthmus in safety.

Forcing their way through a densely forested country inhabited by the most savage and implacable of hostile tribes, undergoing hardships and privations innumerable, weighted down with heavy armor, decimated by fever and the bites of poisonous insects, the Spaniards pressed on. At last, ascending a range of hills, Balboa gazed westward to see an ocean stretching to the far horizon.

Three days later, the Spaniards arrived at the shores of a great gulf. The first man to reach the water was Alonso Martin, who, finding a canoe upon the beach, leaped into it and paddled from shore in order to be the first European to navigate the new ocean. A few moments later Balboa arrived. First drinking of the salt water, he waded into the gulf and took possession of the Pacific in the names of the King and Queen of Spain and of the Pope, boasting that he was prepared to defend it and all its shores against either infidel or Christian.

History does not record what was said or done to Panquiaco when the Spaniards failed to find traces of the rich kingdom of his story. But it is highly probable that Panquiaco, being a youth of intelligence and discretion, took advantage of opportunity and placed himself safely beyond reach of Balboa while that Don's attentions were occupied with the new-found sea.

The other Indians, however, explained to the Spaniards that the land of gold lay farther to the south, and must be reached by way of the sea. But they had a very vague and indefinite idea of its exact locality or its distance, and Balboa jumped to the conclusion that it was near at hand. That he did not doubt its existence, and did not question the truth of the stories of its vast wealth, was typical of the Spaniards of his day.

To them, nothing was too fantastical, too amazing, too strange to be true. Their credulity was astounding, but, after all, we cannot blame them very much. Having discovered a new world, having seen so many strange and wonderful things, having experienced so much that was entirely new, anything seemed possible and probable in this world of wonders. Moreover, in this particular case, Balboa had every reason to believe the Indians' story. He found them using pearls as decorations on their canoes, they possessed many ornaments and utensils of gold, and he even was shown a rude figure of a llama which, to his eyes, represented an Asiatic camel. He was, in fact, convinced that he had reached the Orient, and that the semimythical land of Cipango (Japan) was close at hand.

Elated, filled with enthusiasm as he might well be, he secured some large canoes and recklessly set out for the land of the natives' tales. But he got no farther than the Pearl Islands in the Bay of Panama. Finding no other land visible, he wisely decided not to attempt voyaging farther, and returned to the mainland. He was, of course, greatly disappointed at not finding the land he sought, but he had little cause for complaint. He had secured a vast quantity of pearls and considerable gold, the whole amounting to more than half a million dollars, which was not bad for an expedition of such short duration and which, divided among the one-hundred-odd survivors of the party, was enough to make each man rich for life.

Returning by a different route, Balboa and his companions reached Santa Maria on the nineteenth of January, 1514. His first act on returning to Santa Maria was to send a trusted companion, Pedro de Arbolancha, to Spain with a great quantity of pearls and gold for the Sovereigns, and bearing a request that Balboa should be rewarded for his discoveries by being made commander-in-chief of the Castilla de Oro.

The messenger arrived too late, however. Enciso had told his tale of Balboa's revolutionary activities, and the King had appointed a new governor who had sailed for Panama with one thousand five hundred men and with specific instructions to proceed against Balboa and either to take him prisoner or destroy him. The new governor was a monster in human form whose name was Pedro Arias de Avila, but who was more commonly and popularly known as Pedrarias the Cruel. He was received with all due respect and hospitality by Balboa, who probably was not aware of the new executive's character or purposes until he was seized, chained and imprisoned.

Such was the manner in which the ex-stowaway was rewarded for his momentous discovery, the discovery that was to lead to Spain's acquisition of the most stupendous treasure in its history, and the acquisition of a territory far larger than the whole of

Europe. But we cannot have much sympathy for
Balboa. Without reason, he had doomed poor
Nicuesa and his men to their deaths, he had fomented insurrection and had forcibly deposed and
deported the authorized governor of the colony and
he had been guilty of innumerable cruelties to
the Indians. His imprisonment, his fine—which
stripped him of all his hard-won possessions—his
degradation and his ignominious end were scarcely
more than he deserved. Yet he was no worse than
some others of his fellows who rose to fame, riches
and high honors, but who were more fortunate or
more clever, than the discoverer of the Pacific.

Had Pedrarias the Cruel possessed the initiative
or the vision to follow up Balboa's discoveries, instead of devoting his energies to subduing the territory under his control and earning the hatred and
distrust of his countrymen by his oppressions, he
might have risen to great heights, and Peru might
have been conquered and added to Spain's possessions in the New World before Mexico was discovered.

But while Pedrarias was squabbling with his disaffected settlers, and was establishing the City of
Panama and carrying on a sporadic warfare with
the Isthmian tribes, momentous and amazing events
were taking place in countries far to the north of
Panama.

Hernandez de Cordova had sailed from Cuba for
the Bahamas, there to capture Indians for slaves,
but driven out of his course by gales, and literally
and figuratively at sea for three weeks, he at last

found himself off the coast of a new and unknown land. The natives at first appeared friendly and, on being asked the name of their country, replied *"Ouyukatan"* (We do not understand). The visitors, however, as was so often the case, quite overlooked the obvious fact that the Indians could not understand the Spanish language, and assuming the word was the name of the land, corrupted it to Yucatan.

Astonished at finding the inhabitants clad in finely woven cloth garments instead of being naked savages, and still more amazed when he saw the immense stone buildings and elaborate sculptures of the Mayas, Cordova assumed—and rightly—that he had accidentally come into contact with a civilized race very distinct from the Indians the Spaniards had hitherto met. The fact that the inhabitants of Yucatan were highly cultured did not, however, interest Cordova as much as the fact that they wore innumerable articles of gold. But the Mayas showed no disposition to part with their possessions and, when the Spaniards attempted their usual high-handed methods and tried forcible means of securing the coveted metal, they discovered to their sorrow that the Mayas differed from other Indians in more ways than one. From friends they were changed to the most deadly foes, and attacked the Spaniards with a fury, a daring and a militant skill that was as astonishing as it was disastrous. Cordova himself was wounded in a dozen places and narrowly escaped death, and only one member of the party escaped unhurt. Over one hundred Spaniards, more than half the total number, were killed. Glad to get away with their lives, the survivors managed to reach their ships, and set sail with all haste to Cuba, where Cordova died from the effects of his wounds a few days after his arrival.

But the tales of the new land, the strange valiant race, the great temples and the gold so near at hand and separated from Cuba by less than two hundred miles of open sea, set all Cuba agog. The governor, Don Diego de Velasquez, was of a different stamp from Pedrarias, and fully realizing the importance of Cordova's chance discovery, he immediately fitted out a squadron of four vessels to explore the new country and placed his own nephew, Juan de Grijalva, in command.

Grijalva's observations confirmed all Cordova had reported, and he reaped the harvest of his forerunner's indiscretions, being everywhere accorded a warm reception by the thoroughly aroused natives. He was a diplomatic, rather decent sort of chap, however, and after some difficulty partially won the confidence of the Indians and succeeded in trading with them. Rapidly acquiring gold and gems in exchange for glass beads and hawks' bells, as he cruised northward along the coast, he reached a territory inhabited by another race, even more highly civilized than the natives of Yucatan, who welcomed the strangers with every sign of reverence. Although Grijalva was ignorant of it, for he could converse with the Indians by signs only, he had reached the country under the rule of the Aztec emperor, Montezuma, and he and his men had been mistaken for semidivine beings whose coming had been foretold centuries before. From these Aztecs, the Spaniards received a vast treasure in gold, precious stones, feather mantles and fine fabrics, many of which were bestowed upon them as gifts—treasure, in fact, beyond their wildest dreams. But despite the flattering reception he had received, Grijalva hesitated to attempt establishing a settlement in a land so densely populated by such obviously cultured and valiant people. Continuing on his voyage of exploration, he sent one of his captains, Pedro de Alvarado (a blond, whose fair hair and ruddy cheeks had earned him the Mexican sobriquet of *Tonatiuh* or "Child of the sun"), back to Cuba with the precious cargo he had obtained.

CHAPTER IV

THE RESULT OF A LOVE TRYST

IT was close to the midnight hour in old Seville. In a deserted side street a Spanish youth slipped furtively into the shadows as the heavy footfalls of the approaching *Sereño* approached. That he was no ordinary footpad or night prowler was evident by his personal appearance and his dress. The fairness of his skin was accentuated by his large dark eyes; his high forehead, thin, high-bridged nose and oval face were those of the aristocracy, and upon his upper lip he wore a perky, upturned black mustache. Though slender, and above the average height, his broad shoulders and deep chest were those of an athlete. He was plainly dressed for the style of the times, when men arrayed themselves in all the colors of the rainbow, but his hose and trunks of dark blue were of the finest silk and satin, and his maroon doublet was of the richest velvet. A slender gold chain about his neck and a single solitaire diamond on one finger were his only jewelry, and upon his crisp black hair was a jaunty cap of blue velvet adorned with a scarlet feather held in place by a small gold clasp.

Silent and motionless he waited in the deep shadows of the jasmine-covered wall until the night watchman had passed, and his reassuring cry of

33

"Sereño! Sereño! La media noche y todo sereño!"
("All's well! Midnight and all's well!") sounded
from the next street.

Then, stepping from his hiding place, the youth
hurried to the end of the narrow, cobbled street and
stopped where a detached house rose black against
the sky in a garden beyond the wall. After a quick
glance about, he uttered a low whistle, and, in re-
sponse to the signal, a shutter was cautiously pushed
back and from the invisible casement above a woman's voice spoke in an almost inaudible whisper.

With the agility of a cat the young cavalier commenced to scale the wall. It was the old, old story,
an amorous youth keeping a midnight tryst with his
ladylove—a common enough incident in itself, but
destined to lead to most momentous results in the
present case.

As he neared the summit of the ancient wall, the
vine to which he clung parted from the stones; he
clutched wildly at the coping; the crumbling masonry
gave way, and with a crash and a half-smothered cry
the youth was hurled to the pavement below.

Alternately cursing his luck and groaning with
pain, he lay there awaiting the arrival of the *Sereño*
who, at sound of the crash, was hurrying towards the
scene. Here was a pretty how-do-you-do to be sure.
All his plans had been knocked to bits. He was to
sail at dawn with Don Nicolas de Ovando for New
Spain, and here he was with a broken ankle that
would prevent him from leaving for the New World.
A duel with the fair lady's outraged husband would
unquestionably be in order as soon as his ankle had

mended, and—this galled him worst of all—the lady herself was probably laughing at the plight of the amateur Don Juan.

Little did he dream that his mishap was to lead him to fame and fortune far beyond his wildest dreams. But of such trivialities is destiny shaped, and the escapade of romantic young Hernando Cortes resulted in the conquest of Mexico and changed the history of the New World.

At this time Cortes was barely eighteen years of age. The son of an ancient and respected family of means, Hernando, being a far from robust boy, had been educated for the law. But he was a romantic soul, and despite his physical handicaps he dreamed of a life of adventure, and law failed to appeal to him. And, like many another dreamer, he found much solace and satisfaction in writing prose and verse which, if we are to credit contemporaneous critics, was most excellent at that. This, however, did not satisfy his cravings. Determining that he should see something of the world and have a part in the exploits of his countrymen in the new-found lands across the seas, he devoted himself to a rigorous system of training, adopted a strict diet, abstained from drink, and as a result, he was transformed from a weakling to a muscular, athletic youth, an expert swordsman, a splendid horseman, and the envy of his companions. Full of high spirits, possessing a keen sense of humor, and of a carefree, devil-may-care temperament, he was ever in mischief, and was seldom out of one scrape before he was in another. And his fondness for the ladies was proverbial. Before he was eighteen he had faced more than one lover and husband on the dueling field, but his uncanny mastery of the rapier had stood by him each time.

Finally he had seen the opportunity he had been awaiting, and had joined the forces of Don Nicolas de Ovando who was preparing to sail for America, only to be prevented by his ignominious fall which altered the entire course of his life

Abiding his time, at the first opportunity he set sail for Hispaniola, and upon arriving at once visited the governor of the colony whom he had known in Spain. He was hospitably welcomed by His Excellency, who expatiated on the opportunities presented for accumulating a fortune by husbandry rather than adventure. This was not at all to Cortes' taste. He had set out with romantic ideas of carving his way to fortune by the sword, and to abandon the sword in favor of the plow did not appeal to him. However, he finally decided to follow the governor's advice, and was given a large tract of land, a *repartimiento* of Indian slaves, and was made Notary of Azua. His life as a planter was not entirely a humdrum existence, however. There were still hostile Indians in the interior of the island, and, to vary the monotony of a farmer's life, he joined several expeditions against the natives and rapidly acquired a knowledge of Indian warfare and showed marked military ability. So, when Velasquez set out to conquer Cuba, Cortes went with him, and when Velasquez became governor of Cuba, Hernando was made his secretary. But his fondness for the opposite sex soon got him into difficulties once more. He had become enamored of Catalina Juarez, one of the four sisters of an adventurer, Juan Juarez, who, it would appear, had brought them to Cuba with the hope of marrying them off. Cortes was not looking for the responsibilities of marriage, and broke the engagement, thereby breaking with his friend Velasquez who, it was rumored, was on intimate terms with one of the Juarez sisters.

Cortes thereupon joined the malcontents who were opposed to Velasquez's régime and as he threw himself heart and soul into whatever he undertook, he soon became as ardent a revolutionist as a lover. As a result he was chosen for the dangerous and delicate mission of voyaging to Santo Domingo in an open boat, there to lay complaints of Velasquez with the Governor of Hispaniola. The wily Velasquez was not to be caught napping, however. Hernando was seized, chained and imprisoned, and would have been hanged had his numerous friends not interceded on his behalf. But he did not remain long in chains. By some means he escaped, sought sanctuary in the church, and defied the governor. Then, attracted by a trim figure and a fair face that passed the portal wherein he was safe, he incautiously stepped into the street, only to be seized and pinioned by the guards constantly on watch. By a strange coincidence the man who took him was Juan Escudero who was, long afterwards, hanged by Cortes in Mexico.

Once more laden with chains, Hernando was placed aboard ship to be deported, but once again he managed to free himself—he seems to have been a veritable Houdini—and dropping over the vessel's side, swam to shore. Later on, he agreed to marry Catalina Juarez, and thereby received a full pardon from Governor Velasquez.

Once married, he resigned himself to a quiet life, settled near Santiago de Cuba, and was made Alcalde of that important town. He appears to have been most successful as a planter, for he prospered amazingly, introduced the first cattle into Cuba, and in a few years, was in possession of a tidy fortune of nearly twenty-five thousand dollars—a very large sum for a planter in those days. He had apparently given up all ideas of fulfilling his youthful dreams of a wild life of adventure, and was regarded as a most staid and stable citizen, a man of sterling character, of inflexible determination; a man possessing a remarkable amount of personal magnetism, keen judgment, a dominating nature, yet ever patient, good-natured, kindly, and ready to lend a helping hand to any one. He treated his slaves far better than his fellow planters, he seemed wedded to domesticity and his productive lands, and he appeared to be quite happy with his wife. But deep within his heart there must have been a spark of the old adventurous longing left.

Pedro de Alvarado had recently returned from an expedition to the coast of Yucatan; tales of a land of gold were being circulated, and Governor Velasquez, having sent the gold obtained by Alvarado to the King, had received royal permission to explore and conquer the newly discovered territory.

Here was Cortes' chance. The old dreams came back, the spark was fanned to flame, and the prosperous planter found himself appointed admiral of Velasquez's little Armada. Without hesitation he devoted every *peso* he possessed to securing supplies and equipment; he disposed of his estate, his cattle, his slaves and everything else to swell his funds, and practically all the costs of fitting out the expedition were paid from Cortes' pockets. His experiences in skirmishes with the natives now bore fruit. He knew the disadvantages and the hindrances of heavy steel mail in a jungle campaign, and he had seen the advantages of the quilted cotton armor used by the Indians, so he ordered hundreds of similar protective garments made for his own men. Cool, calculating, resolute, Cortes, now a mature man of thirty-four, was very different from the reckless youth who had been precipitated from the wall in Seville. But he still retained much of his youthful appearance and many of his youthful habits. His figure was still slender but splendidly muscled, and the sun of Cuba had not tanned the pale skin of his face that was now partly hidden by a black Vandyke beard. Never had he allowed himself to become soft or out of condition. He was still the supple, agile athlete, still the master of fence, still the unexcelled horseman. His life of comparative ease had not changed his habit of avoiding liquors and of eating lightly, and his position and prosperity had not altered his taste in dress. Though always well and richly clad, he avoided the gaudy show so popular with his countrymen, affected dark, modest colors, and confined his adornments to the single gold chain and diamond ring that he had worn at eighteen. And he was still as fond of the ladies as ever.

What the Señora Catalina thought of her husband's sudden change, and his approaching departure for parts unknown, history does not relate; but it is probable that, like most Spanish Señoras, she was far more interested in her finery, her bonbons, her gossip and her ease than in the coming expedition and, in all probability, she had become fat and ugly and had a shadow of a mustache on her lip and had little in common with her energetic, active and still physically youthful lord and master.

At all events, she was well provided for and had no need to worry over her future when Cortes received his final instructions embodied in a voluminous and formidable-looking document. According to this the first object of the expedition was to search for six Spaniards said to be held as prisoners by the Indians of Yucatan, and supposed to be survivors of Nicuesa's ill-fated expedition. The main object of the Admiral, Don Hernando Cortes, was, as set forth in the papers, trade, and he was specifically instructed to treat the natives humanely, to respect their lives and property (though this, it added, was a matter of policy to further trade and profit) and finally, and above all things, to convert the natives to Christianity.

Like most of the Spaniards of his day, Cortes was deeply religious, and like his fellows, he felt that he was a true Crusader, persuading himself that the real purpose of conquest was to spread the Christian

Faith rather than to win treasure by fire and blood.
But Cortes, unlike the others, was not of a cruel
or vindictive nature, and though he could be severe
and heartless in what he felt was justice, yet he seldom lost his temper, wrought dire vengeance, exacted reprisals, as did the others. For his day and
race, he was most kindly, courteous and forgiving.
Fate had thrown him into his present position, and
it is doubtful if in all the Spanish possessions there
was another man so well fitted for the task before
him, even though that task would of necessity include
bloodshed, the loss of countless lives, cruelties beyond measure, and the destruction of an empire.

His expedition, when at last all arrangements had
been completed, consisted of eleven ships—the largest was less than one hundred tons—one hundred
and ten sailors, and five hundred and fifty-three soldiers, including thirty-two crossbowmen, thirteen
arquebusiers, and two hundred Indian slaves. He
had but sixteen horses, and his armament consisted
of ten heavy cannon and four small falconets. But
to the people of the island, and more especially to
the governor, Velasquez, it appeared a vast array of
armed men, a veritable Armada. Velasquez, his suspicions aroused by whisperings and hints of trouble-
makers, began to fear that Cortes might play him
false and, with such a powerful force at his command, declare himself independent and grab Mexico
for himself. Authorities differ as to the precise relations of Velasquez and Cortes in those last days,
one declaring that the governor decided to depose
Cortes and give command to another. At all events

Cortes hoisted anchors and sailed at once, though the baffled Governor rowed out to the flagship and asked why the Admiral was in such a hurry. But the vessels were gathering way, and with a smile, Cortes waved His Excellency farewell.

Putting in at the port of Trinidad (Cuba) Cortes was joined by Pedro de Alvarado and several other cavaliers. Taking possession of all the available supplies and provisions in the town he paid what he considered them worth. When the people expostulated, he laughingly told them to go to the governor for redress, and when the local Alcalde approached, bearing the Velasquez's commands to seize Cortes, the latter dared him to do so.

Needless to say the poor Alcalde did not accept the dare, and was grateful when the fleet at last sailed away. The next stop was Havana, where Cortes defied the Governor's officers to interfere with him, laid in more necessary supplies, and from the masthead of his tiny flagship unfurled his colors, a black flag bearing a scarlet cross surrounded by blue and white flames—truly a most appropriate banner, symbolic of death and destruction under the shadow of the Cross.

At last, with everything complete, with his little vessels deeply laden, and with visions of fame and fortune ahead, the fleet sailed out from Havana's harbor and headed to the west. Soon after leaving Cuba the vessels were separated by storm, and when Cortes reached Cozumel Island he found that Alvarado had already arrived. Possibly the sunny-faced, fair-haired Don Pedro was unaware of the royal instructions given to Cortes, or perhaps he considered the document merely as a scrap of paper to be disregarded at will. At any rate he had shown his "respect" for the Indians by looting their temples, by ill-treating the inhabitants until they had fled to the jungles, and by making prisoners of a number of men and women.

Incensed at this high-handed action on the part of Alvarado, Cortes reprimanded him severely, freed the slaves he had taken, and sent them back to their friends loaded with presents and with assurances that he was friendly and that they need have no fear of molestation.

This humane and fair policy won the Indians' trust and confidence, and a number appeared and commenced trading with the Spaniards. But Cortes constantly had in mind his paramount duty to convert the heathen, and most eloquently expounded the doctrines of Christianity to them. As he was obliged to do so through the medium of a Maya youth, whom Alvarado had brought back from his previous voyage, and who had picked up a smattering of Spanish, it is very doubtful if the natives got any idea of what he was talking about. But having done his duty, Cortes insisted that the idols in the temples should be removed and the cross substituted. Much to his amazement and wonder he found the Cross already there, though it was merely the Indian symbol of the god of rain and had no connection with the Christian Cross, as Cortes imagined.

But the heathen idols were there also, and despite the protests of the Indians, Cortes tumbled these from their pedestals and broke them to bits while the terrified natives waited trembling for dire calamities to follow. But as none came, and as their gods appeared powerless to protect themselves or their temples from sacrilege, they decided that, after all, the strangers' gods must be the most powerful, and unanimously consented to being baptized and dubbed Christians, much to the delight and satisfaction of Cortes and his followers.

No doubt much of the kindly treatment accorded these Cozumel Indians and their conversion to Christianity was due to the priest, Bartolome de Olmedo, a most humane and charitable man, who, throughout Cortes' career, did all in his power to mitigate the sufferings and cruelties brought upon the Indians by the conquest. Like Las Casas, Olmedo's name stands out as a shining example of the true Christian priest, the patient, kindly, humane bearer of the Gospel who, however misled by his zeal he may have been, sought ever to lead the pagans to the fold of the Church, and whose life and deeds stand out the more sharply in contrast to the majority of his fellow priests.

Leaving Cozumel, where to his disappointment he had received no news of the Spanish castaways, Cortes sailed for Yucatan. While anchored off the coast repairing a leak in one of the ships, a canoe was seen approaching and, coming alongside, its occupant hailed the Dons in Spanish. To their amazement the unkempt, painted, wild-looking, half-naked man proved to be a Spaniard, Geronimo Aguilar, who had been shipwrecked eight years previously and had been living with the Indians. His comrades, so he said, had been killed and eaten but, for some reason, he had escaped their fate. He had been well treated and had been offered the chief's daughter in marriage. But, having studied for the clergy and having taken vows of celibacy, he refused the offer, and the Indians, unable to understand this and thinking he must be a superior being, had venerated him and had regarded him as inferior only to their caçique.

Unknown to him, however, another of the castaways still survived, and later Cortes' men were to meet him under very different circumstances. Like Aguilar, he had escaped being killed, and like him, too, he had been well treated by the Indians among whom he sought refuge. Gonzalo Guerrero as he was named was no cleric but a soldier. Far from refusing to wed the chief's daughter, he had married three women, and had a numerous progeny. Moreover, his knowledge of warfare and of weapons had won him the position of war chief, and under his training his adopted tribe had become so versed in military tactics that they had conquered the neighboring tribes and had won a reputation for savagery throughout the district. Having found greater happiness and better fortune among the Indians than had ever fallen to his lot among his own countrymen, he refused to be rescued by Cortes, and even warned the latter that, if he attempted to invade his territory, he would lead his Indians against the Dons, a promise which he kept to the letter, and with such complete success that the Santa Cruz Indians were never subdued and still maintain their independence.

But at the time, when Aguilar paddled to Cortes' ship and was rescued by his countrymen, nothing was known of the other Spaniard's presence in the neighborhood, and the fleet sailed away to Tabasco. Here the Indians received the strangers with arrows and spears instead of with gifts and hospitality. After a sharp but brief engagement the Spaniards took the town and occupied the temple. During the night, however, the interpreter, Melchorejo, slipped away, and an Indian captive informed Cortes that the entire country was in arms and prepared to resist the invaders.

He had not exaggerated, and the following day saw the Spaniards battling fiercely with hordes of the Tabascans. Many of the former were wounded, a number were killed, and despite the terrible execution caused by the cannon of the Spaniards the Indians seemed to increase rather than to decrease in numbers. It began to look as though the natives would be the victors when Cortes, leading his cavalry, charged from the rear accompanied—so the credulous Spaniards averred—by Santiago, whose supernatural apparition brought consternation to the Indians.

The Spaniards' victory was dearly bought. Over one hundred of their company were wounded or killed—or nearly one-fifth of the entire force.

Yet despite this and the apparently unprovoked attack of the natives, Cortes, instead of exacting reprisals and murdering his prisoners, liberated the captive chiefs and warriors, gave them presents, and sent word to the others that he would overlook the past if they would submit at once to Spain. Otherwise, he added, he would destroy all. Presently a party of Indians approached and asked permission to bury their dead. This being granted, and further expressions of friendship expressed by Cortes, the caçiques soon arrived bearing gifts or peace offerings, prominent among which were twenty female slaves.

Throughout Cortes' career the most trivial incidents appear to have governed his life and his destiny, and the caçiques' gift of these slave women was to prove one of the most important events in the life and success of the conqueror of Mexico.

Having patched matters up with the Tabascans, and having traded to advantage, the Spaniards sailed northward and landed at a spot they christened San Juan de Ulloa, the site of the present city of Vera Cruz. Here they were received with the most friendly and reverential regard by the natives who were of a wholly distinct race from those the Dons had hitherto met. They were, in fact, Mexicans, people subject to the Aztec emperor, Montezuma, and in the white-skinned, bearded strangers they saw the children of their ancient hero-god, *Quetzalcoatl,* who, so their traditions said, had been a bearded white man who had promised to return when, ages before, he had mysteriously vanished.

But of this Cortes and his men were entirely ignorant at the time, for the Indians spoke a language that not one of the Dons' interpreters could comprehend. At a loss, trying by signs to make his wants and purposes understood by the Indians, Cortes was astonished to hear one of the slave women from Tabasco conversing with the natives. When questioned, she replied that her name was Malinche, that she was a native of the Mexican town of Coatzalcualco, and that she had been sold into slavery by her unnatural mother who had wished to be rid of her in order to secure her inherited rights to bestow them on a son by a second marriage.

Probably Malinche's family history held no interest whatsoever for Cortes, but the fact that she spoke her native Nahua as well as the Tabascan Mayan dialect was vastly interesting as well as gratifying to him. With Malinche to help, negotiations went on apace, and presently Cortes became conscious of the fact that his new interpreter was a most attractive young person. In fact she was really beautiful—as beautiful, according to a contemporary writer, as a goddess—and her charms were fully revealed by the brevity of her costume—or lack of costume— which left little to the imagination.

Surprised that he had overlooked such a thoroughly charming creature hitherto, and delighted that she could be of such service to him, Cortes was completely won over by the girl. She was, however, as shy and as elusive as she was beautiful, and Cortes, to his credit, proved his courtesy, his decency and the sincerity of his affections by refraining from forcing his attentions upon her. Instead, he declared her freed from bondage, provided her with the finest of cloths and materials with which to clothe herself, saw that she was given proper quarters and privacy, and treated her in every way like the princess she was.

He appointed her his secretary, employed Padre Olmedo to instruct her in Spanish and the Christian Faith, and did everything possible to win her. Marina, as she was christened by the priest, was quick to learn. In a surprisingly short time she mastered the Castilian tongue, and before long Cortes was rewarded for his kindness and attentions by her love. From that time until the end of the campaign the two were never parted. Marina shared the hardships, the dangers, the terrors with her lover throughout the entire conquest. She remained absolutely faithful to the Spaniards. More than a dozen times she saved them from calamity and destruction, and through her influence with Cortes and his steadfast love for her she aided her own people and mitigated their sufferings beyond measure.

So inseparable were Cortes and his Indian mistress, and so greatly was she respected and adored by the Mexicans, that they bestowed her Nahua name upon Cortes and, throughout Mexico, the conqueror was universally known as Malinche. By Cortes she had a son, Martin Cortes, who held a not unimportant place in later Mexican history, and on more than one occasion Cortes expressed his regret at not being able to marry her. But he was a good Catholic, Doña Catalina still lived, and in the end the conqueror, who owed so much to his Indian sweetheart, was obliged to part with her. But he saw to it that Marina was not cast adrift. With his blessing—and with moist eyes at thought of the final parting—he bestowed her upon a Spanish hidalgo, Don Juan Zamarillo, to whom she was lawfully married, and as a wedding gift Cortes presented her with vast estates in her native province where she passed the remainder of her days in happiness.

CHAPTER V

A MESSAGE FROM MONTEZUMA

ALTHOUGH Grijalva and Cortes had appreciated the fact that the natives of Yucatan and Mexico were highly cultured and of a different type from those tribes hitherto met, and although they had gathered some ideas of an emperor who ruled the entire country from his seat of government in a city far in the interior, yet they had not the faintest idea of the extent, the wealth or the civilization of Mexico. But to enable the reader more easily to understand all the events and happenings that were incidental to the conquest, a brief description of the Aztecs, their customs, their religion and their civilization is necessary.

The origin of the race is uncertain, and is lost in the dim and distant past, although Aztec traditions and their pictographic records or codices told of their having come to Mexico from some land to the north and west. There were also traditions of a semimythical, highly cultured or civilized race known as Toltecs, who had preceded the Aztecs, traditions which are borne out to a certain extent by remains of a very ancient civilization in Mexico.

At the time of its discovery by the Spaniards, the Aztecs, or more properly the Nahuas, occupied a large portion of what is now Mexico, with the Aztec capital of Tenochtitlan where Mexico City now stands. The empire was not, however, composed of a single race of people, but was a confederation of innumerable tribes rather loosely held together and controlled by the dominating Aztec tribe whose ruler was known as Montezuma.

In some ways the condition of the Aztec Empire at the time of the arrival of the Spaniards was very similar to the conditions in Europe in medieval days. Each tribe or state was semi-independent, and was ruled by its own king or feudal lord, who in turn owed allegiance to the emperor, to whom tribute was paid. And just as in the days of the feudal barons of Europe, these city-states were frequently at war with one another, a condition which, as will be seen later, had a most important bearing on the Spaniards' almost incredible success in conquering a vast territory and millions of inhabitants with a mere handful of men.

The Nahuas were conquerors, who, while attaining great heights in some directions, were sadly deficient in others, and their civilization was far behind either that of the Mayas or the Incas. Their government, though well organized and rigidly enforced, was a despotic monarchy by which the common people were oppressed, and were little better than slaves, whereas the ruling class lived a life of ease, indolence and luxury. An immense army was always maintained, there were innumerable priests and still more nobles and officials, and all of these, together with the court, the public works, the religious ceremonials and all other expenses of the entire empire were supported by the industry and toil of the masses.

Being a warlike race, with well-trained and well-equipped armies, the Aztecs had extended their conquests to embrace much of Mexico, had conquered Yucatan and portions of Central America, and had impressed their religion, culture, customs and language upon the subjugated races until, to the Spaniards, all were Aztec. Like the majority of American races, they were, primarily, sun-worshipers, although like the Incas and others they adored the sun, not as a god in itself, but as the visual manifestation of a divinity known as Teotl or Ipalneomohuani, literally ''The Life-giver'' (the sun-god). Their religion was, however, very involved and complicated, and their mythology included a vast number of deities, many of whom were borrowed from other tribes and races. All of these were worshiped with the greatest devotion, but at the time of the conquest, the Aztecs were tending towards the adoration of a single deity, the air-god or Tezcatlipoca. The sun-god, however, was the background of the religion, the supreme being, and was regarded as above all the other gods and divinities. Very important among these was their hero-god, Quetzalcoatl or the Plumed Serpent, who, according to Aztec mythology, was a bearded white man who had suddenly appeared in the distant past, had taught the people arts, religion and civilization, and had then vanished. According to some versions of the myth he had arrived from the east in a ship and had landed at the point where Vera Cruz now

stands, while according to others he had come from
the skies. Likewise the stories of his departure did
not agree. He was variously stated to have sailed
away on a raft composed of magic serpents, to have
been transformed to a bird, and to have ascended to
heaven where he became the morning star. But in
one respect the myths agreed. Before he had left
the Nahuas he had prophesied that he would return
at some future time, that he and his sons would arrive in a ship from the sunrise, and that his descendants should conquer and rule the land.

Whether, in the hazy past, some European had
found his way to Mexico and had been deified by the
people, whether Quetzalcoatl was purely a mytho-
logical being, or whether he was a true divinity or,
as the Spanish priests believed, a saint, no one can
say. But it is most remarkable that both the Mayas
and the Incas had very similar, in fact almost identical, traditions of a bearded white man having
visited them, the first being known as Kulkulkan or
the Plumed Snake and the latter as Wirakocha
(symbolized by a jaguar and serpents) and who were
credited with having made identical prophecies.
And it is still more remarkable—almost astounding
—that the prophecies should, in the case of the
Aztecs and Incas, have been borne out to the letter.
Moreover, it was this myth and prophecy which
caused the Mexicans (as well as the Incas) to greet
the Spaniards with hospitality and reverence. In
the conquerors, arriving at the appointed spot and in
the appointed thirteenth age, the Mexicans saw the
sons of Quetzalcoatl, and regarded them as divine,

a fact that was of the utmost value and importance to the Spaniards.

But perhaps the most noteworthy and remarkable feature of the Aztec religion was its cruelty and the gruesome rites it demanded. Human sacrifices were an essential part of all religious ceremonies, and probably in no other religion in the world's history were human sacrifices carried to such cruel extremes.

There were two principal forms of sacrifice in vogue—though others were practiced on certain occasions to satisfy certain gods. Ordinarily the victim was stretched upon the sacrificial stone or altar, and the priest, ripping open the victim's chest with an obsidian knife, tore out the living, palpitating heart with his hands and held it aloft as an offering to the gods. In the other form, reserved for certain days dedicated to the god Zipe, the victim was flayed alive and his skin was worn for a period of ten days by the high priest. Cannibalism also entered into the Aztec religion, and it was customary for the priests and the nobility to devour the flesh of the victims of sacrifice, partly to show their respect for the deceased and partly as it was believed that, in so doing, they acquired merit with their gods. It must not be supposed, however, that because the Aztec religion demanded such atrocities and cruelties that the people were either cruel or bloodthirsty. On the contrary, they were normally a gentle, quiet, kindly people, passionately fond of music and flowers, almost childish in their amusements and diversions, and unusually light-hearted and gay for Indians.

Neither must we waste too much sympathy upon the victims of the sacrifice. Believing firmly in the religion themselves, and fully convinced that by being sacrificed they were being deified and would forever live with their gods, they sought rather than avoided their fate. Originally those selected for sacrifice were prisoners of war, but as the empire was extended and its power increased and wars became fewer, the supply of victims dwindled.

This brought about a most remarkable state of affairs and resulted in what was probably the most amazing and unique form of warfare that ever existed anywhere on earth. Each year, at a prearranged time, an army of the Aztecs and an army of the Tlascalans, their hereditary enemies, met at a selected spot. No weapons were carried by either side, for the contestants had no desire to inflict wounds or deaths upon one another, their sole aim being to secure prisoners to provide victims for sacrifice. Rushing forward, each warrior strove to overthrow and carry off a member of the opposing army and the field became a chaotic, swaying, shouting, struggling mass of humanity as the two tribes wrestled and fought to capture and to escape, until at last, exhausted, and with their prisoners securely bound, the two forces drew apart and retired to their respective territories. The prisoners thus obtained still had a chance—though a very slender one—of escaping the fate for which they were intended. Each captive was secured to a huge stone disk by means of a short rope attached to one ankle, and was given a light shield and a wooden sword. He was then attacked by six fully armed and equipped warriors in succession. If—as he sometimes did—the prisoner succeeded in defeating all six of his opponents, he was released, loaded with honors and presents and restored to his people. But if he received the slightest wound he was doomed to be sacrificed.

Nor were the captives reserved for this horrible fate illtreated, tortured or abused in any way. On the contrary, they were treated like honored guests, were provided with every luxury and delicacy, were clad in the finest of garments, were served and waited upon, and were catered to in every way. Those destined for certain ceremonials were revered almost like the gods themselves, and were believed to be under the special protection and favor of the god to whom they were to be sacrificed. They were attended by a retinue of servants, were given the most beautiful maidens as wives, and were carefully trained for the part they were to fulfill. And they no doubt mounted the steps of the sacrificial pyramids feeling that they were being greatly honored, that they were going to eternal happiness, and as exalted in spirit as the old Christian martyrs.

In their arts and in science the Aztecs were far advanced. They were expert metal workers, they fashioned the hard, brittle obsidian or volcanic glass into innumerable ornaments, utensils and weapons; they wove cotton and other fabrics, as well as feathers, into textiles of marvelous beauty and fineness; they erected enormous buildings, were adept sculptors, and produced splendid pottery.

They possessed a very perfect and complete arithmetical system and a calendar that was very nearly as accurate as that of the Spaniards. Throughout the empire they had constructed a network of excellent roads over which messages were sent by means of relays of couriers, and they had perfected a form of written or rather pictographic language by which they recorded events, history, accounts, and, in fact, anything of importance. These records or codices were painted upon parchment, cloth or paper made from the fiber of the Maguey plant, and were made up of numerous pages that were sometimes folded on themselves, but usually were mounted on a stout cloth foundation and folded to form books. Originally these codex records consisted of pictures representing objects and personages, often highly conventionalized; but at the time of the arrival of the Spaniards, the Nahuas were developing a phonetic system in which symbols replaced the real pictures. Thus *Ixcoatl* was represented by a snake (*Coatl*) pierced by knives (*Itzli*). At times entire syllables were indicated by an object whose name began with it. At other times a letter or sound was represented by the same drawing, but in every case the idea was to convey a thought or an idea by a sketch that conveyed the sound.

While Cortes was carrying on his conversation with the first Mexicans he had met, with Malinche, of course, acting as interpreter, he was surprised to see one of the Indians busily drawing pictures upon a sheet of papyrus. And he was still more astonished when he found that the pictures were greatly conventionalized though unmistakable portrayals of the Spaniards, their weapons, armor, clothing and every detail of their equipment. In fact the artist was preparing a codex describing the arrival of the Spaniards, and all data in regard to them, which was to be sent to Montezuma. This was the first time that the Dons had seen the Aztec pictographs, but it was by no means the first time that codices recording the arrival of the long-expected white men had been made and sent to the Aztec emperor. From the time when Grijalva had first appeared off the Mexican coast, every movement of the Dons, every detail of their numbers, equipment and actions, had been recorded, and Montezuma had been kept fully informed of the events on the coast of his empire. It was here, too, that Cortes first learned something of the details of the Mexicans' government and religion, of Montezuma and his capital.

When Cortes announced that he was an envoy from a great monarch over the sea, who had heard of Montezuma's greatness and had sent him to carry a message to the Aztec monarch, the natives were more than ever convinced that the visitors were the long-expected sons of the Plumed Serpent. Their chief, Teuhtlitl, declared that he had no doubt that Montezuma would be pleased to receive the white men, and that he would send couriers to the emperor conveying Cortes' message and presents from the Spaniards. These consisted of a few cheap and tawdry articles—an armchair, a cloth cap, a quantity of cheap glass jewelry and a few hawk's bells— a poor enough return for the presents the Spaniards

had received from the chief, which consisted of
ten loads of fine cotton fabrics, a number of feather
mantles, a basket filled with gold ornaments and a
number of semiprecious stones.

As these exchanges were being made, Teuhtlitl
noticed one of the Spaniards wearing a helmet of
polished brass, and, remarking that it resembled that
worn by Quetzalcoatl, he asked Cortes if he could not
include it with his gifts to Montezuma. To this the
Spanish leader agreed, adding as an afterthought
that he would be pleased if the casque were returned
to him filled with gold dust, as the Spaniards were
afflicted with a disease of the heart for which gold
was the only remedy.

Just what Montezuma's reactions were when he
received Cortes' messages and presents, and studied
the codices, is problematical. But it is certain that
he believed the Spaniards were semidivine, that he
was greatly worried as he realized the ancient
prophecy might be fulfilled, and that he was unde-
cided whether to propitiate or to attack them. If,
he argued, the visitors were truly supernatural and
the sons of Quetzalcoatl, then it would be useless to
attempt by force to evade Destiny. If they were
mere mortals but ambassadors of another monarch
sent on a peaceful mission it would be unjust and
undiplomatic to treat them otherwise than as friends.
But, on the other hand, the Spaniards' behavior had
not been altogether reassuring nor such as might
have been expected from either friends or gods, and
they had used high-handed methods to destroy the
Aztecs' religion. Yet, the ancient prophecy had

stated that the descendants of the Plumed Serpent would do these very things.

One cannot envy Montezuma in his predicament. He was literally between the devil and the deep sea, and whichever course he followed he was faced with doubt and disaster. So, being uncertain which course to follow, he did exactly what might have been expected and adopted halfway measures by sending a princely present with friendly greetings to the Spaniards, and at the same time using every wile and excuse to prevent them penetrating to the capital, meanwhile strengthening his army and his defenses in case hostilities became inevitable.

Meanwhile Cortes and his men were enjoying themselves among the friendly subjects of Teuhtlitl. By the chief's orders, the Indians had erected huts for the Spaniards, they provided them with food and supplies, and they lavished presents upon them. And although these coastal people possessed comparatively little gold, the Spaniards succeeded in obtaining a far from inconsiderable amount of the precious metal by means of barter. In a little more than a week, word was spread that Montezuma's messengers were approaching, and presently they arrived, a long train of more than one hundred cargo carriers bending under the loads of presents sent by the Aztec monarch, and accompanied by two Aztec nobles of high rank. One of these bore a most striking resemblance to the Spanish leader, a likeness that was so pronounced that the soldiers then and there christened him the "Mexican Cortes," a nickname that stuck to him throughout the conquest.

Having saluted Cortes and humbled themselves before him as though he were a great king or deity, the nobles presented the gifts sent by Montezuma. There were shields of feather and mosaic work; casques, breastplates, armor and ornaments of gold; feather garments and mantles; textiles embroidered with gold and pearls; precious stones, golden and silver figures of birds and animals; gem-encrusted vessels and vases; serapes and robes of the finest cotton. But most important and gratifying of all to the visitors were two immense disks as large as cart-wheels, one of solid gold and worth more than two hundred thousand dollars, and the other of solid silver. In addition, Cortes received the Spanish helmet, filled, as he had diplomatically suggested, with gold dust. Assuredly Montezuma had sent enough of the desired remedy to cure the heart troubles of every Spaniard in the camp! Unfortunately for the Mexicans, however, the disease from which the Dons suffered was incurable and, the greater the doses of the golden "remedy," the more virulent the disease became.

Having duly delivered their monarch's presents to Cortes, the messengers informed the Spanish commander that Montezuma was greatly pleased to learn that such a mighty emperor as the King of Spain should have honored him by sending an envoy to his land. But much as he would enjoy a personal interview with the strangers, it would be impossible, as the distance to the capital was too great and was beset by too many dangers for the Spaniards to attempt the journey. The only course, therefore, was for the visitors to return to their king with the gifts they had received as proof of Montezuma's friendship.

Little did he know the Spaniards. His courteous and cleverly worded refusal to permit Cortes to visit the capital, and his thinly disguised hint that the visitors were not welcome in Mexico, only added to Cortes' desire to penetrate the country and made him the more determined to march to the capital.

He was, however, a man of discretion, possessing diplomatic ability, and while quite willing to carry out his plans and desires, by forcible means if necessary, he preferred peaceable methods and a friendly policy to hostility and war. So, concealing his chagrin at Montezuma's refusal to see him, he assured the emissaries that he would not dare to return to his own king without having had a personal interview with the Aztec ruler, adding that, having traversed more than two thousand leagues of ocean and having braved so many perils for that express purpose, the distance to the capital and the dangers by the way were nothing. He besought the messengers, therefore, to again request Montezuma for an interview, thanked them for the gifts, and in return sent a present to the emperor. This consisted of a gilt tankard, a few shirts and some baubles—the whole worth less than fifty dollars.

To the Spaniards the visit of the nobles, their message from Montezuma and the magnificent treasure they had brought, proved both a promise and a threat. The treasure spoke eloquently of the riches of the land and of the vast stores of gold awaiting their rapacious hands. But, on the other hand, they saw in it, and in the attitude of Montezuma, indications of a power and a king with resources far too great for such a small force to attempt to overcome. Almost immediately two factions arose in the Spaniards' camp. One was for marching inland and taking possession of the country and its riches at once. The other was as insistent that Cortes should return to Cuba and not undertake the conquest until a larger expedition could be fitted out. As for Cortes, he refused to express an opinion until after the envoys' return with a reply to his second message; but there is no doubt that from the first his mind had been fully made up to see Tenochtitlan or die in the attempt.

CHAPTER VI

CORTES BURNS HIS BRIDGES BEHIND HIM

WHILE the Spaniards argued and quarreled and waited for the return of Montezuma's envoys, nature took a part and allied herself with the Aztecs. The climate and its tropical maladies began to take their toll of the Dons. They sickened and died, and to such a small company the loss of every man was a disaster. To add to their troubles and fears, the attitude of the Indians underwent a great change. They became cold and aloof, no more presents of food were forthcoming, and only by trading and paying exorbitant prices could the Spaniards secure provisions. Moreover, the vessels in the offing were in constant jeopardy from the first northerly gale that arose and, fearing to lose his ships, Cortes sent them to explore the coast to the north and to seek a better harbor.

By the time the envoys returned, ten days after their departure, over thirty Spaniards had succumbed to the climate, to noxious insects and to disease, and the message brought from Montezuma was not at all reassuring. To be sure, the presents the emissaries brought were almost as rich as on their former visit, but Montezuma's answer was even more plain than before. In fact, he definitely forbade them to attempt to approach the capital and declared that, now they had accomplished their averred purpose in visiting his country, and had obtained that which they most desired, he expected them to lose no time in returning whence they came.

Replying to the envoys with outward courtesy, Cortes turned to his men, and for the first time expressed his decision. "This Montezuma is a great and a rich king," he exclaimed. "He rules a great land and commands thousands, yet it shall go hard with us if we do not pay him a visit." Little did he dream how hard it would go for his company before his words were borne out.

Having thus delivered himself, Cortes took the opportunity to endeavor to impress the people and the royal envoys with the Christian Faith and had Father Olmedo expound the Gospel to the wondering Indians, after doing which he assured them that it was the intention of the visitors to destroy the idols and the temples of the Aztecs and to replace their religion with his own.

The padre then presented the envoys with figures of the Virgin and of Christ, requesting that they should be placed in their temples and the Aztec deities cast down. This was most impolitic on his part, for a nation's religion is its most revered and cherished possession, a thing to be fought for to the end, and to be defended with the last drop of blood.

The immediate result of the priest's dissertation was the complete desertion of the Indians that night, and the conquerors thus thrown on their own resources, moved bag and baggage to a more suitable locality discovered by Cortes' captains on their voyage of exploration. Discontent, however, increased. The soldiers, forced to forage for themselves, suffering from the heat of the torrid coastal district, now fully realizing that to remain in Mexico meant war with a vastly superior and powerful force, clamored for return to Cuba. But Cortes was adamant. He was ever a man to whom the overcoming of seemingly insurmountable difficulties held the greatest appeal, and he used every argument to instill enthusiasm and determination in his men.

They were an untrained, undisciplined lot, however; they regarded their leader as no better than themselves, and Cortes might have been forced to accede to their demands had not an unexpected event completely altered conditions. This was the arrival in camp of five natives who were very different from any of the Mexicans previously met. Large gold rings were in their ears, they wore labrets and ornaments of lapis lazuli in their lips and noses, their dress was distinct from that of the Aztecs, and Marina was unable to understand their dialect. Two of their number spoke the Nahuatl or Aztec tongue, however, and announced that they were Totonacs, natives of the city of Cempoala, and were sent by their caçique who requested the Spaniards' presence in his capital. They then explained that the Totonac nation had only recently been conquered by the Aztecs, and that the people were anxious to regain their independence and would gladly ally themselves with the visitors.

Here was an opportunity that was eagerly seized by Cortes. Hitherto he had been ignorant of the

conditions existing among the dependent states of
the empire and had assumed that the entire country
was Aztec and united under Montezuma. But now
he realized that in the disaffection of the Totonacs,
and, as he rightly guessed, other tribes, there was a
means of achieving his desire to overthrow the
Aztec emperor. He received the Totonac delegation
most hospitably, loaded them with presents, and
assuring them of his aid and friendship, promised
to visit their capital at once.

Before starting for the land of the Totonacs,
Cortes decided to establish a colony, and founded
the settlement which he christened "Villa Rica de
Vera Cruz" (The Rich Town of the True Cross).
Having appointed necessary officials and authorities,
he presented himself before them, cap in hand and
tendered his resignation as Captain-General under
Velasquez, remarking that, as "the power of the
governor of Cuba was now superseded by that of
the municipality of Vera Cruz," he could no longer
hold a superior position unless appointed by the local
authorities. This rather theatrical move on Cortes'
part was a master stroke of diplomacy. Many of
his men had declared openly that he had been disobeying Velasquez's orders in not returning to Cuba,
and in not having established settlements. But by
thus founding a town and resigning his commission
he effectually put an end to any such charges. And,
as he expected and as was inevitable, the newly appointed city officials, in behalf of Their Catholic
Majesties, appointed Cortes Captain-General and
Chief Justice of the colony. He was also authorized

to draw, on his own account, one fifth of all gold and silver thereafter obtained. In other words Cortes was invested with supreme military and civil authority which no one, other than the Spanish Crown, could dispute or revoke. His knowledge of the law, which he had acquired in his youth, had now proved most useful to him. He had been clothed with full authority to found settlements and towns in Mexico and to appoint civil authorities. And these officials, in their turn, not having taken oath of office under Velasquez, had a perfect right to appoint whomsoever they saw fit as their governor and chief justice. And they had been most careful to appoint Cortes, not in behalf of the Governor of Cuba, but in behalf of the Crown. Hence Cortes had *legally* shed his allegiance to Velasquez and was now amenable only to his sovereign. He was, to all intents and purposes, and legally, the Governor-General of Mexico, despite the objections and denunciations of those of the forces who were partisans of Velasquez.

The new Governor-General was not slow in proving his power. Several of the malcontents, among whom was a kinsman of the Cuban governor, were clapped into irons and placed under guard aboard ship while the rest were placed under command of Alvarado and sent into the interior to forage for supplies. Hunger is a wonderful panacea for many evils. By the time the foraging party returned to the new settlement, empty stomachs had stilled all other complaints and, after having satisfied their appetites, the men's good spirits were restored, the rival factions forgot their differences, and even the imprisoned cavaliers gave in and pledged their allegiance to Cortes.

Having thus firmly established himself and settled all difficulties, Cortes sent his heavy guns and more bulky baggage aboard the ships and ordered the captains to proceed by sea to the Totonac territory while he marched overland with his troops. As they proceeded, they entered far better country and found several deserted villages. In the temples of some of these they came upon the bodies of recently sacrificed victims, and for the first time learned of this phase of the Mexican religion. According to their own statements, the Spaniards were filled with horror and loathing at this exhibition of butchery, though why it was any more horrible or cruel than their own custom of burning infidels at the stake in belief that such acts found favor with God, or was more inhuman than lopping off the noses or hands of Indians in punishment for petty offenses, is hard for us to understand.

Passing through this delightful country—which appealed so strongly even to the rough adventurers that they called it "Terrestial Paradise" (*Tierra-paraiso*) they neared the city of Cempoala and were met by a deputation of twelve Indians sent by the cacique to escort them. As they neared the town, marching through well-tilled fields, trim gardens and extensive orchards, they were greeted by crowds of Indians bearing branches and garlands of flowers which were hung about the necks of the horses and the shoulders of the men. Both sexes were well clad in cotton robes elaborately worked and embroidered, all wore innumerable jewels and ornaments of gold, and all had nose rings and labrets of precious metal or semiprecious stones.

Entering the town they found it a large city of from twenty to thirty thousand inhabitants, with many imposing buildings of stone, although the homes of the masses were of adobe. But all were far superior to anything which the Dons had hitherto seen in the New World and bespoke a culture and civilization that astounded the Spaniards. The caçique met them in person, a tall and stout man of advanced years who was supported by two attendants, and greeted Cortes effusively, assigning the Spaniards quarters in a nearby temple. Food and supplies were brought to them, Cortes received a present of gold and fine fabrics, and the inhabitants vied with one another to show their friendship and hospitality.

Cortes, however, took no chances and maintained a strict guard throughout the night. The following day he paid a visit to the caçique and, as he felt bound to do, expatiated on the Christian Faith and endeavored to convert the old Indian. But the latter was not interested. He declared that his own gods were entirely satisfactory to himself and his people, and he was far more interested in Cortes' assurances that he would aid the Totonacs in throwing off the Aztec yoke, if they became his allies, than in matters of theology. He assured Cortes that he could muster more than one hundred thousand warriors, that there were other disaffected states which could be counted upon to join the alliance, and he mentioned

the republic of Tlascala which, though in the heart
of Aztec territory, had always maintained its independence and whose inhabitants were deadly enemies
of the Aztecs. He also added that he had already
heard of the terrible power of the Dons as demon-
strated in their battle with the Tabascans, but he
seemed rather doubtful of the chances of success in
a war with Montezuma's legions.

Leaving the friendly old caçique, after repeating
his assurances of help and support, and accompanied
by four hundred Indians, Cortes started for Chia-
huitztla, the Totonac capital, where he was joined
by the caçique of Cempoala. During his conference
with the natives, Cortes was interrupted by the arrival of five Aztec nobles who, Cortes was informed,
were the tribute collectors for Montezuma. At their
appearance the Totonac chiefs became cowed and
terrified, and informed Cortes that the tax collectors
resented the way in which the Totonacs had welcomed the visitors without Montezuma's authority,
and had demanded, as a penalty for so doing, twenty
young men and women to be used as sacrifices to the
Aztec gods.

Highly indignant, Cortes commanded the chiefs
to refuse the demand and to place the Aztecs under
arrest and imprison them. Terrified at thus laying hands upon the representatives of the emperor, the chiefs hesitated, but they feared the Spaniards more than the Aztecs, and at last carried out
Cortes' orders.

Then Cortes played another of his master strokes.
Secretly releasing two of the prisoners during the

night, he expressed his regret at the treatment they had received at the hands of the Totonacs, promised to aid them to escape, assured them of his friendship for Montezuma and his representatives, loaded them with presents, and sent them aboard his ships. Naturally the Totonacs were greatly excited at find-ing two of their captives had regained their liberty, and they were all for sacrificing the two others im-mediately. But Cortes still had another card up his sleeve. He reminded them that the prisoners belonged to him as he had ordered their seizure, declared they were not to be killed and, having secured possession of the Aztecs, he sent them to his ships and to safety with their comrades.

The effect of this clever if underhanded proceed-ing was exactly what Cortes had foreseen, and more than offset the bad impression he had made on Montezuma by allying himself with the Totonacs. Having thus rid himself of the Aztecs, and paved the way for a very different tale of his activities than was the truth, he sent word to the various Totonac towns ordering the chiefs to refuse any further tribute to Montezuma. But news of what had been done had already spread throughout the country, and the natives, amazed at the daring of the Span-iards and cheered with the hope of regaining their own independence, hastened to ally themselves with Cortes and to swear allegiance to the King of Spain.

In a short time another embassy arrived from the capital. Two of Montezuma's nephews and four nobles of the highest rank appeared, bringing rich gifts and a message from the emperor. He was, he said, surprised that the Spaniards should have shown friendship for the rebellious Totonacs who deserved the most severe punishment for their acts, but, as he was convinced that the Dons were the divine beings who had so long been expected, he would, out of deference to them, spare the Totonacs for the present, though full vengeance would be exacted later.

Truly Cortes' schemes were bearing fruit.

A short time after the envoys had departed with a few gifts and Cortes' compliments to their emperor, the caçique of Cempoala called upon the Dons to make good their pledges and aid him in a dispute with a hostile state. Thus obliged to prove his good faith, Cortes lost no time in marching for Cempoala and on the way he displayed his fairness and his regard for the Indians' rights which so markedly distinguished him from the other conquerors. One of the common soldiers, a fellow named Moria, raided a native house and stole some fowls. Learning of this, Cortes ordered him hanged by the roadside as an example to the men. The sentence was carried out, but Alvarado, realizing that the loss of every man counted, lingered behind and cut down the body before life was quite extinct.

Cortes also showed his remarkable diplomacy when he arrived at Cempoala. Without fighting or bloodshed, he managed to reconcile the people of the two dissenting states, and thus averted a struggle that, as he was quite aware, might kindle a war that would embroil all his allies, and at the same time he won the friendship of those who, previously, had been

hostile. Feeling that he was now sufficiently firmly
established to resume his proselyting efforts, Cortes
once more attempted to convert the Totonac chief to
Christianity. But the caçique could not see it. To
Father Olmedo's amazement, he explained that he,
too, believed in a Supreme Being, an Infinite God
who created the earth and all upon it. But he added
that he could not believe that such a Being would
take the form of humanity and allow himself to be
persecuted and put to death by the very mortals he
had created. Also, he very plainly informed the
Spaniards that he would resent any sacrilege to his
own gods, who would avenge themselves by destroying the strangers.

This was enough for Cortes. Ordering the caçique
and the high priests seized, he anounced that if a
hand was raised against the Spaniards the priests
and ruler would instantly be put to death. Then, at
a signal from Cortes, fifty soldiers rushed up the
stairway of the pyramidal temple, tore the idols from
their places and tumbled them down the steps and
burned them in the presence of the Indians. Cowed,
awed, and amazed that their gods were powerless to
avenge themselves, the people lost all faith in their
deities and clamored to become Christians. Upon
the temple's summit a cross was erected, an altar
was built, and an image of the Virgin installed.
There Father Olmedo celebrated Mass, and one
might have witnessed the strange sight of the Mexican priests, who but a short time before were tearing
the hearts from living victims of sacrifice, clad in
white robes, carrying candles in their hands and

chanting the responses to the Christian priest. Having thus converted the entire community to Christianity, and having placed a devout and disabled old soldier named Juan de Torres in charge of the sanctuary and as religious instructor to the Totonacs, Cortes departed for his settlement of Vera Cruz.

Realizing that Velasquez had in all probability sent his version of Cortes' actions to Spain, he resolved to checkmate him by dispatching one of his own ships with a letter to His Majesty, together with a present such as would win the full support of the Crown. Outlining his plan to his officers and men, Cortes announced that he was prepared to forego his share of the accumulated treasure in order to win the favor of the King, and asked that every member of the force should do likewise. Any who objected should, he assured them, have their rights respected, and the matter was left entirely to them. But not a man refused to comply with the request; a marvelous proof of the power Cortes exerted and of the men's allegiance to him. The treasure that was thus made available was enough to excite the cupidity and to earn the favor of any king, and Cortes' letter was not sparing in its praise of his own acts and of what had been accomplished in Mexico. To this was added a document signed by the officials of the little settlement, in which they lauded Cortes and vilified Velasquez, finally imploring the Crown to grant full authority to Cortes to conquer and control the country.

It was soon after the vessel bearing the letters, the

treasures, a collection of Mexican handiwork and some captive Indians had departed for Spain, that fresh trouble broke out among the Spaniards.

For some cause, either real or fancied, one of the priests, Juan Diaz, became dissatisfied with Cortes' administration. Gathering a group of Spaniards about him, he plotted to seize one of the ships, sail away to Cuba and there acquaint Velasquez with all that was taking place in Mexico. Everything was conducted with the utmost secrecy, and the vessel was provisioned and ready to sail when, on the very night planned for its departure, the plot was betrayed by one of the party who repented of his part in it. Every member of the conspiracy was arrested, a fair trial was held, and their guilt was proven beyond a doubt. The priest, though the acknowledged ringleader and the most to blame, was spared owing to his cloth, but the others were severely punished. Two were sentenced to death, another—the pilot—was sentenced to have his feet chopped off, and the others were to be flogged. Oddly enough the first man hanged was Escudero who had, years before, seized Cortes when he had incautiously stepped from his sanctuary in the church to gaze after a pretty señorita.

But the most amazing outcome of the plot was yet to follow. Realizing that if there was one conspiracy others might be formed as long as the vessels afforded a temptation to the men to desert, Cortes determined upon what was perhaps the most drastic and daring act of his entire career. Stripping his vessels of all their rigging, armament and gear, he had nine of the ships sunk. Only one small vessel remained. He literally had burned his bridges behind him. There was no choice left. They must conquer or perish!

CHAPTER VII

WAR

LEAVING a portion of his forces to garrison the newly established town, Cortes, with four hundred men, fifteen horses, seven guns and thirteen hundred Indian warriors, in addition to one thousand porters, marched inland towards the distant capital of the Aztecs. Leaving the coastal plain, they commenced the ascent of the foothills towards the mountains. Many villages were passed, but everywhere the Indians were friendly. As the higher altitudes were reached the poor natives, accustomed to the hot climate of the coast, suffered severely from the cold winds, although the Dons, in their armor and heavy equipment found the change most welcome. At times large towns were found, but in many cases these had been deserted upon the approach of the Spaniards, while at others the Aztecs treated the Dons like honored guests or were aloof and cold, but showed no open hostility. In one of the latter, a city of some twenty thousand inhabitants, the Dons found a temple wherein were fully one hundred thousand human skulls, trophies of human sacrifices, and Cortes with his customary religious zeal, declared that the idols must be thrown down and a cross erected in such a benighted spot. Fortunately for the Spaniards, the wiser counsel of Father Olmedo

prevailed. He argued that to erect a cross would
only expose it to sacrilege, that to forcibly impress
Christianity upon the natives would result in war,
and that it was wiser to await a more propitious
time.

Here, too, Cortes learned much of Montezuma and
the Aztec government. The cacique of the town informed the Spanish leader that he was running into
the lion's mouth if he persisted in marching to
Mexico, as Montezuma could command fully one
hundred and fifty thousand trained soldiers, and he
hinted that the Dons' skulls would soon be added to
the collection that increased at the rate of thirty
thousand each year. But as he had received no definite instructions as to how he was to receive the
Spaniards, he could neither declare himself their
enemy nor their friend. He therefore gave them
some small presents, provided them with food—
which after their long and weary march was far
more welcome than gold—and allowed them to remain in the city until they were ready to proceed on
their way.

A little later they reached Cholula, whose people
appeared mild and gentle, but, being warned by his
Totonac allies that they were not to be trusted,
Cortes proceeded towards the country of the Tlascalans whom he counted upon to form an alliance
with him. At the borders of Tlascalan territory
they were astonished to come upon an immense wall
constructed of huge blocks of stone, and barring a
passage fully ten miles in width. This fortification,
which was nine feet in height and twenty in thick-

ness, was pierced by a single narrow entrance less than ten feet in width and commanded by an inner wall. Had the Indians seen fit to contest the Spaniards at this point, the entire history of the conquest and of Mexico would have been altered. But for some reason or another, the wall was undefended, and the Dons passed into Tlascalan territory without hindrance.

Cortes had already sent an embassy, consisting of four Totonacs, to the Tlascalan government with a request to be allowed to pass through the republic, and assuring the natives of his friendship; but doubtful as to the reception he would receive from this valiant and independent nation, he was unremitting in his vigilance and made his weary men sleep in full armor and with their weapons by their side. And, as it happened, it was fortunate for them that they did so.

The arrival of Cortes' envoys in the Tlascalan capital aroused the greatest excitement. The people had been fully informed of the arrival of the Spaniards and of all their movements. They knew of Cortes' alliance with the Totonacs, but their suspicions of the Dons' good faith were aroused by the fact that Cortes and Montezuma had exchanged communications and presents. Their rulers were divided as to the treatment they should accord the Spaniards, and while some insisted they should be received as friends, others were just as insistent that they should be regarded as enemies. The old chief, Xicotencatl, in particular, was all for war. Taking a leaf from the Spaniards' book of treachery and perfidy, he suggested that the Tlascalan army should fall upon the Dons at once. If, he explained, they were victorious all would be well, while in case the Dons triumphed, the Tlascalan officials could express regret at the attack, declare it was an unauthorized act, and make peace. He was supported in this by his son, the war chief of the same name, and in order that the Totonacs should not carry word of the plans to Cortes, they were held as prisoners.

Ignorant of what was taking place in Tlascala, but troubled because his emissaries did not return, Cortes pushed on, and the next day came upon a small body of Indians who fled at the Spaniards' approach. Spurring their horses in pursuit, the Spaniards in advance soon overtook the natives. But to their confusion and surprise the Tlascalans, instead of tamely submitting, turned and fought viciously. In itself the skirmish would have amounted to little, but as the Dons were battling with this small party they were terrified to see a swarming horde of warriors bearing down upon them from every side. Furiously, desperately, they fought for their lives. One Don was dragged from his horse and killed. Two horses were decapitated by the jagged-edged swords of the Tlascalans. Scores of the Spaniards were wounded, and the Dons were on the point of being wiped out when their companions and Totonac allies came to their rescue. Mowed down by the artillery and cavalry, filled with superstitious terror of the thundering cannon that they had never before seen, the

Indians retreated and the Spaniards were only too glad to rest on their victory. The next day they were met by Tlascalan envoys, with two of Cortes' Totonac envoys, and were promised a friendly reception, the Tlascalans assuring Cortes that the attack had been unauthorized.

But when, on the following day, the other two Totonacs met the Dons and told of being made prisoners and threatened with sacrifice, and declared that the Tlascalans were in arms and massed to attack the Spaniards, the Dons began to realize the jeopardy in which they had placed themselves. Realizing that to wait would only arouse greater forebodings in his men, Cortes determined to advance and when, a little later, the Dons met the warriors of Tlascala and charged them, the Indians retreated with little resistance. Elated at their victory, unacquainted with the subtlety and military resourcefulness of their enemies, the Spaniards dashed after their foes, until entering a narrow ravine, they found themselves surrounded by thousands of warriors. With the sun glinting on their cuirasses of silver and gold, with their gold helmets flashing fire, with the waving plumes of their headdresses, wearing the white and yellow feather mantles, the white and yellow garments and bearing the white and yellow shields of Xicotencatl's army, and with his banner—a heron upon a rock—waving above them, the host of Tlascalans shouted their war cry and fell upon the ambushed Dons. In an instant it had become a hand-to-hand struggle. At such close quarters bows and arrows, crossbows and arquebuses were of little use. The lances and flashing swords, the battle-axes and daggers of the Dons, and the javelins, clubs, obsidian-edged swords of the Indians thrust, hewed, slashed and battered on steel mail and quilted cotton. Indians fell by hundreds; Spaniards were wounded, killed, torn from their horses, but the Indians' desire to take prisoners for sacrifice, rather than to kill outright, saved the Spaniards from annihilation. Even as it was, it seems incredible, almost miraculous that any escaped, and still more miraculous that, literally cutting their way through the Indians' ranks, they managed to reach an open plain beyond.

Once in the open, guns and cannon could be brought into play, and finding themselves at a disadvantage, the Tlascalans withdrew in good order. Just what the losses were on both sides will never be known. According to the Spaniards less than a dozen Dons were killed and less than half their number wounded, while more than five thousand Tlascalans were killed. But the Spaniards invariably exaggerated the losses of their foes and underrated those of their own forces. It was, however, the most desperate battle they had yet fought, but worse was to follow. Now, for the first time, the Spaniards fully recognized the hard row they had to hoe, the fact that they were not pitting themselves against unorganized, untrained savages, but against disciplined, well-armed, valiant and resourceful soldiers of a civilized race.

Many a Don, as the forces rested and patched and plastered their wounded bodies, felt misgivings as to the future; many were for then and there turning back; and many would have given all their chances for future riches to have been safely back in Cuba. But to dream of return was hopeless. Cortes had seen to that, and forward was the word, even though to go forward they went to their deaths. And the message brought to them by envoys from their enemies was not reassuring. The Dons might pass through the country whenever they chose, declared the Tlascalan general, but, he added, it would be to have the hearts torn from their bodies on the sacrificial altars of Tlascala.

Cortes, however, was undaunted. The greater the odds, the greater a struggle appealed to him, and without hesitation he decided to take the bull by the horns and attack the enemy before the Indians were ready to receive him. But even Cortes felt in doubt of the issue when, on the following day, the Spaniards came in sight of the Tlascalan army, an army of fifty thousand Indians covering a plain over six miles square. No longer were the Dons to face the legions of Xicotencatl alone. Above the thousands of waving plumes, of feather mantles, of grotesque headdresses in the form of animal heads, and the vast array of gleaming spears, swords, and war clubs, waved the golden eagle banner of Tlascala, the white heron of Xicotencatl, the plumed serpent of Quetzaltenango, and many another standard of the Tlascalan and Otomic chiefs.

The shock, as the two forces met, was terrific. The conquerors, four hundred strong and now backed by more than three thousand Indian allies, hurled

themselves upon a solid mass of their foes. Clouds
of arrows, harpoons, stones from slings, and javelins, hurled by the power of the throwing-sticks or
atlatls, rained upon the Dons. Many a missile found
its mark and penetrated the joints of the Spanish
mail. Many an obsidian-edged sword sheared deep
into Spanish flesh. Many a heavy war club thudded
on a Spanish helmet and knocked the senses from its
wearer. But for every blow three were given, and
the superior weapons of the Spaniards wreaked terrible vengeance. So closely packed were the Tlascalans, so numerous, that those in the rear forced
those in front upon the Spaniards with irresistible
force. Even had they wished to retreat they could
not, and as fast as those in the front ranks fell others
stepped into their places. Slowly, surely, the Dons,
fighting as they had never fought before, were driven
back. All seemed lost. Then the tide turned. The
Indians were too closely formed, too crowded to use
their weapons to the best advantage, and as, rallying
for a moment, the Spaniards brought their cannon
into action, the ranks of the Tlascans were mowed
down by hundreds. Still they pressed forward
oblivious of wounds, oblivious of death, intent only
on wiping the Dons from the face of the land. And
in a short time more they would have succeeded had
not dissensions arisen between their leaders. A
chief, piqued at being reprimanded by Xicotencatl
for the manner in which he handled his men, withdrew his forces from the battle. Others followed
him, and presently Xicotencatl with his army alone
remained. Realizing that he was losing, he withdrew

after five hours of steady fighting, and the wearied, wounded Dons were only too thankful to retire to their camp.

Scarcely one of the Spaniards escaped without injuries, every horse was wounded, their Totonac allies had been decimated, and a number of the Spaniards had been killed. Burying their dead secretly, for Cortes wished to keep up the Indians' belief that the Spaniards were immortal, he sent another message to the Tlascalans asking if they were ready for peace.

The rulers all urged a cessation of hostilities, but Xicotencatl and the other war-chiefs, anxious to retrieve their defeat, and now convinced that the Dons were human beings like themselves, stood out for war. In their dilemma the caçiques called upon their priests for advice to decide whether or not the Spaniards were men or gods. Having consulted their omens and gods, the priests declared that the Dons were not gods but were the sons of gods, and that as they drew their power and their invincibility from the sun they were helpless and weak after sundown, and should be attacked at night. Although this was contrary to all the natives' rules and customs of warfare, yet it was agreed that Xicotencatl should secretly approach the Spanish force that night and destroy the supposedly helpless white men.

Unfortunately for the Indians, their approach was seen, and Cortes, silently arousing his men, ordered them to remain noiseless as though still asleep until the signal was given to charge. Cautiously and as

silently as shadows the Tlascalans crept forward
until, when on the point of rushing the supposedly
sleeping camp, the soldiers sprang from the earth,
and with flashing swords and blazing arquebuses
charged down upon them. Surprised, terrified, disorganized, with all their superstitious fears aroused,
the Indians turned and fled, only to be pursued and
cut down by the Dons.

The following day Cortes sent still another message to the Tlascalans by means of the captive chiefs
he had taken, offering forgiveness if peace was
declared, but threatening to destroy every Tlascalan
and every Tlascalan village if his offer were not
accepted. There was nothing for the Tlascalans but
to submit. Messengers were sent back assuring
Cortes of friendship and free passage through the
country, and in order that there might be no mistake,
these messengers were ordered to visit Xicotencatl
and instruct him to surrender and to send supplies
to the Dons. That gallant warrior refused to comply
with the orders, however, and seizing the messengers,
held them prisoners. Admirable and magnificent as
was his bravery and his determination to defend his
country and his people to the last, yet, under the
circumstances, it was a foolish act. Its immediate
result was to bring down the vengeance of Cortes
upon the heads of the innocent country folk, for
when the envoys failed to return with an answer to
his message, Cortes, though so ill with fever that he
scarcely could keep his saddle, led a raiding party
into the country and pillaged, burned and murdered
without mercy. Inexcusable as these brutal reprisals

were, yet Cortes wrote to the King of Spain that, as he "fought under the Cross for the True Faith, multitudes of infidels were slain with little loss to the Christians." But he failed to add that the "multitude of infidels" were unarmed, defenseless peasantry.

At this time, too, discontent again broke out among his men. They had secured little enough gold since leaving the coast, they had found only hardships, hard knocks and weary fighting in place of treasure, and had it not been for Marina they would have broken into open mutiny. But the Aztec girl cheered them and urged them to abide by Cortes' orders and will, until the men, ashamed to show their fears and to complain of their hardships when a frail woman had endured as much as they without a complaint, became once more reconciled.

A few days later several Indians approached wearing white badges as a sign of a truce. But Marina suspected them of being spies, and when her suspicions were proved true, Cortes ordered their hands cut off and sent them back to their chief. Barbarous and cruel as such an act may seem, we must remember that a much worse fate was usually in store for spies, and that, in the time of the Conquest, amputating hands or limbs was a recognized legal punishment for minor offenses. The Tlascalan chief, horrified—as he well might be—at this mutilation of his men, and amazed that the Dons could "read their very thoughts," felt himself obliged to surrender.

Attended by his captains, he appeared before

Cortes and offered his allegiance and friendship, at the same time frankly assuming all responsibility for the continuance of hostilities. Even Cortes was forced to express his respect and admiration for this valiant, heroic Indian, whose appearance and personality were in keeping with his bravery. Tall and muscular, with a fine head and erect carriage, he had a commanding presence. His features were regular and fine, and, to the Spaniards' surprise, he wore a thin beard and mustache. He was magnificently clad in a costume of finest cotton embroidered with gold; a gold breastplate covered his chest, a leather casque plated with gold and set with gems was upon his head, and leather boots with gold ornaments covered his feet and legs. Ornaments set with large green gems were in his ears and about his neck; a splendid feather mantle of yellow and white fell from his shoulders, and a tall plume of white and yellow feathers rose above his helmet.

Having made obeisance to Cortes, he drew himself up proudly and haughtily, declaring that he knew the Dons were mortal and the enemies of his people, although, he added, the Spaniards might be the sons of Quetzalcoatl. For himself, he told Cortes, he had only the desire for the freedom of his people and his country. He bowed to superior powers, but he hoped the Spaniards would use their victory and powers in moderation and would not make reprisals for his act upon the people who were not to blame. He then tendered Cortes a present of a number of gold objects, apologizing for such a small gift by explaining that the Tlascalans were poor, as Monte-

zuma had left them nothing but their freedom and
their bravery.

Cortes, stern soldier that he was, could recognize
bravery in another, and he assured Xicotencatl that
the past was over and was forgiven, that he was
honored to have the Tlascalans as allies, and as for
the gift, he prized it more coming from such a brave
man than a house full of gold from any other—a well
turned and complimentary speech indeed for a victorious Don to make to an infidel chieftain.

The war with the Tlascalans was over. The most
valiant and warlike of the Mexican tribes were allies
of the Dons, and Cortes felt that he could now march
on Mexico with far more chances of success than
ever before.

CHAPTER VIII

ONWARD TO THE CAPITAL

UNKNOWN to the Spaniards, every move in this war with the Tlascalans had been watched with interest and then with forebodings by Montezuma. Daily reports, both by messengers' lips and by means of codices, were brought to him and when, at last, he heard of the Dons' victory over the Tlascalans, he felt his worst fears realized. Men who could so easily overcome that nation with apparently no loss to themselves must indeed be more than mortals. In his mind there was no longer a doubt that they were the sons of Quetzalcoatl. In that case the doom of his empire was sealed, a conjecture in which he was perfectly right, for the doom of the Aztecs had been sealed from the moment the Spaniards set foot on Mexican soil.

Why the Aztec ruler should not immediately have bowed to Destiny and the will of his gods is a mystery. The Indian, whether savage or civilized, is invariably a fatalist, and seldom or never does he attempt to resist in the face of what he believes is Destiny. But Montezuma, though he had been a high priest before he had ascended his throne, and though intensely religious and superstitious, still hoped to evade the fulfillment of the ancient prophecy.

He no longer thought of war as a means to thwart
Fate, but he foolishly believed that he might succeed in propitiating the divinities in human form
who were marching on his capital.

So, selecting five of his highest nobles, he sent
them to Cortez, together with two thousand slaves
laden with more than half a million dollars in gold,
with the richest of feather mantles and with every
prized object of Aztec workmanship, and, moreover,
with his congratulations on the Spaniards' victories.
But at the same time he expressed his regret that it
would be impossible for him to receive the Spaniards
in Tenochtitlan, where he claimed a rebellion had
broken out. However, he added, if the Spaniards
would forego their intended visit he would send a
great treasure to the King of Spain as tribute and to
show his friendship for his fellow-monarch.

This was Montezuma's greatest mistake. He
showed at once his weakness and his fears, and he
revealed to the avaricious visitors that he possessed vast riches.

None of this was lost upon the astute Cortes. He
fully realized that the Aztec king was trembling
upon his throne, but he had no desire to put him on
his guard. For the time his policy was suavity and
pretended friendship, and he sent back word that
while he could not hope to equal the emperor's gift
by a present in return, he would "repay him some
day with good works!"

Then, as another clever stroke of genius, he invited two of the Aztec envoys to remain with him,

accompany him on his march and observe how matters went.

Thus having checkmated Montezuma's moves, and now fully determined to lose no time in making for the capital, Cortes marched towards the city of Tlascala. As the Spaniards approached the city the people welcomed them as enthusiastically as they had attacked them a few days previously. Crowds thronged the roads to meet and accompany them. Women decked the men and horses with garlands of flowers. Priests scattered incense and called upon their gods to protect and favor them, and, like the conquering hero he was, Cortes led his motley army into the ancient city. Everywhere the houses were decorated and hung with flowers. People packed the streets and the flat roofs of the houses, and the air was a tumult of songs, music and shouts of welcome. Through the close-packed, rejoicing throng the Spaniards marched to the house of the elder Xicotencatl, one of the four rulers of the republic, where Cortes dismounted and embraced the old and blind chief. A splendid banquet was then served, and the Dons were given quarters in the principal temple.

Even the Spaniards, who were now becoming accustomed to marvels, were astonished at the size and magnificence of Tlascala. Cortes, in his letter to the King of Spain, declared it was larger, finer and more populous than Granada, and while this may have been a bit of exaggeration, there is no doubt that it was an imposing city. Its population at that time was in the neighborhood of one hun-

dred thousand, and while the majority of the houses
were of adobe, they were large, well-built and covered with ornate stucco work which gave them a
substantial and rich appearance. But the principal
buildings, the temples, the palaces and the great
pyramidal *teocallis* were of sculptured stone. Moreover, the town possessed an excellent police force,
there were hot and cold public baths, and as the
Tlascalans (as well as the Aztecs) possessed fairly
heavy beards, there were a number of barber shops
in the city. The town was in reality four cities, each
originally the home of a distinct tribe and built at
different periods, but now confederated and ruled
by four caçiques or chiefs. Cut off from all inter-
course or commerce with the rest of the country by
the ever hostile Aztecs, Tlascala much resembled the
little European republic of Andorra, for its whole
extent was comprised within the city and its re-
stricted surrounding fields. Primarily agricultural-
ists, noted for their arts and especially their fine
pottery, the Tlascalans, hard-working, industrious
and hardy, were proud, independent and intensely
patriotic.

Among these people, who now seemed as fast
friends as they had before been implacable foes, the
Dons passed some time in a round of festivities, at
the end of which Cortes decided it was time to attempt to convert them to Christianity. The time
seemed especially right—almost as if Providence
had arranged it—for the chiefs, hoping thus to show
their allegiance and to secure the friendship of the
Dons, suggested that Cortes and his officers should

marry the princesses. To this Cortes replied that
such an alliance was impossible as long as the Tlascalans remained infidels. Then, with Father Olmedo's help, he expounded the Faith. Having duly listened to the discourse, the chiefs declared they had
no doubt of the power of the strangers' God and
they were quite willing to give Him a prominent
place among their own, but that they could not and
would not dispense with deities who had served them
and their people so well and faithfully for countless
generations. In fact, they added, the Tlascalans
were as fond of their religion as of their liberty and
were prepared to defend it just as strenuously and
zealously.

This opposition as usual only made Cortes the
more determined to accomplish his purpose, and had
not Father Olmedo almost literally thrown himself
in Cortes' way the fanatical leader might have become a martyr instead of a conqueror. It was useless, the good padre declared, to establish the Faith
outwardly if the people remained pagans at heart.
As soon as the Spaniards left the spot any images
or crosses they erected would be desecrated and destroyed. To throw down the idols and defy the Tlascalans would be to transform them from powerful
allies to implacable foes. And he reminded Cortes
that the patriotic warriors of the little republic
were not to be so easily cowed and trifled with as the
Totonacs. Even then Cortes was obdurate, but when
Alvarado, De Leon and others added their remon-
strances to those of the priest, he at last agreed to
let the matter drop for the present, although he

eased his conscience by insisting that all the prisoners reserved for sacrifice should be freed.

It speaks volumes for the allegiance of the Tlascalans that they consented to this, and even permitted the Dons to erect a cross for themselves and to hold their own services in the plaza. In return for this toleration, Cortes agreed to his officers accepting the Tlascalan brides, provided they embraced Christianity, and, after having been baptized, the princesses were married with all the pomp and ceremony of the Church. One of these princesses, who was christened Doña Luisa, became the bride of Alvarado. She was a daughter of Xicotencatl, and the descendants of the couple became nobles of Spain.

Hardly had the wedding bells ceased—metaphorically, of course—to ring when another embassy arrived from Montezuma, this time bearing an invitation for the Spaniards to visit the emperor in his capital, assuring them of a cordial reception, and suggesting that Cortes should take his route through Cholula. To the friendly Tlascalans, the whole matter savored of a trap, and they earnestly advised Cortes to avoid it and most especially to be wary of the Cholulans whom, they declared, were fanatical adherents of Montezuma and were noted for their treachery. While these discussions were taking place, another embassy arrived. This, however, was not from the Aztec monarch but from one of his deadliest enemies, a prince named Ixtlilzochitl who, before Montezuma's enthronement, had been an aspirant for the throne.

He now offered Cortes his friendship and support,

and another ally was added to the Spaniards' cause.

About the same time, messengers arrived from Cholula inviting Cortes to visit them, and this only aroused more suspicions in the minds of the Tlascalans. But Cortes, feeling secure in his own resourcefulness and power, decided to disregard their advice and to march to Cholula.

Cholula, the greatest commercial center of the empire, was a large and magnificent city of extreme antiquity, and was the center of many of the most important arts and manufactures of Mexico. Metalworking, weaving, paper-making and various other industries flourished in the city, which, like Tlascala, was a self-contained republic but was under Aztec rule. Like most industrial and commercial races, the Cholulans were averse to war and were regarded as weak and effeminate by their more warlike neighbors. But the principal importance of the city lay in the fact that it was a religious center, an Aztecan Mecca, for, according to tradition, it was at Cholula that the Plumed Serpent (Quetzalcoatl) had passed twenty years while teaching the people their arts, religion and civilization. And here had been built the stupendous pyramidal temple in his honor, an edifice that was hoary with age when the first Aztecs had overrun the country. Its base covered nearly fifty acres, it was nearly two hundred feet in height, and on its summit was a magnificent temple containing an immense image of Quetzalcoatl laden with golden ornaments and jewels. From every quarter of the land, and from distant points in Central America, pilgrims journeyed to this revered spot to make offerings to the hero-god, while around his great temple were clustered the shrines and lesser temples of scores of other gods and divinities. Cholula was the Holy City of Anahuac as the Mexicans called their country, and from six to ten thousand human sacrifices were annually offered upon the altars of the city's three hundred temples.

Towards this city of temples marched the conquerors, accompanied by their horde of Totonac allies and six thousand of the Tlascalan warriors—an imposing army indeed. Reaching the city, near which he was met by a Cholulan escort, Cortes ordered the bulk of the allies to remain outside, and entered with only his own countrymen and a handful of Indian porters. For a time the Dons were shown every courtesy and hospitality, and Cortes' suspicions were allayed.

But presently a messenger arrived from Montezuma, and unknown to Cortes, held a conference with the chiefs, after which the attitude of the Cholulans completely altered. The people became cool and aloof, the supplies of food were reduced, and when streets were found barricaded and women and children daily left the city, Cortes' fears were again aroused. At this time Marina again proved her value and her faithfulness. From the wife of a cacique with whom she was on friendly terms, she learned all the details of a conspiracy to destroy the Spaniards as they left the city. Cortes for once seemed to have been caught in a net from which there was no escape. The city was filled with armed men and twenty thousand Aztec troops lay in wait

outside.   Every house was a potential fortress.
Either to fight or to flee meant irreparable loss, perhaps annihilation. But Cortes was not discouraged.
Where force was of no avail, guile might triumph,
as he had repeatedly proved, and once more he resorted to diplomacy, trickery and subtlety. Rebuk-
ing the priests and caçiques for their coldness, he
informed them he would leave the city the following
day, but requested as a last favor that they should
provide two thousand men to transport his baggage
and artillery to the camp of his Indian allies. He
then summoned Montezuma's emissaries, told them
he was aware of the plot but declared he was loth to
believe that the monarch could have incited such a
nefarious scheme, and placed them under guard so
they could not communicate with the Cholulans. At
daybreak the next morning he arranged his troops
and guns in accordance with the plans he had
formed, having meantime sent word to the Tlascalans to advance on the city at a prearranged signal.
With the plaza wherein he was quartered surrounded
by his men concealed in the buildings, and with his
cannon commanding all the streets leading to it, he
awaited the arrival of the caçiques and the two thousand porters he had demanded. Scarcely had they
gathered in the square when, at the signal of a gunshot, the massacre commenced.

Packed closely in the plaza, unarmed as they were,
the Spaniards' hail of crossbow bolts and musket
balls mowed them down by scores. Then with drawn
swords the Spaniards fell upon them. Those who
tried to escape by way of the avenues were de-

stroyed by the cannon, and in the midst of the butchery the fierce Tlascalans fell upon the rear of the defenseless Cholulans. Few escaped. All but one
small group were slaughtered, and this handful of
survivors sought sanctuary on one of the nearby
pyramids under protection of their gods.

But their deities had no power to guard them from
the relentless Dons. Finding it impossible to scale
the hundred and more steps of the *teocalli* in the face
of missiles hurled from above, the Spaniards by
flaming arrows set fire to the wooden temple on the
summit. Still the Cholulans refused to surrender
and be put to death. Some hurled themselves to the
earth far below, others with prayers to their gods
threw themselves into the flames.

But the Dons were not yet satisfied. Through the
city they and their allies raged; murdering, muti-
lating, burning, looting; but in all the wild riot and
confusion Cortes' commands not to molest women
and children were obeyed.

At last, satiated with bloodshed, loaded with treasure, the Dons paused in their destruction and Cortes
ordered the sacking of the city to cease. It had been
a terrible, an inhuman reprisal; but Cortes was ever
a magnanimous victor and he now assured the
caçiques that all who acknowledged their allegiance
would be pardoned and protected. He then ordered
his Tlascalans to release all the prisoners they had
taken. By these pacific measures he restored confidence, and presently the city was as peaceful as ever
despite the fact that from five to six thousand of its
inhabitants had been slain.

Brutal, inhuman, treacherous and unfair as was this massacre at Cortes' orders, yet it was by no means as cruel nor as destructive as would have been the struggle that would have ensued had the Cholulans been successful in carrying out their designs. And while we cannot forgive the conqueror for wreaking vengeance on unsuspecting, unarmed and probably wholly innocent noncombatants, yet we must remember that self-preservation is man's first instinct and most important duty, and that Cortes saw no other means of preserving the lives of himself and his men.

Moreover, Cortes permitted no acts of individual violence, abuse or excesses that he could prevent. He expressly forbade all acts of violence against women and children; he prohibited resorting to tortures, and he did not countenance looting. Naturally, among such a horde of Indian allies and almost equally savage Spaniards, many acts of wanton violence were committed. But in every case that was brought to Cortes' notice prompt and severe penalties were dealt out to the offenders.

We cannot vindicate Cortes—for that matter there is no vindication for his conquest in the first place—but we can at least find mitigating circumstances for his actions while, in comparison with his contemporaries and those who followed after him, he was humane, admirable and almost gentle in his conduct.

And whatever may have been the moral aspect of Cortes' act its results were most satisfactory, as far as the Spaniards were concerned. Combined with the superstitious fears of the natives was dread of the vengeance the Dons could exact, and no individual in the entire empire was so filled with both dread and superstitious fears as Montezuma.

Each day his predestined fate and the fate of his empire was drawing nearer. Already he saw himself dethroned, his empire destroyed, the religion of his ancestors overthrown and the white strangers—the sons of Quetzalcoatl—ruling the land. Feeling himself doomed, realizing his own helplessness, yet he still deluded himself with hopes of somehow averting the impending catastrophe, and sought wildly, impotently for some means of saving his empire from its fate.

Meanwhile, with little opposition, the Spaniards were rapidly approaching the capital. They crossed the Sierras, reached the high interior tableland, and at last, emerging from a mountain pass, looked down upon the fair valley of Mexico and the capital of the Aztecs.

CHAPTER IX

THE CONQUEROR MEETS THE EMPEROR

TENOCHTITLAN as viewed by Cortes and his men was an imposing sight. It was more than twelve miles in circumference and contained upwards of sixty thousand houses with a population close to half a million, while other towns clustered about the shores of the gleaming Lake Tezcuco—suburbs we might say—were nearly as large, the total number of inhabitants being several millions. Built as it was upon the shores of the lake, and much of it extending over the water, canals took the place of many streets. Bisecting the city at right angles were four broad avenues that were carried across the lake on causeways of masonry with numerous bridges to permit the passage of canoes and boats to and from the city. The houses of the poorer classes were of adobe, but the majority of buildings and homes were well built of red stone, often elaborately sculptured, and coated with white stucco. They were mainly one story in height with flat roofs or *azoteas* and were gay with potted plants, vines and flowers. Towering high above these were the immense pyramidal temples or *teocallis* (literally High Places) built of stone in a series of terraces or platforms with winding stairways leading to the summits. On the tops were the temples proper, stone or elaborately carved wooden structures, within which were the images of the god or gods to whom the pyramid was dedicated.

Largest of all these was the temple of Huitzilopochtli, the war-god, with its enclosing walls nearly five thousand feet around and decorated with sculptures of festooned snakes—the *coetpantli* or sacred serpents. Within the court thus formed the mighty pyramid rose, in a series of six terraces, to its summit three hundred feet and more above the earth, and topped by two three-storied towers sixty feet in height. Here were the sacred fires, the statues of the bloodthirsty god, and the great sacrificial stone of jasper drenched with the blood of thousands of victims. As in every other temple throughout the empire, the fires of the temple burned continuously, and it was firmly believed by the Aztecs that the extinction of the sacred fire would bring the power of the Aztecs to an end.

Surrounding this largest pyramid were more than forty others, among them the Pyramid of the Skulls, wherein were stored the gruesome souvenirs of the human sacrifices that, at the time of the Spaniards' arrival, numbered over one hundred and thirty-six thousand.

Even though their minds were filled with thoughts of the gold and riches so nearly within their grasp, though they were despoilers intent on destroying and ravishing the city, yet the visitors halted and gazed in admiration upon the vast, magnificent capital and the shimmering blue lake in its setting of rich and verdant gardens and tilled fields. And as they mentally estimated the city's size and the millions who dwelt within it, even their hearts sank, and they felt far less confidence in their success than they had heretofore. Compared with the multitude that dwelt in the city and its environs, their force— even with its thousands of Indian allies—seemed puny indeed, a force woefully inadequate for the conquest of the Aztec capital and a contest with the armies of its ruler. Indeed, their forebodings were such that many were for turning back even at this late hour, and they begged Cortes to retreat from the verge of what, to their minds, was certain disaster.

But Cortes, his avarice and religious zeal aroused by the rich and populous valley before his eyes, had no misgivings. No fear of the outcome crossed his mind, and by arguments, threats, cajolery and by appeal to their gallantry, honor and avarice in turn, he won over the more timid of his followers and continued his march. Everywhere, as the Dons passed through the many villages of the valley, they were met with tokens of friendship, and everywhere, too, Cortes heard complaints of the tyranny of Montezuma and of the oppression of the Aztecs. Realizing that this disaffection would all be in his favor, Cortes returned courtesy for courtesy, and assured the people of his friendship and aid.

Long before they reached the city itself the Spaniards were met by embassies from the emperor who, now fairly quaking with terror, was making a final mad effort to prevent the Spaniards from entering the city.

MONTEZUMA

He sent rich presents, he offered to send Cortes
four loads of gold and to give a load to each officer,
and he offered to pay a stupendous annual tribute
if only they would turn back. But in so doing the emperor only made his situation the worse, and the
conquerors the more determined to attain their goal.
Finding bribes and promises had no avail, he summoned his councilors for advice, but found them
worse than nothing. Some were for peace at any
price, others were for war to the last, and still others
advised accepting whatever fate Destiny had in store
for them. Finding he could secure no aid and no
support from these men, he decided to receive the
Spaniards with every courtesy and honor and trust
to his friendship being held sacred, and to this end
he sent the King of Tezcuco, second only to himself,
as an envoy to Cortes.

He arrived, carried in a palanquin covered with
plates of gold and encrusted with gems, above which
was a canopy of green feathers of the Quetzal or Re-
splendent Trogan, the sacred bird of the Aztecs.
Dismounting from his litter he bowed before Cortes,
presented him with three enormous priceless pearls,
and bade the Spaniards welcome. Embracing him
like a brother, Cortes presented the prince with
some glass beads, and assured him of his esteem and
friendship.

The Dons had now come to the shores of the lake,
and marched forward, eight abreast, upon the broad
stone causeway stretching towards the distant city
that gleamed like silver in the sunshine. On all sides
the Indians, decked in their gayest finery, poled or

paddled their canoes, singing and laughing, keeping pace with the Spaniards, and tossing flowers and fruits at their feet. Presently, too, they passed the floating gardens or *chinampas*, ablaze with flowers, bearing patches of intensively cultivated earth, adjoining the tiny thatched huts of their owners in the shade of banana trees. Charmed, amazed, wondering at each new sight and scene, the Spaniards pressed forward until they entered the suburb of Itzapalapan, governed by Montezuma's brother, Cuitlahua. Here the Spaniards were received in royal style by the prince and his nobles; a wonderful gift of gold and other treasures was presented to Cortes, and a magnificent banquet was served.

Although a comparatively small town, of only four or five thousand houses, yet architecturally and in its arrangement it was even superior to the capital.

The buildings were all of stone, with roofs of aromatic cedar, and in the heart of the city were the royal gardens, a great park of several acres filled with plants, trees and shrubs from every corner of the empire, traversed by walks and paths, irrigated by canals, and among other things including an immense aviary filled with bright-plumaged birds, a menagerie of beasts and reptiles, and a huge aquarium. Amid these delightful surroundings the Spaniards spent the night.

At daybreak the next morning, the eighth of November, 1519, the trumpets called the soldiers to form, and leading his army of nearly seven thousand men, Cortes resumed his way to Tenochtitlan. About two miles from the city they came to a wall of solid rock twelve feet in height that crossed the dyke. On either side were battlemented towers and in the center was a fortified doorway that was thrown open as the Dons approached. As they stared at this evidence of the Aztec's military knowledge, the Spaniards realized how well the city was protected. But little did any of them dream how important a part this fort of Zoloc was to play in their future.

Here the cavalcade was met by several hundred Aztec chiefs and nobles, dressed in their finest garments and feather robes, wearing the red, white and green colors of Mexico, and loaded with ornaments of gold, silver, jade, precious stones and mosaic work. Having received the homage and the respects of these nobles—a process that required more than an hour—the Dons entered the city gates and crossing the drawbridge that spanned a wide canal stood within the streets of the Aztec capital.

Presently shouts, music and songs announced the approach of the Aztec emperor, surrounded by his retinue and bodyguard. Seated in his royal litter ablaze with gold and silver, and carried on the shoulders of nobles, the emperor was sheltered from the sun by a red, white and green canopy of feathers, borne by four princes. As he approached Cortes he dismounted, and attendants quickly spread mats of finest cotton cloth before him so that his imperial feet might not touch the earth, while the common people prostrated themselves upon the ground. He was clad in the costume of his race, a single one-piece garment of cotton secured about his waist by a girdle of woven fiber and gold threads. From his shoulders hung a magnificent feather cloak in the national colors. Gold-soled sandals were upon his feet, and cloak, girdle and sandals were decorated with pearls, emeralds and turquoise. Upon his head he wore a fillet of gold, bearing the royal insignia, the long fernlike tail plumes of the sacred Quetzal. Taller than the average, lean but well built, Montezuma was fair-skinned for an Indian—fairer in fact than the majority of Dons who gazed curiously at him—and a thin beard and mustache covered his chin and lip. He moved slowly, majestically, and the visitors were surprised to see that, instead of the savage, malignant-looking potentate they had expected from the accounts of the Tlascalans, the Aztec emperor was a quiet, benign and pleasant-looking man who, clad in European dress, might have passed for a Spanish grandee or a member of the aristocracy of Italy or France.

Who can picture, who imagine the sensations of the two, as Cortes and Montezuma met? Before Cortes stood the Aztec king of whom he had heard so much, from whom he had received princely gifts, whose subjects he had fought and vanquished and whose kingdom and power he intended to destroy. Before Montezuma stood the semisupernatural being who had defied him, who had overcome all obstacles, who seemed invincible, whose coming had been foretold centuries before, and who, he felt in his heart, was to cause his own death and the destruction of his empire.

But he showed no sign of any bitter thoughts that might have been in his mind. He expressed his

pleasure at seeing the Dons in his capital, compli-
mented Cortes upon his safe arrival and his victories, and expressed his friendship.

Cortes, actually impressed and deeply moved, expressed his most profound respect for the monarch,
thanked him for his many gifts, assured him of his
friendship, and placed a string of colored glass
beads about the emperor's neck. Montezuma then
delegated his brother to conduct the Spaniards
through the streets to the residence prepared for
them, and entering his golden litter, was carried to
his palace.

As the Spaniards passed onward they were more
and more impressed with the size, the magnificence
and the perfection of the city. On all sides of the
broad straight avenue were splendid residences;
here and there were open plazas and market places.
People thronged everywhere; canoes filled with Indians choked the canals. Stone bridges spanned the
waterways and, looming high against the blue sky
and the distant snow-capped mountains, were the
lofty pyramidal temples of sacrifice. At the great
central plaza the Dons halted. Before them, on the
spot where now stands the cathedral, rose the temple
of the war-god, and, facing this, were the low spacious buildings that had been the palace of Montezuma's father, Axayacatl. This had been prepared as
the barracks for the Spaniards, and Montezuma in
person was awaiting them in the courtyard.

As Cortes approached, the emperor held in his
hands a magnificent gold collar set with shells and
gems, from which depended golden crayfish eight

inches in length. Placing this precious gift about the Spaniard's neck, Montezuma assured him that the palace belonged to him, and, advising him to rest after the long journey, he promised to return and visit him again in a short time.

Having allotted his men to their various quarters —and with his invariable foresight placed his guns so they commanded all approaches—he issued orders forbidding any soldier to leave his quarters without permission under penalty of death. Then, having assured himself that everything was in order, he partook (as did his men) of a bountiful meal provided by his hosts. True to his promise, Montezuma returned in a few hours and found Cortes much refreshed after his siesta. A long conversation ensued, each trying to obtain all possible information regarding the other, at the close of which Montezuma signaled for his attendants to bring the presents for his guests. These consisted of enough fine cotton to supply every man, including the Indian allies, with a suit; a vast quantity of golden chains and other ornaments; and an abundance of feather-work, gems and other choice specimens of Aztec art. He then withdrew, expressing his wish that Cortes should visit him in his palace the following morning.

Attended by Alvarado and several other cavaliers, Cortes made his way to the royal palace, a vast pile of red stone with Montezuma's arms—an eagle bearing an ocelot in its talons—over the doorway. Within were spacious courts with sparkling fountains that supplied water for more than one hundred baths.

The low, immense rooms were carpeted with reed mats and skins of wild beasts. Incense burners gave out the exotic odors of sandalwood, jasmine, orange and other scents, and upon the walls were richly painted and embroidered tapestries and the choicest pictures and panels of delicate feather-work.

Scarcely had Cortes completed the first formal greetings to the emperor, who sat upon his magnificent gold and jeweled throne, before he plunged into his favorite subject—religion. Having expounded most voluminously all the tenets and beauties of the Christian Faith, he calmly informed Montezuma that he and his people were worshiping Satan, that their religion and its bloody sacrifices would condemn them to everlasting damnation, and that his real purpose in visiting Mexico was to snatch the people's souls from the jaws of Hell and to convert them to Christianity.

Even if Montezuma comprehended the meaning of Cortes' words, as interpreted by Marina, the doctrines were far too involved and abstruse for him to grasp. Moreover, Marina, though an excellent mouthpiece for Cortes, had some remarkable ideas of the religion she had so recently embraced. Her explanation of the visitors' partaking of the Host was such that the emperor declared he could see little distinction between the Aztec custom of devouring the flesh of the sacrificed and eating the flesh of the Lord himself. Moreover, as I have said, he had been a priest before he had become an emperor; he was the head of the church as well as of the state, and he was not at all likely to cast aside his own faith on a moment's notice or on the word of Cortes. Yet he listened respectfully until the Spaniard had ceased speaking.

He knew, he informed Cortes, that wherever the visitors went they repeated these words. He had no doubt that their God was a good God. But his gods were as real and as good to him as the Spaniards' God was to them. Moreover, the Don's story of the creation was so similar to what the Aztecs believed—even to the story of the flood and of Sodom and Gomorrah—that he felt sure there was little choice between the two faiths, so why discuss the matter further? Moreover, he continued, he and his people were not the original occupants of the country and neither were they the originators of their religion. They had been taught their present faith by the god Quetzalcoatl, who, upon his departure, had promised to return and with his sons take charge of the empire. He was convinced that the Dons were those sons of the Plumed Serpent and as such he bowed to their will and to Destiny. "Your king beyond the sea, the great Quetzalcoatl, is, I know, my lord and master," he declared. "I rule only in his name. You, Malinche, are his ambassador and shall share all things with me. I will see that your wishes are obeyed in every way. The city, the nation, is yours to command, and all things shall be provided for you."

Even the stern and avaricious Spanish cavaliers were touched by this speech of the monarch, but they were still more deeply touched by the wealth of gold he then bestowed upon them, enough, so says a contemporaneous chronicler, "to provide the poorest soldier with two heavy collars of gold."

Nevertheless, the old Dons possessed many excellent traits, despite their lust for gold, their cruelty and their religious fanaticism, and prominent among these was a deep respect for position, a reverence for bravery, an admiration for nobility of character, and a love for punctilious courtesy and good breeding.

Montezuma had proved he possessed all these and more; he had proved he could swallow defeat and yet remain proud and unbroken; he had proved he was equal in courtesy and breeding to any Spanish grandee, he had proved himself noble in every sense of the word, and he had proved himself generous to a degree.

As the cavaliers, hats in hands, rose to leave, they bowed to him as to their own sovereign and backed from his presence.

And yet these same Spaniards who, to quote their own words, "could talk of nothing else but the courtesy, the culture and the liberality of Montezuma," were even then planning to encompass his ruin. Not satisfied with his allegiance, his humility, his friendship and his generosity, they were ready and willing to destroy his cities, massacre his subjects, rob him of all he possessed and, if need be, murder him in cold blood, in order to obtain his possessions.

CHAPTER X

THE CONQUEROR SHOWS HIS HAND

DURING the days that followed, the Spaniards led a life of ease, indolence and luxury. Everything was provided for them as the emperor had promised; they were waited upon, catered to, treated like royalty. Wherever they went the people accorded them almost the same reverence as shown Montezuma himself, and, daily, rich presents were sent to them by the emperor, the nobles and the princes.

Each day, too, they were more and more impressed with the high civilization of the Aztecs and with the beauty and the admirable features of the city. The streets and canals ran at right angles, dividing the entire city into perfectly symmetrical squares as even as a checkerboard. The entire capital was patroled by efficient police, and more than one thousand persons were constantly employed in sprinkling and sweeping the streets. As the lake on which the city was built was salt, fresh water was brought by means of a huge aqueduct from Chapultepec, and in order that there should be no failure of the supply, there were two conduits, each more than two feet in diameter. In the various sections of the city were market places, reached both by the streets and by canals, while west of the center of the town was the great central market or *tiangez,* where traders, dealers, artisans, farmers, hunters, tradesmen, merchants and purchasers gathered from all parts of the land to sell, trade and buy. Here was every product, every manufacture, every type of handiwork of the innumerable tribes and races of Mexico. From Azcapozalco came the famed gold-workers with their delicate filagree-work and ornaments and utensils of precious metal. Cholulans had their stalls where they displayed their finest pottery and unique jewelry. There were sculptured stone chests and marvelously carved crystals and semiprecious stones from Yenahocan; feather pictures from Tezcuco; gorgeous woven serapes from Saltillo and Oaxaca; silver-work from Queretaro; wonderful opals from the hills in the north; hides of jaguars and wild beasts brought in by the savage hunters of Xilotepec; woven mats and straw raincoats from Quahtitlan. Deerskins filled with the native beverage, *pulque,* made from the maguey plant's juice, filled one section of the market; another was devoted to flowers, another to fruits, another to live birds, another to vegetables and others to meats, grains, etc. Among the strange edibles that the Dons saw here were cakes made from the eggs of a fly and considered a great delicacy by the Aztecs. There were also tiny cages filled with huge fireflies that the Aztec women used as living decorations for their black hair. Great piles of cotton cloth towered above the venders' heads; magnificent feather and fur mantles were displayed; there were garments, headdresses, sandals, toys and miniature idols of the various Aztec gods; carved woodenware, cooking utensils, weapons and tools of stone, obsidian, copper and even of precious metals. Here the farmer, the householder, the carpenter or even the soldier could purchase all the tools or equipment of his profession. There were spears, bows and arrows, clubs, throwing-sticks or *atlatls,* obsidian-edged swords or *machahuitls,*[1] helmets of wood, leather, gold, copper and silver; quilted cotton armor, cuirasses of various metals and of rawhide; shields of wood, metal or hide; plumed headdresses and every warlike accouterment.

Sections of the huge market were also given over to booths wherein men plied their various trades. There were feather-workers, goldsmiths, leather-workers; makers of hair rope and ornaments; carpenters, weavers, painters and representatives of every art and profession. There were apothecary shops filled with strange medicines, cures, and charms. There were bookmakers who prepared codices or wrote messages to order, and, as in Tlascala, there were numerous barber shops where the natives, who as a rule affected smoothly shaven faces, could have their beards removed by means of obsidian razors. And in order that the vast throng that crowded the market might not go hungry there were countless restaurants, as well as small stalls, where all manner of native viands—maize tortillas,

---

[1] From the Aztec name of this weapon was derived the word *machete,* now universally applied to the long-bladed bush knives used throughout tropical America.

savory stews, steaming *chocolatl,* honey-cakes and other delicacies—were being cooked and served.

Much of the business of the market was carried on by exchange, but to the Spaniards' surprise most of the purchasing was done with money. This consisted of copper bells and of bits of metal stamped with a character resembling a letter "T." For higher values small bags of cacao beans were used, the bags varying in size according to value, and quills filled with gold dust also served as currency.

Despite the crowds of Indians and the seeming confusion, perfect order was maintained by the police, who settled disputes, saw to it that full measure was given, collected duties on certain merchandise; and when a case of fraud or a disturbance arose, they hailed the offenders before a tribunal of twelve judges or jurors who held court within the market itself.

Wonderful and interesting as was this great market to the Spaniards, they were still more amazed when they visited the emperor's palace and were shown over it. It covered several acres of ground and its roof was of such width that, as one of the cavaliers declared, "Thirty knights might hold a tourney upon it." Connected with the true palace was the royal armory filled with weapons and uniforms. Another building was a granary for the supplies of corn for the army in time of war, or to relieve the city in case of famine. Other edifices were stored with clothing, supplies and various utensils. There was an immense aviary wherein were confined bright-plumaged birds that supplied the feathers for weaving feather cloaks, as well as a poultry yard with more than five hundred turkeys destined for the royal table. And there was a very complete menagerie or zoo filled with the beasts and reptiles of the country. There was also a collection of another sort—a museum or side-show, as we might call it, of human freaks—dwarfs, giants, armless and legless persons, monsters and midgets.

Surrounding the buildings were extensive gardens in which fruits, flowers and medicinal plants were grown, while canals and fountains furnished a constant supply of fresh cool water.

Despite the magnificence of this city residence of Montezuma, it was nothing compared with his favorite palace on the hill of Chapultepec. Here, in the shade of immense cypress trees, and commanding a magnificent view of the valley and the mountains with the cone of Popocatapetl shimmering against the sky, the emperor passed most of his time. He lived on a sumptuous scale that would have shamed many an Oriental potentate. He maintained a harem with several hundred inmates, and a vast retinue of servants. According to Aztec religious and court rules he bathed at least twice each day and changed his garments four times, never wearing the same clothing twice. His personal attendants were all nobles, and his table service was of gold and silver for state occasions or of the finest Cholula pottery for ordinary meals. He was a gourmand in his way, and the rarest and finest of viands were served him. According to the Dons, his ordinary meal consisted of not less than ten courses, while state banquets often included more than fifty. Moreover, with every variety of climate from the frigid to the torrid zone within his empire, Montezuma could dine on a greater variety of fruits, vegetables and other foods than any monarch of the world of his day, and the Spaniards declared that to sip iced drinks, eat fish from the distant sea, devour turkey from the uplands, and taste the luscious oranges and bananas of the tropics together with strawberries from the lands of eternal spring, was as if some magic wand had provided the repast. Although the emperor was a voracious eater, he was strictly temperate in his drinks and never partook of any beverage other than chocolate. But he was an inveterate smoker, and at the close of each meal several pipefuls of tobacco were smoked.

Having visited the various interesting places in the city, and the palaces of the emperor, Cortes requested permission to ascend the great pyramid or *teocalli*. This wish was readily granted by Montezuma, who offered to accompany the Spaniards in person. From its lofty summit the city lay spread like a map below them, with the vast panorama of the lake and valley beyond.

But Cortes was far more interested in the temple as a site for a Christian shrine than in the view, and he suggested to Father Olmedo, who accompanied him, that they should erect a cross upon the summit of the pyramid without further parley. Fortunately the friar's common sense prevailed, and no attempt was made to desecrate the temple at the

time. In one of the small structures on the summit
of the pyramid the Dons found an immense image of
the war-god, Huitzilopotchli, adorned with pearls,
precious stones and gold, and with a chain of alter-
nating silver and gold hearts about his neck, while
resting on the altar before him was a still warm
human heart from the last victim of sacrifice. The
other shrine was dedicated to the Supreme God,
Tezcatlipoca, whose black stone image represented
a young man richly adorned with gold and bearing
a polished mirror in which he was supposed to see
reflected all the doings of mankind. Before him was
a gold platter on which were five human hearts, and
the Dons shuddered and drew back at the gruesome
sight. Turning to Montezuma, Cortes declared that
if he were permitted to erect a cross on the spot the
emperor would "soon see how the false gods will
shrink before it."

Shocked at these words uttered in the presence of
his deities, the emperor merely replied that they
were the gods who had led the Aztecs to victory and
who had always served the people well, and added
that, had he dreamed Cortes would offer them such
an insult, he never would have permitted the Spaniards to visit the temple.

Nevertheless, the monarch graciously gave permission for the Spaniards to convert one of their buildings into a church, and he furnished the artisans to
make the necessary alterations. While this work
was progressing, the Dons came upon a hidden door
in one wall, and on forcing this they found an immense room filled with gold and silver ingots, boxes

of jewels, precious stones, bags of gold dust and treasure which to the Spaniards seemed "all the riches of the world gathered together there." It was, in fact, the reserve treasury of the empire, the accumulation of tribute in excess of governmental needs, and the private property of the emperor who had inherited much of it from his father. Oddly enough, the Spaniards for once seem to have had scruples about helping themselves to others' property, and after feasting their eyes upon the wealth within the chamber, the door was again sealed by the orders of Cortes who commanded that no one should mention having seen it.

A week and more had now passed since the Spaniards arrived at the Aztec capital, and while everything possible had been done to please them and to prove that the emperor and his subjects were truly friendly, yet Cortes was no nearer his desired ends than ever. From the first he had been bent on conquering the nation, on enriching himself, his men and the Spanish Crown by looting the empire, and in converting the people to his own religion. In order to do this he must take possession of the capital, and he was in constant fear that unless he did so very soon his king or even Velasquez might send a larger force than his own to dispossess him and wrest the empire from his grasp. He was not quite unprincipled and underhanded enough to fall upon the unsuspecting people and massacre them by thousands, and he was wise enough to realize that such a step would in all likelihood result in his ultimate defeat and death. So he formed another and fully as treacherous a scheme, which was to seize the emperor's person, hold him a prisoner, and force the people to submit to Spanish rule on threat of putting Montezuma to death.

His plan was to frighten the monarch into placing himself in the Dons' hands without resorting to force, but he was quite prepared to employ any means to accomplish his purpose. As a plausible excuse for this daring and underhanded action, he raked up an incident that had occurred weeks before, the killing of four Spaniards by Indians in a remote district on the coast. Having requested an audience with the emperor, which was of course granted, he ordered thirty-five picked men to follow him to the palace— as if merely on independent sight-seeing visits which they were accustomed to make—and to remain in groups of three or four together ready to spring to his aid at a signal. Then, accompanied by five cavaliers: Alvarado, Sandoval, Lujo, Avila and De Leon, all clad in full armor, he made his way to the throne-room of the palace. Receiving him with his usual courtesy, Montezuma presented him with the customary gifts of gold and jewels, and paid Cortes the special honor of offering him one of his daughters as his wife, an offer that Cortes respectfully declined, explaining that he already had a wife as well as his Indian sweetheart—quite enough for any man. For a time the conversation was gay and pleasant. Then, as Cortes saw that his soldiers had gathered about as ordered, he suddenly altered his tone and accused the emperor of being responsible for the affair near Vera Cruz.

Amazed and shocked, Montezuma disclaimed all knowledge of the outrage and offered to send for the caçique of the district and to punish him as he deserved. To prove his good faith he drew a ring from his finger—in which was set a stone engraved with his royal arms—and handing it to one of his nobles ordered him to lose no time in bringing the caçique before his emperor.

No sooner had the messenger left than Cortes assured the monarch that he personally had complete confidence in Montezuma's good faith, but that in order that the King of Spain should be assured of it, it would be advisable for Montezuma to transfer himself to the Spaniards' palace until the offending caçique had been duly punished.

Montezuma was astonished, insulted, frightened. He indignantly protested against becoming a prisoner, and expressed in no measured terms his amazement that Cortes should dare suggest such an indignity. Cortes, however, assured him he would not be considered a prisoner. He would be treated like an honored guest, surrounded by his own household, and in fact would merely change his residence temporarily.

Montezuma, though realizing he was in the power of the white men, still refused to listen to the proposal, but he offered to send one of his sons and a daughter as hostages. This, of course, did not suit Cortes in the least. Still, he wished if possible to avoid force and bloodshed, and for two hours he tried to induce the emperor to accede to his demands.

Finally one of the cavaliers, Velasquez de Leon,

losing patience, exclaimed: "Why waste time talk-ing with this infidel? Let us seize him, and if he resists, put him to the sword!"

Alarmed at the savage tone of the impatient ad-venturer, the monarch asked Marina what he had said. She repeated his words, at the same time urg-ing Montezuma to accompany the Spaniards, and, in all probability, added warnings of what might hap-pen if he persisted in refusing. At any rate her words had far more weight than those of Cortes, and realizing at last that his supposed friends were deadly enemies, that the fair words and promises of Cortes were merely to disguise his true objects, but helpless in the face of the mail-clad, armed Span-iards, Montezuma agreed.

Immediately the royal litter was ordered, and Montezuma, unable to admit his degradation to his nobles, announced that he was visiting the Spaniards of his own free will. Even so a rumor spread that he was being abducted, the crowds in the streets be-came threatening, and it would have gone hard in-deed with the Spaniards had not the emperor him-self calmed them and assured them he was among friends, at the same time ordering them to disperse. He was received by the Spaniards as though still a free monarch; his quarters were furnished with whatever he desired, and his wives, attendants, serv-ants and entire household were installed in the sec-tion of the buildings he selected. As far as outward appearances went he was as much the king as ever.

He held audiences, gave commands and ruled his people, and even the soldiers had strict orders from

Cortes never to approach Montezuma without removing their hats or helmets and making obeisance, nor to be seated in his presence unless he requested them to do so. But he knew, as well as did the Spaniards, that this was merely show, that he was as much a prisoner as though in fetters, and if he had any doubts on this score he had only to glance outside his doors where a guard of sixty armed Spaniards paced back and forth day and night. Notwithstanding this, Montezuma appeared contented, pleased to be among the Dons, and entertained the leaders and loaded them with gifts exactly as he had done when in his own palace.

In a few days, the messenger sent to bring the cacique Quahupopca, from the coast, returned with the chief and several of his sub-chiefs. According to his promise, Montezuma turned the cacique over to Cortes for trial. He did not deny his responsibility for the murder of the Dons—if indeed killing the men in a battle could be called murder—but when asked by his pitiless judges if he were a subject of Montezuma he replied by asking, "What other sovereign could I serve?"

That was enough. He and his fellows were condemned to be burnt alive, and the flames were to be fed by javelins, bows and arrows from the royal arsenal. But the whole affair was merely a cleverly planned and devilishly devised scheme for humbling the Aztec monarch and reducing him to the status of a vassal if not, in fact, a slave. As preparations were being made for the execution, Cortes entered Montezuma's apartment, charged him with being the instigator of the whole affair, and ordered a soldier to rivet irons on the monarch's ankles.

This affront, this degradation, struck the monarch speechless with indignation and misery. Tears welled to his eyes, he groaned as if in physical agony, but he offered no resistance and uttered no word of reproach or anger. No longer was he a monarch. His head had been humbled in the dust; he had been treated like a common felon, and death would have been more welcome than his fetters.

When at last the unfortunate caçique and his comrades had been burned to cinders in view of the wondering public, Cortes again approached the manacled emperor and removed the shackles, expressing his regret that he had been obliged to inflict this indignity. He then embraced the Aztec monarch, declared he loved him as a brother, and gave him permission to return to his own palace. A hollow mockery, meaningless words, as Montezuma well knew. Realizing that he could never resume his place among his people who had witnessed his degradation, he declined Cortes' offer, and declared he would remain with the Dons.

Cortes had shown his hand. He had stripped the emperor of his power, had crushed his spirit, had left the Aztecs without a ruler who could issue an order, a command, or even a request that was not put onto his lips by the Spaniards. He was a mere puppet—the mouthpiece of Cortes.

CHAPTER XI

THE TURNING OF THE WORM

THOUGH Cortes had conquered the Aztecs' king he had not conquered the Aztecs, and no one appreciated this fact better than himself. He realized that, should the people defy him and risk the Dons taking reprisals upon their emperor, they could completely cut him off from the rest of the country. To avoid any such casualty arising he built two small vessels which, if necessity arose, could be used to transport his forces across the lake even if the causeway were cut off by enemies.

Meanwhile, Montezuma was treated with the same deference as ever and, outwardly, seemed contented with his lot. Anyhow, he made the best of it, gambled with his captors—often winning large amounts which he gave as presents to his servants, or losing even larger sums with no regrets. He even presented the contents of the secret treasure room to the Spaniards, remarking as he did so that they were welcome to all in the land if they would only spare the gods. In fact he became a real favorite with the Dons, and was particularly friendly with Alvarado and De Leon. He was even permitted, though under heavy guard, to visit the temple and worship before his gods, and several times he took part in hunts accompanied by Cortes and his men.

But he well knew, and had been repeatedly warned, as had his people, that the first attempt at escape or rescue would bring about his instant death.

Though Montezuma had apparently resigned himself to his fate, others had not. Among these was Cacama, the King of Tezcuco, a young man of noted bravery and intelligence who was a nephew of Montezuma. Second only to Tenochtitlan in importance, size and beauty, Tezcuco was a city-state of half a million inhabitants with buildings and temples that rivaled those of the capital. Although at first on the friendliest terms with the Spaniards, and among those who had most strongly urged receiving them with honors and courtesy, yet their treatment of his uncle had transformed him into their most bitter and dangerous enemy. Secretly, and unsuspected by Cortes and his men, Cacama had formed an alliance with a number of other chiefs, among them Montezuma's brother, the ruler of Itztapalapan, and the King of Tlacopan, and, had other nobles and rulers whom he approached been willing to join him without authority from the captive monarch, it is probable that Cortes and his men would have been wiped from the face of the earth. But as it was, word of the conspiracy reached Cortes, who was only prevented from attacking the Tezcucans by Montezuma who offered first to order Cacama to abandon all ideas of rebelling against the Spaniards' rule. Cacama, however, refused to recognize the commands of a captive king, and when Cortes threatened him, the proud and independent young man informed the Spaniard that he did not recog-

nize his authority to command, that he knew nothing about the King of Spain or his subjects, and
that he cared even less.

Montezuma then endeavored to induce his belliger-
ent nephew to come to Mexico and talk over matters;
but Cacama was wise and wary enough not to fall
into any such trap, and replied that when he visited
the capital it would be to rescue it from bondage,
not to be enslaved. But Cortes' treachery did not
fail him. He forced Montezuma to employ natives
of Tezcuco to betray Cacama, and while in a conference with these supposed friends, he was seized,
bound and brought to Mexico. Refusing even then
to humble himself before Cortes, he was heavily
ironed and chained and cast into a cell, and at
Cortes' orders, Montezuma announced that he was
deposed and that his younger brother Cuicuitzca
was to take his place. The other chiefs who had
joined with Cacama were also secured and imprisoned, and Cortes felt that he was master of the
situation. To complete his ascendancy, he forced
the Aztec monarch to make public proclamation that
he and his subjects were henceforth vassals of the
Spanish king. Without a dissenting voice the
princes and nobles swore allegiance to the Spanish
Crown, for not only was the word of Montezuma
still law, but all implicitly believed that the prophecy
of Quetzalcoatl had been fulfilled, that, as foretold,
the descendants of the Plumed Serpent had returned
to take possession of the land, and that, exactly
as stated in the age-old prophecy, the reigning house
of the Aztecs would end with Montezuma.

Having thus secured the allegiance of the rulers of Mexico, Cortes informed them that it was customary for new subjects of his king to send their ruler overseas a fitting present as proof of their loyalty, and, at his suggestion, Montezuma ordered collectors to visit every city and province in the empire (accompanied, of course, by armed Spaniards), and to collect tribute in the name of the King of Spain. The resultant treasure, though enormous, fell far short of the Spaniards' expectations. Objects that the Mexicans prized most highly were of no value to the conquerors. Fine cotton cloth, magnificent feather-work, beautiful pottery—treasures worth more than gold to the Aztecs—were merely rubbish in the eyes of the Spaniards. Even the turquoise mosaic work was worthless to them, and the green Mexican jade—to the Mexicans the most precious of precious stones—was of no intrinsic value in Spain. The only treasures worth having, from the Dons' point of view, were gold, silver and gems, and of these there was comparatively little. Still the gleaming heap of precious metals and precious stones far exceeded anything the Spaniards had hitherto seen in the New World, and some idea of the quantity of gold may be obtained from the fact that it required more than three days for a score of expert goldsmiths to reduce the treasure to bullion.

When at last this task was accomplished and the spoils were divided it was found that the value amounted to nearly one and a half million dollars, while the pearls and jewels totaled two million dol-

lars more. From this were deducted Cortes' fifth,
the royal fifth, large sums for the cost of the expedition and for the Governor of Cuba, and by the
time the shares due the common soldiers were dis-
bursed it was found that the men received less than
five hundred dollars each! It is little wonder that
they became surly, complained bitterly, and even
accused Cortes of taking the best and most for himself. With difficulty Cortes quieted them. He even
offered to divide his own share with his men if they
thought there had been any unfairness, an offer that
would have done him great credit, had he not known
perfectly well that the men would not accept it.
Moreover, as he cunningly pointed out, there was
much more to be had, while if they quarreled among
themselves it would only result in their own deaths.
As a matter of fact it made very little difference to
the rough soldiers whether they had much or little,
for within the hour many had lost all they possessed
by gambling and were as poor as ever.

Having secured the greater portion of all the
treasures in the city and the country, Cortes now
decided that it was high time to rob the Aztecs of
their gods and religion. These were all that Montezuma and his people had left, and the captive emperor begged Cortes to refrain from this last step,
declaring that to interfere with their faith would
arouse the people to madness and result in insurrection. Very probably Cortes realized the truth of this,
and he finally compromised by forcing Montezuma to
prohibit human sacrifices and by being given permission to use one of the shrines on the temple top

for a Christian chapel. Never perhaps was there a more incongruous spectacle, a more amazing ceremony than the first Mass celebrated on the summit of the great *teocalli*. In one sanctuary was the Christian altar, the images of Christ and of the Holy Virgin, with the emblem of the Cross. In the other, a few yards distant, was the hideous image of the Aztec war-god decked with gold and precious stones. Before the one knelt the mail-clad Dons with bowed heads as the priests elevated the Host. Before the other the Aztecs prostrated themselves and chanted their prayers to the bloodthirsty gods of their forefathers.

But in establishing the Cross upon the sacred pyramid, Cortes had overstepped himself, had stretched the submission of the Aztecs to the breaking point. They had allowed him to take possession of their country and their capital, they had raised no outcry when he had made a prisoner of their monarch, they had given him their most precious possessions without a murmur, but the profanation of their temple was the last straw.

Montezuma himself underwent a change. He became morose, aloof, melancholy, and avoided the Dons whenever possible. Then one day he sent for Cortes, and with a coldness and hauteur very different from his usual deferential manner, he informed Cortes that his prediction had come to pass. "The gods have been offended," he declared. "They have threatened to forsake us if you and your men are not destroyed and sacrificed upon the altars. It is only because of my regard for you that I warn you. If you value your lives leave at once. Remember I have only to raise my finger and the land will rise against you."

Even Cortes and his generals realized the sincerity and the truth of his words. But he controlled his feelings of alarm and amazement at the revelation, and assured Montezuma that he was willing to depart as soon as ships could be built, although he hinted that the monarch might be taken along when he departed.

Anxious to save the lives of the visitors, whom he regarded as superior beings, and for some of whom he had formed real friendship, Montezuma offered to send as many artisans as were required to aid in building vessels on the coast. But Cortes, while accepting this and dispatching the laborers, together with some of his men, ostensibly to build the ships, gave secret orders to delay matters, for he had no intention of playing fair or of leaving the land he had been to such pains to take and that he was so near conquering. We may be sure, however, that neither Cortes nor his men felt at all comfortable or too sure of themselves after that warning of the emperor.

And they would have been far more uneasy had they known of events transpiring on the distant coast. Velasquez, the Governor of Cuba, had not been idle. He had fitted out a large and powerful force, and under command of Pánfilo de Narvárez his fleet had set sail for Mexico to wreak summary punishment on Cortes and to wrest Mexico from him. It was the most powerful army and the largest fleet that had ever been raised in the New World, and consisted of eighteen ships, nearly one thousand men, eighty of whom were mounted, nearly one hundred arquebusiers, one hundred and fifty crossbowmen, and fifty cannon, besides one thousand Indian slaves.

The first intimation that Cortes received of this hostile force of his own countrymen came from Montezuma. Inviting him to an interview, the monarch informed Cortes that there now remained no obstacle to his immediate departure, as a number of ships were waiting and ready for him. Amazed, not comprehending, the Spaniard demanded an explanation. Unfolding a codex, Montezuma handed it to the Don who, with wondering—and no doubt startled—eyes, saw every detail of Narvárez' fleet and equipment accurately portrayed upon the paper.

Quickly recovering himself, Cortes assumed an air of thankfulness and assured the monarch he would lose no time in taking advantage of the opportunity so providentially provided for his departure. He was, however, vastly disturbed. He was not for one moment deluded into thinking—as did his men—that his countrymen had come to augment his forces. He felt sure the fleet was hostile, and his worst fears were confirmed when, shortly afterwards, a number of Indian cargo-bearers arrived from the coast bringing six Spaniards, bound and trussed, from Narvárez' forces. The unfortunate men, among whom was a priest and a notary, had demanded Sandoval's surrender of Vera Cruz, but instead of acceding to their orders, that worthy and stout old soldier had trussed them up, loaded them on the backs of porters, and sent them to Cortes with instructions for them to present their credentials to the conqueror in person. Needless to say, the wily Cortes sympathized with them, treated them royally, loaded them with presents, won them to his side, and from them acquired a knowledge of all the details of the Velasquez expedition. Realizing that hostilities with such a superior force would jeopardize his career, even if it did not end in his utter defeat, Cortes sent a letter to Narvárez offering to coöperate with him and to share all profits.

The envoy found Narvárez at Cempoala. The message, brought by Father Olmedo, had very different effects upon Narvárez and his men. The latter were all for an alliance with Cortes and a share of the treasure, while their leader was determined to come to blows and take charge of matters himself. The result was a split in the ranks, and though the incipient mutiny was outwardly suppressed, the disaffection still remained, and by twos and threes men deserted Narvárez' forces and joined Cortes. Realizing that delay might mean disaster and that Narvárez' assurances to the Indians that he had come to free Montezuma and restore him to power might win the entire populace to his side, Cortes decided to take the offensive. It is not necessary to relate all the details and incidents that followed. Leaving Alvarado in charge of the capital, Cortes, with only one-third of his force—amounting to barely seventy men—left the city bent on the conquest, not of infidel Indians but of his Christian countrymen.

At Cholula he joined De Leon with his one hundred and twenty men, and at Tlascala he was given six hundred warriors. These, however, were of no use to him, for, having no desire to lose their lives in a struggle between two parties of Spaniards, and in which they had no interest, the Tlascalans soon deserted and returned to their homes. Soon after leaving Tlascala, Cortes' company met Sandoval, who had come from Vera Cruz with sixty soldiers and a number of deserters from Narvárez' forces, and he was also joined by Captain Tobillos, whom he had sent to Chinantla to procure a supply of long spears with double-pointed copper tips. The total forces of Cortes now numbered two hundred and sixty-seven—only five of whom were mounted—who were poorly armed and who had discarded their mail in favor of the quilted cotton armor of the Aztecs— a paltry company indeed to face the trained, well-armed, well-equipped army of Narvárez.

But Cortes counted as usual upon other means than force to win the day. Encamping by the bank of a stream a few miles from Narvárez' camp, Cortes, taking advantage of a raging storm, crossed the river unseen, crept upon the sentries and made them prisoners without giving the alarm, and entered the city. By the time the alarm was given the enemy was in the camp. Too close for the artillery to bear upon them effectively, one party rushed the guns, put the artillerymen to flight or to the sword, and took possession of the cannon, while others attacked Narvárez' quarters. A short hand-to-hand struggle followed. Narvárez was struck with a spear that pierced his left eye. Retreating to a stone building

of the temple where he was quartered, the wounded
general and his guard still fought viciously, until
the thatch above their heads was fired and they were
forced to surrender. The battle was over. A single
discharge of the captured artillery, now turned
against the garrison, was enough to cause them to
capitulate, and Cortes' handful of men had triumphed over Narvárez' troops. The easy victory
was partly due to Narvárez' overconfidence and care-
lessness that resulted in his being taken by surprise,
but largely it was the result of the disaffection
among his men who desired to ally themselves with
Cortes, and made a half-hearted resistance. At any
rate, the result was wholly satisfactory to the conqueror who now had a large force under his command, and who felt at last in a position to defy the
Mexicans and to substitute force for the guile he had
practiced hitherto.

He soon had cause to give thanks that he had thus
augmented his army. Messengers from Alvarado
arrived with the alarming news that the capital was
in arms and that the invaders were attacked, that the
vessels built upon the lake had been burned, that
many Dons had been killed and wounded, and he
begged Cortes to come to his relief.

Hurrying towards the capital, adding to his forces
by levying thousands of Indians who were only too
willing to join any party that was hostile to their
hereditary enemies, the Aztecs, Cortes reached the
borders of the lake. There he was met by two more
messengers, one from Alvarado, the other from Montezuma. The first told of the city being besieged,

the latter disclaimed all responsibility for the uprising. But to the Spaniards' surprise no attack was made upon them, no one attempted to bar their way. They crossed the causeway, passed through the gate, and entered the city without hindrance.

The city was deserted. Everywhere a deathly silence reigned, and the tramp of the soldiers' feet reëchoed from the empty buildings as they marched to the palace and rejoined their fellows.

Cortes was not long in learning the cause of the outbreak which was directly due to the violent and bestial acts of the sunny-faced Alvarado. He had given permission for the Aztecs to hold their annual May ceremonial and dances in the court of the great pyramid, provided there were no sacrifices. More than six hundred Indians had assembled, dressed in their finest, unarmed, bent only on having a gala day to propitiate their gods. Then, at a prearranged signal, Alvarado and his men had fallen upon the happy dancers and had butchered them to the last man and woman. Among the slain, nobles and princes were numerous, and there was not a Mexican family of the aristocracy that did not lose a son or daughter in this utterly ruthless and inhuman massacre. Why Alvarado committed the atrocity has never been explained. His own excuses were flimsy, contradictory and inadequate. In fact he could not explain, and Cortes reprimanded him severely in the presence of the others.

But the harm had been done. The people, horrified, aroused, even their superstitions forgotten in face of this inhuman, wholesale murder, rose in arms and attacked the Dons in a frenzy. Only the prayers and commands of Montezuma saved the garrison from being annihilated and Alvarado from being offered up in sacrifice. The people stayed their assault, but only to institute a siege. They blockaded the quarters of the Spaniards, closed the markets, and calmly, doggedly waited for famine to wreak vengeance for them. Cortes had no reason, no cause to suspect Montezuma of any part in the trouble, in fact the emperor's efforts had all been to save the Spaniards, yet he showed by his attitude that he regarded Montezuma as responsible. When the captive monarch requested an interview, Cortes refused to see him and exclaimed: "What have I do do with this dog who allows us to starve?" This unfair, childish and uncalled for attitude aroused the resentment of the more fair-minded generals, who remonstrated with him, but to no avail.

"Did not this dog betray us to Narvárez?" he cried. "Does he not have his markets closed so we cannot get food?"

Then, turning to the Aztec nobles near, he exclaimed: "Go to that dog you call master and tell him if the markets are not opened by his people we will do it for them at their cost—and that he will be the first to feel my anger."

But despite his bluster and his anger, Cortes had little confidence in being able to frighten the people into submission. He realized that at last they were aroused, and he sent a messenger to Vera Cruz telling the garrison of his plight.

The envoy got no farther than the gates of the

city, however. Covered with wounds, terrified, he dragged himself back to his fellows. The city was all in arms, the drawbridges raised. The Spaniards were trapped within the hostile capital.

city, however. Covered with wounds, terrified, he
dragged himself back to his fellows. The city was
all in arms, the drawbridges raised. The Spaniards

CHAPTER XII

LA NOCHE TRISTE

HARDLY had the dying messenger stammered
out the alarming news, than the roar, the tumult of the approaching Indian thousands reached
the ears of the now terrified Spaniards. Sounding
the call to arms, Cortes ordered every man to his
post. Filling the streets, banners and plumes waving, sun glinting on gold, copper and gems, the Aztec hordes swarmed towards the besieged Dons. A
hail of arrows, stones and javelins rained upon the
beleaguered Spaniards. Then, as the front ranks
of the Aztecs were within pistol shot, the cannon
and muskets of the Dons roared out and mowed
down their enemies by hundreds. But the terrible
slaughter passed unheeded by the Indians. Over
and over again the firearms of the Spaniards decimated their foes, but apparently with no effect.
From the streets, from housetops, from every point
of vantage, they kept up an incessant fire of arrows,
darts and stones. Many of the Dons and scores of
their Indian allies fell dead or wounded. Regardless
of death, the Aztecs clambered over the mangled
bodies of their comrades, and fixing their spears in
the crevices between the stones, used them as ladders
to scale the walls. Though all Indians who gained
the parapet were struck down, others constantly took

their places. They fought madly, fanatically, and turning to the gateways they strove to batter them in with logs and timbers. Finding this impossible, they discharged blazing arrows, and soon the roofs and the woodwork within the Spaniards' stronghold were a mass of roaring flames.

The battle raged until night when, according to Aztec custom, the Indians ceased their attacks and the Dons, wearied, choked with smoke, wounded and filled with the most dismal forebodings, sought to strengthen their defenses and to rest their bodies in preparation for the morrow.

Fully realizing that to remain within the beleaguered courtyard would mean the ultimate end of himself and his men, Cortes determined to take the offensive. At the first break of dawn the gates were thrown open, and following a volley of cannon and musketry fire, the Dons charged the enemy. Instantly the Aztecs broke and fled, but not far. Ducking behind barricades, seeking refuge in doorways, mounting to the flat roofs of the houses, the Indians poured a galling fire upon the Spaniards. From every quarter—even from boats upon the canals— the arrows, sling-stones and *atlatl*-hurled spears fell upon the Dons and their allies. Finding it impossible to dislodge the defenders, Cortes ordered the city put to the torch. Luckily for the city the amount of inflammable material was small, the buildings were separated by wide streets and by canals, and only a few hundred houses were destroyed. Even then the infuriated, valiant Aztecs seemed as numerous, as determined as ever. Though hundreds perished in the flames, though hundreds more lay dead and dying on every side, though the canals were choked with bodies, yet never for an instant did their efforts cease or even diminish. At last, finding he was gaining nothing, that for every Aztec killed a dozen took his place, and realizing his own losses were great, Cortes retreated with the remainder of his men to the fortress-like palace.

So far the Aztecs had been the victors. Though they had lost hundreds to the Dons' one, yet they could far better afford to lose a thousand than Cortes could afford to lose a single Spaniard; though they had not accomplished their objective, yet they still hold the Dons under siege; though they had been temporarily driven back, still, in the end, they had forced the Dons to retreat.

Even Cortes realized that he had but faint chances of success, and he sought Montezuma's aid to intercede with the people and to bring an end to hostilities. But Montezuma, still smarting under the angry and utterly unwarranted words of Cortes, repaid him in his own coin. "What have I to do with this man Malinche?" he exclaimed. "My willingness to serve and befriend him has brought only ruin and disgrace. He mistrusts me and denounces me. It is of no use. I do not wish to hear him nor see him. I wish only to die."

But in the end, hoping to avert further bloodshed on both sides, he agreed to attempt to stem the tide of fury in his people on the sworn promises of Cortes that the Dons would leave the city and the country if they were permitted to depart in peace.

Arraying himself in his state robes and insignia, Montezuma mounted to the parapet of the palace in view of all the assembled people. Many prostrated themselves as they saw him, others made obeisance, and all were hushed and listened expectantly to what he might say.

But when Montezuma pleaded for the Dons, and declared he was their friend, the attitude of the populace underwent a quick change. All reverence for the monarch was swept away. Epithets were hurled at him, and a hail of missiles was aimed at him. Too late, the Dons who were there to guard him threw themselves before the monarch. Montezuma was thrice wounded, and a sling-stone, striking his forehead, stretched him senseless on the pavement. Shocked at their impulsive act, the Indians dispersed, and in a moment not an Aztec remained in sight.

Utterly crushed by this last incident, Montezuma lost all desire to live. He refused aid, tore the bandages from his wounds, refused to speak, and seemed determined to die.

The Dons, actually affected by the plight of the unfortunate emperor, had little time to attend to him. A number of the Aztecs were in possession of the pyramid overlooking the Spaniards' quarters, and from their lofty vantage point maintained a galling and deadly fire.

If any were to survive, the pyramid had to be taken, and Cortes in person led the assault. Fighting every inch of their way upwards, the Dons at

length gained the summit where the determined Aztecs made their last stand.

Back and forth the struggling men swayed, a duel
to the death upon the narrow summit of the great
teocalli, while from far below Dons and Aztecs
watched with bated breath and forgot hostilities for
the time. Swords flashed, *machahuitls* gleamed,
mail-clad cavaliers and cotton-armored Indians
thrust, slashed, cut and stabbed. No quarter was
asked, none given by either side. Again and again
the Spaniards seemed about to be forced over the
edge of the platform to awful death. Again and
again the Aztec warriors recovered themselves on
the very verge of the abyss. Once, Cortes, fighting
hand to hand with a grim-faced Aztec chief, actually
swayed beyond the edge, one foot poised in mid-air,
and his friends below crossed themselves and their
faces paled. But with a superhuman effort he recovered his balance, seized his enemy by the waist,
and hurled him to his death upon the stone steps far
beneath.

For three hours the battle on the temple-top raged.
Gradually the Aztecs were overcome by the superior
weapons of the conquerors. One by one they fell.
At last, realizing their cause was lost, the few survivors, defying the Spaniards, calling on their own
gods, leaped from the platform, preferring death to
surrender. The Dons had not won their victory
cheaply. Forty-five of their number lay dead upon
the summit of the pyramid or upon the stairways
where they had fallen from above, and every survivor was badly wounded. But forgetting their in-

juries, seized with fanatical religious zeal, the
survivors tossed aside their weapons, and rushing
to the sanctuary where the statue of the war-god
still remained, the triumphant Dons tumbled the
image from his throne, and rolling him to the edge
of the platform, hurled him over the edge. Then,
setting fire to the empty sanctuary, they descended
to the courtyard where, so filled with awe were the
Indians, that not a hand was raised to bar the Spaniards' way.

That night the Dons made a midnight sortie, and
burned more than three hundred houses with their
helpless inmates who, when they sought to escape
from the flames, were ruthlessly cut down by the
waiting Spanish soldiers.

Feeling that the destruction of their god and this
holocaust would bring the enemy to terms, Cortes
announced that he would hold a parley with them.
Accompanied by Marina, he mounted to the same
spot where Montezuma had been struck down, and,
through the medium of his beautiful interpreter, he
harangued the multitude. But Cortes had woefully
underestimated the spirit and the character of the
Aztecs. They listened attentively enough to his
ridiculous, bombastic speech, in which he declared
they had brought the troubles on themselves, and
which he concluded with a threat to slaughter every
man, woman and child in the city and burn the capital over their bodies if they did not submit and lay
down their arms.

But their reply was merely to declare that though
all he said was true, they were quite satisfied to be

wiped from existence provided they took the life of one Spaniard for every thousand Mexicans slain. Moreover, they reminded him, though every soul in Tenochtitlan were slain, yet millions more would fill their places from the outlying districts, and finally, they pointed out, the Dons must perish soon from hunger and sickness. "The bridges are broken and you cannot escape!" they cried. "Our gods have delivered you into our hands!" and with this parting taunt they discharged a volley of arrows over the wall.

Only too well the Dons knew the truth of the Aztecs' words. They were already feeling the pangs of hunger. Despite the numbers killed, the Indians seemed more numerous than ever, and the news that the bridges were down filled them with dismay. They saw only death or worse—sacrifice—before them, and they demanded that Cortes lead them from the accursed city at once.

Cortes, however, remained calm, calculating, apparently undismayed, though he realized as fully as any of his men the jeopardy in which he had placed himself. To retreat now would be to lose everything. To remain promised nothing but defeat and death. Yet of the two it was better to sacrifice his ambitions, to lose the city than to sacrifice himself and his faithful men. While there was life there was hope, and to evacuate the city was his only chance. But if the bridges were destroyed how could he expect to escape? His best chance, he decided, was by way of Tacuba, for there the causeway was barely two miles in length. But before he attempted to retreat he must reconnoiter the ground and must divert the enemy from his true purpose.

In preparation for this he had three strange machines built which, to the Mexicans, must have seemed the abodes of vengeful gods. They consisted of towerlike structures with two loopholed chambers, the whole contrivance being mounted on small wheels or rollers so they could be dragged along by Indian slaves. Within the towers were arquebusiers who, from their lofty stations, could rake the roofs of the houses with their fire, or could even spring to the roofs and attack the occupants with their swords.

As long as the movable fortresses were in the paved streets all went well, but at the first canal their limits were reached, for they could not cross, the bridges having been utterly demolished as the Aztecs had said. If the invaders were to escape from the city the waterways must be bridged, and, under a galling fire from the Aztecs, the Spaniards forced their Indian allies to fill the canals with stone, timbers and rubbish from the razed houses in the vicinity. Seven of the canals were thus made passable, each as it was filled being left under guard of strong bodies of soldiers. Everything seemed now in readiness for the evacuation of the city; but Cortes had yet to learn the temper of the Mexicans. They overpowered the guards and demolished the enemies' works, and when, riding at the head of his men, Cortes drove the Aztecs back and repaired the fills, the Indians swarmed in from all sides. The Spaniards barely escaped with their lives. In fact, so remarkable was their escape, that the Spaniards attributed it to a miracle and declared they had seen the Virgin Mary riding by Cortes' side and throwing dust in the eyes of the infidels—a most unworthy act on the part of the gentle Virgin, much as Cortes was in need of her divine aid.

That same night Montezuma died. To the end he retained his faith in his own gods, and in his last moments replied to Father Olmedo's exhortations, that he had but a few moments to live and in that hour would not desert the faith of his fathers. But he had one final request to make. Calling Cortes to his side, he implored him in the name of his own God and in the name of his king to see that his three children were safeguarded and protected and that they should be given some portion of their rightful inheritance. ''They are the most precious jewels I can leave you,'' he whispered. ''If only for the friendship I have shown you—though it has brought me only shame and death—you will do this, Malinche?''

Both Cortes and his cavaliers were really moved by the death of their royal hostage, and Cortes, despite his zealous hatred of all things pagan and his unceasing determination to force Christianity down the Aztecs' throats, consented willingly to Montezuma being buried by his own people in accordance with the rites of his own religion. Where or how his body was disposed of is not known. The dead Montezuma, arrayed in his royal robes, was carried on a bier, borne on the shoulders of nobles, to the emperor's palace, where he was probably interred under the shade of the cypresses on the hill of Chapultepec.

The death of Montezuma was a great blow to the Dons. No longer did they hold a hostage whom they could wield as a weapon, and whose commands had so often served them in their direst extremities. Everything now depended upon their own initiative and their own unaided efforts. Every one was agreed that nothing was left but retreat, and knowing the Aztecs' custom of refraining from hostilities after dark, the time chosen for their evacuation was night. Cortes' first care was to arrange for the transportation of the treasure, for despite his religious zeal he was as avaricious as any of his men. Dividing the bars of gold among his trusted officers, with orders to guard it with their lives, he still found that a large portion of the bullion must be abandoned. Throwing this on the floor, he told his men to help themselves, adding the caution not to overburden themselves. Those who were wise selected light articles whose value lay in the gems they contained, but many of the soldiers, rushing at the gleaming pile of riches, loaded themselves down with the precious metal—an act that they paid for with their lives a few hours later.

All was now in readiness. Two hundred infantry-men led the cavalcade under Sandoval and some twenty cavaliers. Behind these in charge of Cortes was the baggage, much of the treasure, the lighter cannon and the prisoners, among whom were the son and two daughters of Montezuma, Cacama, the deposed king of Tezcuco, and several nobles. In the rear came the bulk of the infantry under De Leon and Alvarado, while the cavalry was distributed here and there.

Certain that he would find his way barred by the open canals, Cortes had prepared a portable bridge designed to be thrown across the waterways and removed after his men had crossed. But Cortes was no engineer, and bitterly did he regret that fact a little later.

At midnight, after a most solemn Mass, the Spaniards set out in a drizzling rain. The city was deserted, and steadily and as noiselessly as possible they held their way to the causeway. Not a sound, not an alarm disturbed them. The entire valley seemed wrapped in slumber. But the Aztecs did not sleep. Here and there keen eyes watched the Dons as they passed. From the summits of the *teocallis,* priests gazed down to see the moving forms threading the streets of the city below them. And as the vanguard of the Spaniards reached the causeway and paused while the movable bridge was placed across the canal that barred their way, the booming of the temple drums, the blaring of shell-trumpets, and the sudden flare of signal fires sounded the alarm. No time was to be lost. Urging his army on, Cortes watched as the forces hurried in safety over his makeshift bridge. But scarcely had half the cavalcade passed over when, from the blackness that hid the lake, came the swish and splashing of thousands of paddles and speeding canoes, followed by a rain of arrows and stones. Panic-stricken, defenseless against these unseen enemies, the Dons raced forward while the hordes of Aztecs, running their craft against the dyke, threw themselves upon the retreating Spaniards. Thinking only of escape, each man bent on saving his own life; the thoroughly terrified soldiers crowded, screamed, fought with one another and made no effort to beat off the shouting, yelling, demoniacal Indians. The cavalry rode ruthlessly over friends and foes alike. Men burdened with gold and unable to keep up with their fellows were seized, bound and carried off in triumph to become victims of sacrifice.

The march became a panic. On that narrow causeway bare of ramparts, the crowding, jostling, struggling men were at the mercy of their foes. Hundreds were dragged down, hundreds more were forced over the brink by their own countrymen in their mad struggle. Scores fell to javelins, arrows and stones, scores were dragged down in the waters by their weight of gold and never rose again. And at every opening in the dyke they were forced to wait until the clumsy bridge was fitted in place. But at the second halt the bridge stuck. In vain those in the lead sent frantic messages to the rear to bring the bridge. The weight of horses, men, baggage and cannon had wedged the affair fast, and the most frantic efforts were powerless to move it. The entire force was held, crowded upon the narrow causeway between the open canal in front and the swarming enemy in the rear!

All order and discipline were cast to the winds. Those in front were forced bodily onward by the pressure of thousands behind. Mounted men spurred their steeds to the brink, leaped into the black waters and swam to the farther shore. Some gained the bank in safety, others were shot down before they could gain the causeway. The foot soldiers, seeing no other hope, crowded onward, sprang into the water and attempted to swim. But their mail, their weapons, their gold dragged them under. Others, struck down by arrows, clubs and spears tumbled into the breach, until the opening became so filled with the dead and dying, the baggage, the arms, the treasure and the bodies of horses that those Spaniards who survived actually crossed over on the horrible bridge thus formed! As day dawned a hideous scene was revealed. Everywhere the struggle continued. Everywhere, as far as eye could see, were the swift canoes filled with armed warriors. Everywhere the mangled and disfigured corpses of Dons and Indians floated upon the waters. In one spot Alvarado, unhorsed, was fighting desperately against a group of Aztecs. Towards him hurried a number of the Dons led by Cortes himself. But their gallant efforts to relieve him were in vain. Attacked on every side they were forced to plunge into the lake and swim their steeds to the opposite bank. Wounded, as he was, Alvarado, with a supreme effort, beat back his assailants, paused for an instant, and then, rushing forward and using his lance as a vaulting-pole, he cleared the gap at a leap. To this day the spot is pointed out as the *Salto de Alvarado* (Alvarado's Leap) in memory of a feat that to both Dons and Indians alike savored of the supernatural. The worst was over. The pitiful remnants of the Spanish forces continued their retreat unmolested, and reached Tacuba in safety. Most of the cavaliers survived, Marina was safe; but many were missing, among them the children of Montezuma, and many a Spaniard of high rank, including De Leon and De Morla, while the loss of the rank and file was terrific. No two historians agree as to the total losses of the Dons, but at the lowest estimate it was not less than four hundred Spaniards and four thousand Indian allies. Scarcely a weapon and not an arquebus nor cannon remained, and the treasure was lost. The conqueror had been conquered. The Aztec gods had wreaked their vengeance. No wonder that, through the centuries, that fateful night has ever been known to the Spaniards as *La noche triste,* the sad night. It was the saddest night to the Spaniards in all the history of their conquests.

CHAPTER XIII

THE CAPITAL BESIEGED

CORTES and the shattered remnant of his forces did not linger longer than necessary at Tacuba. Had the Mexicans followed up their victory, their triumph would have been complete, but they had accomplished their aims and had driven the Dons from their capital, and they foolishly rested on their laurels. Even as it was the Spaniards' retreat was little better than a rout. Throughout the night they hurried on as fast as the condition of their wounded would permit, casting furtive glances in the rear, filled with dread that at any moment the Aztec hordes might appear to resume the attack.

Although local bands and villagers made desultory efforts to harass the Dons, these were little more than skirmishes and scarcely delayed the flight of the fugitives. Far more disastrous than these brushes with the enemy was the lack of food. The country seemed to have been stripped bare. Wild cherries, an occasional ear of corn and their own horses that died for want of fodder formed their only sustenance. Many a Spanish soldier fell dying of starvation and exhaustion by the roadside, to be put to a more merciful death by lurking Indians who ever hung upon the Spaniards' flanks.

No longer did the soldiers think of gold. Those who had come safely through the *noche triste* with their treasures now cast them away to lighten their loads, and the trail of the fleeing army was marked by the skeletons of horses, the emaciated bodies of soldiers, discarded arms and mail, abandoned baggage and glittering gems and ornaments of gold and silver. So slowly did the Dons move, that a week was consumed in traversing a distance of barely fifty miles, and their delay had afforded time for the enemy to outgeneral them. As they reached the summit of the hills about the valley of Otompan, their hearts sank and their wan faces paled in dread. Before them, filling the valley, was a huge army of the Aztecs. Their white cotton armor gave the effect of the valley being covered with snow; hundreds of banners, bearing the arms of as many chiefs, waved above the thousands of plumed casques, of shining breastplates, of gaudy feather-cloaks, and forests of spears.

It was the army of Montezuma's successor, Cuitlahua, awaiting the arrival of the Spaniards, expecting to deal a final blow that would destroy their enemies to the last man. Sheer desperation often triumphs where nothing else will, and the Dons were now in most desperate straits. Either they must cut their way through the Aztec hosts or must perish in the attempt.

Briefly, Cortes addressed his weary, famished men, urging them to take heart, recalling the victories they had so often won over vastly superior numbers, advising them to thrust rather than strike with their swords, admonishing them to strive to kill the chieftains, and exhorting them to have faith in the Cross and their God in the approaching battle with the infidels. Then, at the head of the company, he led the charge. In an instant the Spaniards seemed swallowed up, utterly annihilated. But the flashing swords, the charging horses, the long lances and the steel mail of the Dons began to tell. As usual, the Indians numbers were against them. Hurled aside, cut down by the Spaniards who literally hewed a lane through the densely packed enemy, the Aztecs closed in behind them, surrounded them, until the Dons formed the nucleus of a struggling, surging maelstrom of warriors. But only a few of the Indians could attack the Spaniards at one time. Only those in the front ranks immediately surrounding the Dons could wield their weapons, and the thousands who swarmed on every side were merely spectators, ready to step into the places left vacant by the death of their comrades.

As for the Spaniards, not a man was free from wounds within the first ten minutes of the battle; many of the allies and several Dons were killed, and Cortes himself bore a jagged cut across his scalp. But slowly, steadily the desperate band moved through the mass of warriors. Still their numbers were as steadily decreasing, and Cortes realized that long before his company could force their way through the enemy the last man would have been destroyed. At this moment he caught sight of the commander of the Aztec legions, the Cacique Cihuaca, who was borne on a litter surrounded by his bodyguard of nobles. Turning to his officers, Cortes pointed to the caçique, ordered them to follow him, and spurred his horse towards the chieftain. Trodden under the feet of the horses, dismayed at this sudden change of tactics, the Indians fell back, and the cavaliers reached the caçique's side. Cutting down the chief's guards, Cortes drove his lance through the helpless Cihuaca and pinned him to the ground where he was instantly beheaded by one of the cavaliers.

The loss of their commander caused panic among the Aztecs. The tide had turned, and in a moment they were in retreat. From men battling furiously to save their own lives the Dons were transformed to the aggressors, and, forgetting their wounds and their weariness, they followed the panic-stricken Indians until utterly exhausted and satiated with slaughter. Then, like hungry vultures, they stripped the dead of their golden and jeweled ornaments and armor, after which they piously offered thanks to God and the Virgin for their success. What the losses were is not known. But there is no doubt that this battle of Otompan was the most astonishing triumph of a handful of Spaniards (though aided by several thousand Indian allies), over fully one hundred times their numbers, in the history of the conquest.

The conquerors had now entered Tlascalan territory, the district whose inhabitants were hereditary enemies of the Aztecs and who welcomed the Dons hospitably. Everything was done to make the Spaniards comfortable, and the Tlascalan allies were treated like conquering heroes by their fellow countrymen. Cortes, however, received disquieting news. Many of his men in the district about Vera Cruz had been killed, but the settlement itself remained undisturbed. The men, too, became unruly, insisting upon returning to Cuba, and finding that words had no effect, they prepared a round-robin signed by nearly all the men and duly attested by the notary. Wounded and ill as he was, Cortes refused to accede to the demands. Troubles also brewed between the disaffected troops and the Tlascalans, owing largely to excesses committed by the soldiers, and the Indians bluntly demanded to know how much longer they were to be burdened by the invaders. Truly, poor Cortes was sorely tried during those dark days, and despite our sympathies for the oppressed and betrayed Mexicans, we cannot help being sorry for the Spanish leader, nor can we avoid admiring his steadfast determination, his iron will, his undaunted bravery and his adherence to his purpose during this time when his fortunes were at their lowest ebb. And to add to all his other troubles, an envoy arrived from Mexico urging the Tlascalans to forget their old enmity and to aid the Aztecs in driving the Spaniards from the country. Many of the Tlascalan chiefs were in favor of it, but Mazizca, ever a friend of the Dons, overruled them and the envoys' offer was indignantly rejected.

Cortes' first step, when he was able to take the field, was to lead an attack on the Tepeacans, ancient foes of the Tlascalans, partly to secure booty, partly to subdue them and remove a constant menace, but

largely to still more firmly cement his alliance with
the people of Tlascala. Several savage battles ensued, but as usual the invaders were triumphant and
the Indians surrendered, only to meet with a worse
fate than death in battle. All that had received
severe wounds were butchered like maimed cattle.
All that remained were branded with red-hot irons
and enslaved, and all their property and cities were
confiscated by the conquerors. Cortes also formed
an alliance with the caçique of Quauhquecholan by
driving out and destroying the Aztec garrison of the
town, following up this victory by attacking and
capturing the town of Itzocan. In this way he completely subjugated the entire district and eliminated
all chances of the Aztecs molesting him within the
area. Gradually his influence and his alliances were
extended, until he felt that he could control sufficient
warriors to again march upon the capital. To trust
to the causeways he knew would be dangerous, and
he determined to build a number of vessels, disas-
semble them, carry them to the lake, reassemble
them and attack the city by water.

Meanwhile, the new ruler of the Aztecs, Cuitlahua,
had died of smallpox introduced by the Spaniards,
and Guatemozin had been enthroned to succeed him.
He was a mere youth in his twenties, but noted for
his bravery, his religious fervor, his intelligence and
his hatred of the Spaniards. Not a movement, not a
plan of the Dons escaped his knowledge. He was
kept well informed of their actions, their victories,
and of Cortes' scheme for navigating the lake, and
he made preparations accordingly. All the noncom-

batants of the capital were sent to the outlying villages. All the fighting forces for miles around were brought to the city. Throughout the country all loyal Indians were ordered to beset the Dons wherever possible, and the ruler set a price on the heads of the Spaniards, with thrice the amount for every captive Don brought to him.

Cortes knew nothing of this aside from rumors of the new occupant of the Aztec throne. His force now amounted to nearly six hundred Spaniards, fifty of whom were cavalry; eighty arquebusiers and cross-bowmen and nine small cannon from the garrison at Vera Cruz. But his Indian allies totaled nearly sixty thousand under their own chiefs, and were as perfectly armed and equipped as was possible. Having reviewed his army, Cortes made a long address which was translated to the allies by Marina, the most noteworthy portion of which was his declaration that the conversion of the heathen was the prime object of the expedition, and that, "without that the war would be unjust and merely robbery and an abomination to the Lord." Truly a most astounding statement from one whose prime motive was robbery, and whose treatment of a nation must have been an abomination to the Lord if ever there was one.

He also read his orders, among which was the prohibition of gaming with dice, and of brawls and private duels, and a strict command that no officer should, under pain of death, charge or molest the Indians without orders. Finally, no man, officer or private, was to take possession of any loot for his personal use under pain of death. Moreover, Cortes enforced these rules to the letter, and shortly thereafter, hanged several men for looting the natives.

Having thus addressed his men and read the ordinances that should govern them, Cortes ordered his army to march, and with bands playing and colors flying, the forces of the conqueror passed from the friendly republic of Tlascala and headed for the distant capital.

Without molestation they reached Tezcuco where they were met by an embassy and invited to take up their quarters in the city. Although Cortes gave strict orders to respect the persons and property of the Tezcucans, yet he could not control his Indian allies, and a party of the Tlascalans burned one of the temples and committed many excesses. As a result, the people became frightened and began to desert the city. Immediately, Cortes, suspecting treachery—for he invariably judged all others by himself—ordered the soldiers to force the inhabitants back and to seize the caçique of the city. His orders came too late, however. The ruler, Cianaco, was already far beyond his reach, and, swallowing his chagrin as best he might, Cortes declared the ex-chief's brother the ruler. This prince was a mere tool in the Dons' hands, and having been baptized, was placed on the throne. This was, of course, a politic move on the part of Cortes.

Tezcuco was an excellent point from which to conduct his projected campaign of pillaging and devastating the surrounding country and laying siege to Tenochtitlan, and with a weakling, subservient to him, upon the throne, he was practically ruler of the city-state. Very rapidly Cortes transformed Tezcuco into a veritable fortress. Eight thousand Indian slaves were put to work digging a canal to connect the city with the lake, walls were fortified and moats dug; cannon were mounted on the ramparts, and every weak spot was strengthened. Meanwhile he sent a message to Guatemozin, in which he deprecated hostilities and assured the ruler that as all his late enemies had perished he was willing to forgive the past provided they submitted. Otherwise, he concluded, he would lay siege to the city and would wreak full vengeance for what the Spaniards had suffered. This time, however, there was no friendly, superstitiously fearful Montezuma on the throne of the Aztecs. There was no question of whether the Dons were friends or foes, and Cortes' offer was scornfully rejected.

The first attack of the Spaniards was made on the city of Itzapalapan, and the invaders, beating back the warriors sent to meet them, pursued their enemies into the city. Here a desperate battle ensued, the combatants fighting while in the shoal water up to their waists, and the foreigners, having at last triumphed, commenced a pitiless massacre of every man, woman and child in the city. In vain Cortes endeavored to call a halt. He had turned loose a power beyond his control; the savage, implacable Indian allies were aflame with the lust for blood, and the slaughter did not cease until more than six thousand noncombatants, every inhabitant still in the city, had been killed. In addition, the legionaries had fired the houses, and by the lurid light of the flames the Spaniards commenced looting the dead and the empty houses.

Very nearly their avariciousness cost them their lives. The Indians, mad for revenge, pierced the dykes that protected the city, and a flood of water came rushing in upon the Spaniards. Only by madly dashing from the spot and casting aside the loot did the forces of Cortes escape complete disaster. As it was all of their powder was ruined, much of their equipment was lost, and through a hail of arrows from the hundreds of canoes that swarmed upon the lake, the half-drowned, bedraggled Spaniards barely managed to reach their camp.

In many ways the battle might be said to have been a draw. The Aztecs had lost thousands of lives, much of their magnificent city had been wantonly destroyed, but they had caused the Dons irreparable losses of property and equipment and had driven their enemies to their holes. Despite this, however, the fate of Itzapalapan redounded to the Dons' advantage and several cities offered allegiance to Cortes if he would aid them in throwing off the Aztec yoke. After a few sharp struggles the invaders drove the Aztec garrisons from these towns and added their citizens to their allies. Still Cortes was little nearer taking the capital than ever. He realized the inadequacy of his forces, and he was fully aware of how little trust could be placed in his new allies, composed of numerous tribes each on hostile terms with some of the others. By dint of argument, threats and his remarkable personality,

Cortes succeeded at last in reconciling all their differences—probably his most remarkable and praiseworthy achievement since coming to Mexico —a feat to which he largely owed his final success.

Once more he endeavored to frighten or browbeat the Aztec emperor into submission. But the young Guatemozin was as determined, as dauntless as the conqueror himself. Though he realized the hopelessness of his position, though the entire responsibility for the fate of his people rested on his shoulders, he was prepared to concede nothing to those who had shown themselves the most deadly foes of his race. The result of Cortes' message was merely to arouse a still greater hatred for the Dons, and to cause him to command that every Spaniard captured should be sacrificed upon the altars of the temples.

Soon after this the dismantled vessels built at Tlascala arrived, their individual parts carried by Indian slaves and escorted by twenty thousand warriors. The arrival of these thirteen tiny ships was received with the utmost delight and enthusiasm by the Dons who lined the road and cheered lustily as the array, covering a length of seven miles, passed slowly into Tezcuco. It was in truth a marvelous feat to have constructed these vessels, tested them upon the lake near Tlascala, taken them down, transported them for one hundred miles overland, and reassembled them upon the waters of Tezcuco. While the little ships were being reassembled and rigged, Cortes employed his time by making raids on the suburbs of the capital, massacring, looting,

burning and destroying. Having conquered and
fired the beautiful city of Tlacopan, the Dons, in
pursuit of the retreating Indians, hot-headedly
followed them on the causeway and across the
bridges where the terrible scenes of the *noche triste*
had taken place. Too late the Spaniards realized
their mistake and that they had been decoyed into a
trap. The Indians, halting, turned on their foes with
terrific fury; hundreds of canoes appeared as if by
magic on every side and poured a hail of arrows,
javelins and stones upon the amazed Spaniards who,
fighting every step of the way, with many falling
dead or wounded, with the utmost difficulty extri-
cated themselves from the dilemma into which their
impetuosity had led them.

To add to Cortes' discomfiture at making so little
headway, messages were brought to him, by means
of his allies who had fallen into the Aztecs' hands,
asking him, in mock courtesy, why he delayed so
long in making another visit to the city, and assuring
him of a far warmer reception than he had received
from Montezuma.

Moreover, the Aztecs seemed to have suffered no
diminution in numbers despite the hordes that had
fallen in battle. Their legions were more numerous
and better drilled and equipped than ever. There was
no outward sign that the city itself had suffered from
the previous battles, and the confidence of the
Aztecs greatly disturbed the Dons. And during
their protracted struggles, their victories and their
defeats, the Spaniards had acquired a wholesome
respect for their enemies and had lost much of their

former cocksureness. Cortes had no intention of rushing blindly into a conflict this time. He went warily, cautiously, and he was particularly careful to guard the vessels upon which everything depended.

About this time most welcome reënforcements arrived from Hispaniola, and Cortes' forces were increased by more than two hundred well-armed men with an abundance of equipment, ammunition, cannon and supplies. Also, with these came a number of Dominican friars, one of whom had most thoughtfully brought along a stock of pontifical bulls offering special indulgences to all who took up arms against the infidels. Being a far better tradesman than priest, the padre offered to dispose of these to the soldiers in exchange for gold, and arguing that his supply of the papers was limited, he drove hard bargains—much to the scandalization of good Father Olmedo and regardless of his protests. Having at last exhausted his stock in trade of spiritual wares, he returned to Hispaniola with a tidy fortune, which, it is a satisfaction to know, was promptly confiscated by the Superior of the Order and devoted to the use of the Church.

Volumes might be filled with accounts of the innumerable skirmishes, the many battles, the plots and counterplots, the victories and the massacres that took place in and about the Valley of Mexico during the weeks that followed. Many Aztec cities and towns were captured or destroyed, many cities willingly and gladly became allies of the Spaniards. But the campaigns of the Dons were not carried out without loss. Many soldiers were killed, many so seriously wounded that they were crippled for life, and many were taken prisoners and sacrificed by the Aztecs. In many a temple the dried skins, the ghastly mummified heads, and the armor of sacrificed Spaniards hung on the walls as trophies or were placed before the images of the gods as offerings. Indeed, Cortes came very near meeting the same terrible fate. Thrown from his horse he was seized by the Indians and was being dragged away when a Tlascalan warrior threw himself on the enemies and succeeded in releasing the conqueror. Whether in his extremity, and a bit dazed from being knocked over the head with a club, Cortes mistook the valiant Tlascalan for a supernatural being, or whether he saw in him an instrument of the Lord, we cannot say with certainty, but at any rate, instead of rewarding the warrior or giving credit where credit was due, he attributed his timely rescue to Saint Peter, donated a large sum to the Church for his deliverance, and ordered special prayers and Masses said in gratitude to the Saint.

By the time the thirteen vessels were ready to navigate the lake practically all the Valley of Mexico, all the territory between the capital and the eastern coast, and a considerable area to the north and south, had been—to all intents and purposes—conquered. Only the taking of the capital remained to make the conquest complete, and Cortes now made final preparations for that important stroke.

His forces now mustered eighty-eight cavalrymen, eight hundred and twenty-five infantrymen, of whom more than one hundred were armed with crossbows or arquebuses; and there were three large fieldpieces of iron and twelve light brass cannon. He had more than six tons of powder, a great amount of shot and cannon balls, and his archers were supplied with more than fifty thousand bronze-tipped arrows. It was the largest, best equipped and most powerful force that had yet taken part in the conquest. Each of the twelve vessels—one having been discarded as unseaworthy and a poor sailer—was equipped with a cannon, and, from his army, Cortes managed to secure enough men with some knowledge of the sea to man his fleet. His allies formed a veritable host. There were fifty thousand Tlascalans alone, and the other towns that had allied themselves with the Dons sent twice as many more. Commanded by Alvarado and Olid, the greater portion of this immense army marched towards the capital with the purpose of besieging it by land. Their first act was to destroy the aqueduct that carried water to the capital, and after a severe fight with the Aztecs guarding it—and not without heavy losses to the Dons—this was accomplished. Next, the Dons attempted to take possession of the causeways. But in this they met with utter defeat and, with the heaviest losses they had yet suffered, retreated to their camp. Meanwhile Cortes with his companies had embarked upon the vessels and had set sail for the portion of the capital on the lake. *En route* he was attacked by a flotilla of canoes, but running them down, and mercilessly slaying the natives struggling in the waters, Cortes completely annihilated them and proved himself master of the inland sea. Anchoring in a favorable spot that commanded the causeway with his guns, Cortes landed, drove off the few Aztecs on guard, transferred his heavier cannon to the shore and established his camp. The capital was now surrounded on all sides by the Spaniards and their allies. Tenochtitlan was besieged, and the army settled down to await the ravages of famine and of thirst that, they felt certain, would soon force Guatemozin to surrender.

CHAPTER XIV

THE FALL OF TENOCHTITLAN

THOUGH the city was blockaded, though the Spaniards had no doubt that it must soon capitulate, yet Cortes was too impatient to wait idly for the results. To hasten matters he determined to assault the city, and after dint of severe fighting, succeeded in forcing a way into the suburbs. Steadily, battling at every step, losing a man here, several there, using their cannon to batter down walls and barricades, leveling buildings as they went in order to prevent the enemy from pouring a rain of missiles from the roofs, the Dons at last reached their former quarters in the shadow of the great pyramid.

Amazed, filled with superstitious fears at finding their foes had reached the heart of their city, the Indians retreated. Instantly, a party of Spaniards raced up the steps of the *teocalli,* to find the Cross and shrine they had erected replaced by an Aztec idol. Tearing the gold and jewels from the image, they hurled it over the brink, and seizing the struggling priests, cast them screaming after their god.

But their zeal cost them dearly. With all their fury aroused a hundredfold by this desecration of their temple and their gods, the Aztecs threw themselves like demons upon the Spaniards gathered in the great courtyard.

Taken by surprise, outnumbered, the Dons became panic-stricken, and abandoning their cannon, raced madly through the streets towards their allies. Catching the panic of the Spaniards, the Tlascalans joined in the rout, while from all sides the shouting, triumphant Aztecs poured a rain of arrows and javelins upon them from every point of vantage.

In vain Cortes tried to rally his men. His terror-stricken troops, if they heard his shouted words, gave them no heed, and like a chip on a torrent he was borne onwards with the rushing stream of fear-maddened men.

Just when all seemed lost a party of cavalry dashed from a neighboring street to aid the fugitives. But the invaders had had enough of it. They were far too thankful to escape with their lives to turn on their foes and they made the best of their way out of the city and to their camp. Despite this disastrous repulse a second attack was made on the city the following day. During the night all the barricades had been repaired, and all the Dons had accomplished the previous day had to be repeated. Maddened at the stubborn resistance offered, Cortes now determined to put the city to the torch and to carry on a war of extermination. The first building to go up in flames was the splendid palace of Montezuma. This was followed by the adjoining edifices, but owing to the nature of the materials used in the construction of the buildings this first attempt at ruthless destruction resulted in only a small section of the neighborhood being burned.

Meanwhile, on the opposite sides of the city, Alvarado and Olid, with their forces, were duplicating the assaults, but with less success, though they showed more common and military sense than Cortes, and, having once battered down a defense and secured a position, they held it and prevented the enemy from repairing damages during the night.

Neither was Guatemozin idle. His counter attacks were frequent, severe and conducted with military knowledge, discipline, and often with success, and he gave the besieging Dons no rest, day or night.

For three months the siege continued, the Spaniards making daily attacks but gaining little. First one side then the other could claim the honors of the day. By strategy the Aztecs captured one of Cortes' vessels and killed most of the crew, and by strategy the Aztecs managed to maintain communications with the outside world, and, to the wondering Dons, seemed in no danger of suffering for either food or water. And never once through those long months did the spirits of the Aztecs weaken nor Guatemozin waver from his determination to resist the Spaniards to the end.

Gradually, however, the city's supplies were cut off. The immense stores of provisions accumulated in preparation for this very siege were becoming woefully low, the outlying towns that had furnished the city food under cover of night had been conquered or destroyed, and famine began to stalk through the streets of Tenochtitlan. But if the Aztecs in the city suffered, so did their enemies. It was the rainy season, the Spaniards were constantly drenched to the skin, their provisions, too, were very scant, and their allies frequently satisfied their gnawing hunger by dining on the bodies of the slain. Many of the Spaniards sickened and died, others succumbed to their wounds, and, preferring anything to the monotony and hardships they were undergoing, the soldiers clamored for a bold attack regardless of consequences. Though not approving of the attempt, Cortes was forced to yield to the demands of his men, and on the appointed day a general assault was ordered.

Fighting as they advanced, the Spaniards and their allies forced their way towards the center of the city. And as they advanced the resistance seemed to decrease, the defenders to have little heart in battling with their antagonists, until the Dons found themselves moving with comparative ease and rapidity. They had almost reached the great market-place when from the summit of a *teocalli* the blare of a shell-trumpet sounded. Instantly the retreating Aztecs wheeled, and from every street, every building, every lane, hordes of warriors sprang as if by magic and fell upon the surprised Spaniards. No living men could have resisted that cyclone of savage, exasperated, hunger-maddened Aztecs. The Dons, confused, blinded by arrows, attacked on every side, cut down by swinging obsidian swords, pierced by javelins, fought, struggled, trod upon one another, swayed madly seeking some avenue of escape, and fell by dozens. In their mad flight they failed even to note the openings where their foes had destroyed bridges in their rear.

Into the breaches they poured, screaming, fighting one another as they felt the waters close over them. Cortes, striving to restore order, was injured in one leg, and Olid was mortally wounded. The conqueror, unhorsed, helpless, was surrounded by Aztecs bent on taking him alive, and a ferocious hand-to-hand conflict took place above the prostrate leader. His page was stabbed in the throat, Guzman, his chamberlain, was seized and carried off in triumph, but at last Cortes managed to gain his saddle, and surrounded by his most valiant cavaliers, fought his way to safety, though two of his captains were lost. The rout was complete. Not since the *noche triste* had the invaders suffered such a defeat, and the Spaniards—or those who escaped—had no further thoughts of attacking the city for the present at least.

And it added to their depression and their forebodings of the future when the dull resonant boom of the temple drum broke the silence of the late afternoon, and with horrified faces the defeated Spaniards saw their captured comrades being led up the steps of the *teocalli* to be sacrificed upon the altars of the Aztecs' gods.

This defeat of the Spaniards led to other and most deplorable results. Their allies, no longer filled with the idea that the invaders were invincible, began to desert them, and in a few days only a few hundreds remained of the tens of thousands who had flocked to the Spanish colors. Still Cortes

bore up, and more remarkable still, he managed to
instill a measure of confidence in his men. Presently, too, a large portion of their allies returned,
ashamed of their disaffection, and to the Spaniards'
intense joy and relief they received unexpected reënforcements of their fellow countrymen. The fleet
of romantic Ponce de Leon, bound for the coast of
Florida, where the imaginative cavalier hoped to discover the Fountain of Youth, put in at Vera Cruz.
Willy-nilly the authorities seized the supplies, equipment, ammunition and arms, and forwarded them
on to Cortes. Also, a number of Ponce de Leon's
followers, seeing greater prospects of an easy life in
joining the conqueror than in seeking eternal youth-
fulness, joined Cortes' forces.

Having now in a measure recovered from his disaster, and with plenty of ammunition and supplies,
Cortes decided to make his greatest and final effort
to seize the capital. This time he was to be more
ruthless, more wanton in his destruction than ever.
Every building was to be leveled as the Spaniards
advanced. He was ready to raze the city to the
ground, and though his terrible decision may have
been necessary for his success as a measure of war,
on which grounds it has been excused by many, yet
we must remember that it was a war of unprovoked
conquest, and the necessities that demanded his destruction of the city were the same necessities that
cause the burglar to murder the victim who resists
him.

But Cortes still was, at heart, a gallant cavalier
with a sense of honor. He sent a last message to

Guatemozin beseeching him, for the sake of his people and his city, to surrender, promising forgiveness for all the past.

No doubt, had the conquerors proved their trustworthiness in the past, the Aztec emperor would have capitulated. But he and his people had every cause to mistrust the good faith and fair words of the Spaniards. The fate of Montezuma was still fresh in their minds; they had seen what happened when the Dons had triumphed elsewhere, and the young monarch, his proud and independent spirit unbroken, would not willingly bend his head to the conqueror. However, he was willing to abide by the decision of his councilors, and he left the matter in their hands. But they were of one mind with their monarch. "Peace is good," they announced, "but not with the white men. Wherever we have shown them friendship it has resulted in oppressions and death. Montezuma's hospitality was repaid by imprisonment and fetters. Better that we trust to the promises of our gods or if need be give up our lives than become slaves to the strangers."

"So be it," agreed Guatemozin. "Let no Aztec henceforth think of surrender. We can at least die like warriors."

The answer to the Spaniard's message came in the form of an attack by the desperate defenders of the city. Like a torrent they poured through every street, every gate, and like a deluge they swept in wave after wave upon the invaders. Incessantly the muskets and cannon roared and flamed. Great

furrows were plowed through the ranks of the Aztecs. Arms ached with the thrusting, slashing, stab-
bing, with wielding sword, poniard and lance, until
at last the Aztec host sullenly retreated and vanished in the mazes of their capital.

Cortes now took the offensive. Day after day
his thousands labored, fought and advanced from
every side. Houses, temples, palaces, public buildings; every edifice, regardless of its beauty, its magnificence, its historic value, was mined, battered
down, torn to pieces, utterly destroyed. The débris
was used to fill the canals, and the beautiful city
was transformed to a waste as the Dons slowly
advanced, inexorably, like a devastating, irresistible force.

Undismayed the Aztecs kept up an incessant fire,
shouting taunts, harassing the Spaniards and their
allies constantly. "Destroy!" they shouted. "The
more you cast down the more you will have to build
hereafter. If we conquer you shall build for us.
If you are victorious you must build for yourselves."

Over and over again they threw themselves upon
their enemies, seemingly heedless of results to themselves, and though they were as often driven back,
yet each sortie left dead and wounded among the
Dons and their Indian allies.

In time Cortes' men on one side and Alvarado's
on the other met at the great avenue of Tacuba near
the palace of Guatemozin, a magnificent building.
Though deserted by the emperor it was held by a
garrison of his warriors, but they were soon forced
to flee as the Spaniards set fire to the palace, and

in a short time the splendid pile, one of the finest examples of Aztec architecture in the city, was reduced to fragments. All this had taken weeks to accomplish, and the inhabitants of the city were suffering terribly from famine. A few, too weak to resist, were taken prisoners, and these were kindly treated and fed by Cortes' orders, probably not so much from pity as from a desire to induce others to surrender. Few did so, however, and the bulk of the population continued to exist—if existence it could be called—upon the few roots, the grass, the bark of trees, even on offal, while their only water was the brackish water that seeped into shallow wells from the lake. Hundreds sickened and died daily; dead bodies—little more than skin and bones—were found by scores each day as the Spaniards penetrated farther and farther into the city. In innumerable houses, doomed to destruction, the Dons came upon terrible sights—men, women and children perishing of hunger; men covered with uncared-for wounds, and corpses decomposing, poisoning the foul air but allowed to remain by the emaciated living who were too weak to move the bodies of their companions. But even death in its most terrible forms, the agonies of famine, the sight of their loved ones dying before their eyes, did not force the Aztecs to submission. Better to die than become slaves was their constant cry, and with their last gasps they taunted the Dons by declaring they would have all their labors for nothing, as all the treasure in the city had been hidden where the Spaniards could never find it. Even the women heroically took part in defending their homes and city. They cared for the wounded, worked constantly at making arrows and weapons, and at times took the places of their husbands and sons in battle.

By the time the Spaniards had penetrated to the market-place, seven-eighths of the immense and glorious capital had been laid waste, converted to a wilderness of smoldering timbers, broken stones, shattered walls, and the remaining eighth of the city was a charnel house. Dead lay in heaps; the living, too weak to move, resigned themselves to death amid the festering bodies, and to add to the horrors a pestilence broke out. In the midst of this pesthouse, wherein were crowded eight times the normal population of the quarter, the indomitable emperor remained unmoved by the devastation, the awful scenes on every side.

Cortes made preparations for his final act in this inhuman drama. Summoning all his men, he led the attack upon the famine-weakened, starving people. With what little strength that remained they made a feeble resistance, but many were unable to lift a spear or sword, too weak to bend a bow. Training their artillery upon the houses, discharging volleys of musketry, cutting the helpless people down with their swords, running them through with the lances, the Dons swept through the only portion of the city left standing. The carnage was indescribable; mounds of dead and dying filled the streets, the horses were knee-deep in human flesh, the canals ran crimson with blood. To be sure, Cortes had given orders that all who surrendered should be spared, that women and children should not be killed, but he was as powerless to control his savage allies and his equally savage countrymen as to control a tornado. No quarter was given, neither sex nor age was spared. At last, unable longer to endure such sights, Cortes ordered a retreat, but not before forty thousand Aztecs had been slain. Yet those few who survived remained loyal to their king, loyal to their country, loyal to their decision to die any death rather than be enslaved by the conqueror.

On the following day the terrible massacre of the starving, disease-ridden, helpless Indians was resumed. Bodies soon filled the canals until the cavalry rode across the bridges formed of their victims. Those who sought to flee in canoes were blown to atoms by the cannon of the Dons' vessels. Few in that fated quarter lived to tell the tale of the horrors of that butchery. Among those that, knowing all was lost, took to a canoe, was the emperor. But before his craft had traveled far it was overtaken by the Spaniards, and the arquebusiers were on the point of putting every occupant to death when their captain, Holguin, suspecting the monarch might be of the party, ordered his men not to shoot. At the order a young warrior, who had risen with *machahitl* in hand to die fighting, threw down his weapon. "I am Guatemozin!" he cried. "Take me to Malinche, I am his prisoner. But let no harm come to my wife and children."

Holguin assented, and the occupants of the canoe,

among whom were the emperor's family and a number of caçiques, were taken aboard one of the Spanish vessels. Arriving there, Holguin begged the
captive emperor to command his people to surrender.

"It is not needed," replied Guatemozin. "Now
that I am taken they will fight no more."

Hardly had he spoken when all resistance ceased.
All the Aztecs in the canoes and ashore threw down
their weapons; a wail of sorrow and despair arose,
and the Indians followed like faithful dogs as their
monarch was led ashore and into the presence of
Cortes. The conqueror welcomed him as befitted his
prisoner's rank, and assured him he would be treated
with honor and the respect due a brave and valiant
enemy. To this the still proud and dignified youth
replied that he had done all he could do to defend
his city and his people, that he was now the prisoner
of Cortes to do with as he pleased. Then, with
sudden fire, he added, touching the hilt of the dagger at Cortes' side. "Better kill me at once with
this than allow me to live a slave."

Meanwhile, Cortes had given orders for Guatemozin's wife to be brought to him. She was the
youngest daughter of Montezuma, one of the children of that monarch whom Cortes had been asked
to guard and protect, and the conqueror received
her with every respect and courtesy.

The following day Cortes gave orders—at the request of the emperor—that the few surviving Aztecs
were to be permitted to leave the city without mo-

lestation, and for three days the mournful, starved, sick and wounded people filed out of the ruins of their once-proud capital. Of the half million people who had dwelt within Tenochtitlan—to say nothing of the countless thousands of warriors from the neighboring districts—barely forty-five thousand survived. The Spaniards had conquered, but at fearful cost to both themselves and the enemy, and they had but a shell, a ruined, empty husk for their recompense. As the Aztecs had warned them, practically all the valuables had been secreted. The total loot obtained by the Dons amounted to less than half a million dollars—a mere tithe of what had originally been in the city.

Incensed at thus being cheated of all that had led them to Mexico, all that they had struggled and suffered and fought and died for, the Spaniards were loud in their expressions of dissatisfaction, their ill-founded charges that Cortes had cheated them, and their insistence that the captive emperor should be forced to divulge the hiding place of the treasure. In vain Cortes tried to calm them and to reason with them. They demanded that Guatemozin be put to the torture to wring the secret from him, and Cortes, to save his own face—for he had been accused of being in league with his prisoner—consented, despite his pledges that Guatemozin should be treated with honor and respect.

In all his career Cortes had never been guilty of such an atrocious act. He had been ruthless, at times cruel, unprincipled in his conquest; even inhuman, and he had at times resorted to guile, to

treachery and to double-dealing. But never before
had he stooped to such a despicable act as to deliver a helpless prisoner, whom he had promised
to protect, to the common soldiers to be tortured
into a confession of the hiding place of gold.

But if the Dons thought that suffering would
wring truths or untruths from the man who had
suffered so much, they were mistaken. When a
caçique, who had been subjected to the rack at the
same time, groaned in anguish, the torn, tortured
emperor exclaimed: "Why complain? Do you think
I am enjoying *my* bath?" All that could be wrung
from him by the most excruciating tortures the
Spaniards could invent—and they were past-masters
in the art—was that the gold had been cast into the
water.

At last, realizing the enormity of his action, unable to endure the sufferings of the monarch
longer, Cortes ordered Guatemozin released, in time
to save his life. But he might as well have been
allowed to die, for a few months later, finding his
royal captive a burden on his hands, Cortes accused
him on a trumped-up charge of conspiracy, and
hanged the last of the Aztec emperors to a tree by
the roadside.

Of the two men Guatemozin must ever stand forth
as the more noble, the more honorable, the more
honest and the braver.

His last words were brief, but branded the conqueror forever. "I knew what it would be to trust
one as false as you, Malinche," he exclaimed. "I

knew that you had destined me to this fate when I did not die by my own hand when you entered Tenochtitlan. But why slay me so unjustly? Your God will demand vengeance from you!''

CHAPTER XV

DEATH COMES TO THE CONQUEROR

WITH the fall of Tenochtitlan the conquest of the country was practically complete. To subdue the few remaining states and cities was comparatively easy. The conquerors penetrated north, west and south. Settlements were established by Cortes on the Pacific and as far north as California. Southward, he overran Guatemala and Honduras, though the conquest of those countries fell largely to the sunny-faced but black-hearted Alvarado. Though the conqueror had accomplished his conquest he was not at ease. No word had yet been received from Spain to confirm the position he held by authority of the council of Vera Cruz appointed by himself. No reply had been received to his numerous letters to the king. Troubled by the royal silence, not knowing where or how he stood, he wrote still another letter and sent with it the royal fifth of all the loot he had taken, a rich collection of Mexican handicraft, specimens of products, birds and beasts, and last but by no means least, an immense pyramidal emerald whose base was as large as a man's hand.

Unfortunately the treasure never reached the King of Spain. The ship that bore it was captured by a French privateer and the wonderful emerald, the gold, and everything of worth went to swell the coffers of the King of France.

The letter, however, was in due time delivered to the Court. But the only result, as far as Cortes was concerned, was to bring a commissioner with a royal order for the arrest of the conqueror. The officials at Vera Cruz refused to accept his credentials, however; he was bought off by Cortes and returned to Cuba with much gold and no glory, and Cortes was again in possession of his territory though no more securely established in authority than before.

Meanwhile enemies were working against Cortes in Spain, and had the conqueror known of what was going on there he would have been far more uneasy than he was.

Cortes and Mexico were in fact a burning question at the Spanish Court, and had it not been for the support of his friends, especially his father, Don Martin Cortes and his friend the Duke de Bejar, Cortes' career would have come to a sudden end.

Accusations poured in to the king from one side, the highest praises and most exaggerated plaudits poured in from the other. By one party Cortes was accused of every crime and offense against God, the Crown and his fellowmen. By the other he was pictured as a Crusader, a hero, a defender of the Faith, a miracle-worker and the greatest Spaniard of his day. His enemies declared he had usurped the powers of the Crown, had defied the king, and had robbed the royal treasury of its rightful share of gold. His friends countered by vowing he had enriched the Crown beyond calculation, had robbed himself, had added priceless territory and eternal glory to Spain. One faction demanded that he should be imprisoned, hanged, beheaded. The other claimed that he should be knighted, given every reward within the power of the king. No wonder the poor young monarch was at a total loss as to whom to believe and left the whole matter to a committee appointed for the purpose.

There was much of truth and much of falsehood in the testimony of both enemies and friends. Many of the more serious charges—such as the torture and death of Guatemozin, the seizure of Velasquez's vessels, the oppression of the natives, the wanton destruction of the capital, were perfectly true. But the vindications of his friends were equally weighty and just. The main argument, however, the one point that really interested the council, was the undeniable fact that Cortes had won a new empire and vast treasures for Castile. The acts of Cortes were all confirmed. He was made Governor, Captain-General, and Chief Justice of New Spain with the powers of a Viceroy.

Meanwhile the capital was being rebuilt—the prophecies of the Aztecs were being fulfilled, and toiling Indian slaves labored under the unrelenting eyes of their masters to rebuild the city they had destroyed. Four years after its fall, Tenochtitlan was replaced by the City of Mexico and was much the same as it is to-day. Throughout the country the Spaniards were settling, the Indians had become little more than slaves and only the Tlascalans —as a reward for the invaluable aid they had rendered Cortes—were exempted from being forced into slavery.

Although the conquerors had little regard for the bodies of the Indians, they were possessed with the utmost regard for their souls, and Cortes begged that numbers of missionaries might be sent to Mexico, but cautioned: "See to it they are not pampered bishops and prelates, but goodly men of pure and unblemished lives. Thus only can they exercise influence over the people who have been accustomed to see the least departure from morals in their own priests punished by the utmost penalties and death."

Among those who arrived in Mexico as soon as peace had been established was the Señora Cortes— the former Doña Catalina Juarez of the long-past intrigue in Cuba. But the arrival of his wife gave little cause for satisfaction to the conqueror. She was a petulant, shrewish woman, and the conqueror, who had never quailed before the legions of the Aztecs and had faced every danger and every foe with equanimity, cowered and became a craven under the lashing of her vitriolic tongue. The temperate climate of Mexico did not agree with the hot-tempered lady of a tropical land, however, and within three months of her arrival she relieved the henpecked conquerer by an opportune death. Indeed, that event was a bit too opportune, and tongues wagged and malicious enemies of the governor hinted that something more rapid than asthma had carried her off—hints that were probably without foundation.

Matters did not go altogether smoothly in Mexico, however. While Cortes was absent on his expedition to Honduras, dissensions broke out in the capital, the various officials committed outrages and excesses and an insurrection was threatened. Hearing of this, Cortes made all haste to return to Mexico, but Fate seemed to have turned against him. Twice he was driven back by tempests and storms, and, remembering the last words of Guatemozin, the conqueror felt sure that he was about to pay the penalty for his sins. So certain of his death did he feel that he actually prepared the shroud in which to be buried. But with fresh word of the trouble in the capital he determined to once more attempt to reach his colony. Again he was buffeted by storms and, driven far off his course, was forced to land in Cuba, where he remained for some time to recoup his exhausted strength. Finally, however, he reached Mexico but, as his contemporaries declared, more like a corpse than a living man.

His arrival settled the difficulties almost at once. But the conqueror was a changed man. Whether his conscience troubled him and he worried over his despicable treatment of Guatemozin, whether he was actually suffering from some disease, or whether it was his recent campaign and his conviction that the hand of God was turned against him, it is hard to tell. But he was no longer the strong, determined, dominating Cortes of old. He was weak and vacillating, seeming to have lost all interest in life. And his condition was not improved when a vessel arrived from Spain bearing a Residential Judge with royal warrant to take over temporarily the government of Mexico. Cortes' enemies had been at work, word of the internal troubles in the capital had sifted to Spain, and the Crown had deemed it wise to investigate matters. The only comfort that Cortes could glean in this dismal hour was the confidence he had in the honesty and justice of the official, who was none other than Luis Ponce de Leon, son of the famous seeker after perpetual youth, a man of unquestioned integrity and judgment.

But Cortes' ill luck seemed to dog him everywhere. De Leon died within a few weeks and was replaced by a feeble-minded old man named Estrada.

Puffed up with his own importance, already on the verge of his dotage, and glorying in making other people uncomfortable, Estrada did everything in his power—which was large—to insult, mortify and degrade every one with whom he came in conflict. Cortes was treated like a menial; a servant who displeased the irascible old fellow was sentenced to lose his hand, and when Cortes remonstrated he was expelled from the city.

At last, unable to bear his disgraces and his ill-treatment further, Cortes embarked for Spain, accompanied by a few old friends, several Aztec and Tlascalan caçiques and the surviving son of Montezuma. He did not forget to take along a vast treasure in gold, silver and gems to the value of more than a million dollars, in addition to huge emeralds worth as much more, while in addition, he carried a very complete collection of plants, ores, birds, beasts, pottery, textiles, feather-work, in fact

a veritable museum of Mexico's products and resources.

At Palos, where he landed, the conqueror of Mexico met the future conqueror of Peru. Cortes and
Pizarro, who were distant kinsmen and old friends,
talked long and earnestly over their pasts and fu-
tures, and from the returning conqueror of New
Spain, Pizarro learned much that aided his future
career.

Cortes was graciously received by the king, who
was deeply interested in the specimens—and more
particularly in the treasure—that the conqueror presented to him. He announced publicly that he had
every confidence in Cortes. He showed the conqueror marked attention, visiting him in person
when he was ill, and investing him with the exalted
title of Marquis of Oaxaca. With this title went
a vast grant of land in Oaxaca, other estates in the
Valley of Mexico and over twenty large towns, together with twenty-five thousand vassals, all of
which were bestowed because of "the good services
rendered by Cortes and the great benefits resulting
therefrom, both in respect to the increase of the
Empire of Castile and the advancement of the Holy
Catholic Faith," as the voluminous document be-
stowing the honors on Cortes put it.

But despite these honors and the avowed confidence of the sovereign, the king absolutely refused to reinstate Cortes as Governor of Mexico.
As conqueror he was in favor, as governor in disgrace. Yet Cortes had no need to complain. He
was rich beyond the dreams of avarice, he had re-

ceived the highest of honors, he was still Captain-General of New Spain.

He found a new interest in Spain, in the shape of the Doña Juana de Zuñiga, niece of the Duke de Bejar, a lady of nobility and royal lineage as well as of great wealth, and quite suited to become the bride of the millionaire-marquis-conqueror. Among the presents bestowed upon his young and beautiful bride were five huge emeralds carved by the Aztec artisans in the forms of flowers, fishes and birds.

But life in the humdrum capitals of Old Spain soon became monotonous to Cortes, and in the spring of 1530, he embarked for Mexico where he was received with enthusiasm by the people and where he maintained the court of a potentate. He took up his residence at Cuernavaca and devoted his time to husbandry, exchanging the sword for the plow and succeeding in conquering the soil as well as he had conquered the country. He was the first to introduce sugar cane to Mexico, the first to introduce merino sheep and blooded cattle, and the first to introduce silkworms. In addition, he developed many rich mines on his property, drawing a fortune in gold from Tehuantepec and several fortunes in silver from Zacatecas.

Still, a little of the old adventurer was left in him, and he embarked on a venture to explore and colonize Lower California, a venture that proved most disastrous and in which the conqueror nearly lost his life.

This did not dismay him, however. A second expedition was sent out, but it was even more unfortunate than the first and was never heard from. Apparently convinced that his adventuring days were over, Cortes decided to resign himself to a quiet life. In fact necessity forced it on him, for he had lost the neat sum of nearly four million dollars by his attempt to add to his domains, and was forced to pawn his wife's jewels to raise money. Even then, he was heavily in debt for the rest of his life.

But if his ill-starred expeditions had brought him no financial returns, they were noteworthy for the geographical knowledge gained by them. For the first time the Pacific coast had been explored from Panama to the Rio Colorado, Lower California had been circumnavigated, the Gulf of California had been explored, and much had been learned of the flora and fauna, the natives and the resources of those new lands and seas.

From time to time the Marquis became involved in quarrels with the officials; and finally, determined to lay his side of the story before the king, he bade farewell to his wife, and accompanied by his son Martin, then eight years of age, sailed for Spain. He found the king absent and, at the end of a year, seeing redress no nearer than ever, joined a company of volunteers in an expedition against Algiers. But ill luck or the curse of Guatemozin still pursued Cortes. A terrific tempest scattered the naval vessels, the flagship was driven upon a reef and lost, and Cortes and his son barely saved their lives by swimming ashore. But the famous jewels of the Marquesa, the emeralds that had once adorned the regal person of Montezuma, went to the bottom of the sea.

Upon his return to Spain he laid his troubles before the king, but he met with little more than civility. Mexico was a thing of the past. The treasures of the looted Incas were pouring in from Peru, and the monarch cared little for the plaints of one whose conquests were over while another conqueror was in the ascendant. For three years Cortes lingered, striving pathetically to induce the king to redress his wrongs, real or imaginary. At last disheartened, filled with bitterness at the neglect and ingratitude of his sovereign and his country, he decided to leave Spain forever and return to Mexico.

But he got no farther than Seville. He was taken ill with dysentery and sank rapidly. Convinced that his end was drawing near, he made all arrangements for the disposal of his property, provided for all his offspring, legitimate and illegitimate, left a large portion of his holdings to be devoted to charity and to endow a hospital, a theological college and a convent. He also left instructions as to his funeral and burial, and attended to every business detail with the utmost care. In the rather remarkable document by which he disposed of his multitudinous interests and holdings, he inserted the following still more remarkable paragraph: "It has long been a question," he wrote, "whether one can conscientiously own Indian slaves. Since this point is not determined I enjoin my son Martin and his heirs to come to an exact knowledge of the truth as it concerns their consciences as much as my own."

Obviously certain matters were troubling the conscience of the dying conqueror. But with all the black marks that can be checked up against him, with all his misdeeds and his crimes, Cortes had far less to trouble his mind than any other Spanish conqueror. Very soon he discovered that many who had treated him coldly in life became most solicitous of his welfare as he neared death. But the dying Cortes would have none of them. To avoid his unwelcome visitors, he had himself removed from Seville to the village of Castilleja de la Cuesta. There, having confessed his sins and received the Sacrament, he calmly faced the future, as he had so many times faced the unknown. He breathed his last on the second of December, 1547.

Thus death came to the conqueror in the sixty-third year of a life which for adventures, victories, achievements and conquest has few equals in history.

CHAPTER XVI

A STRANGE PARTNERSHIP

WITHIN a secluded room on the outskirts of Old Panama, three men sat in earnest conversation. Three men, whose conference was to result in the greatest conquest of the New World, the destruction of an empire and the looting of the greatest treasure the world had ever known. Three men, obscure, unknown beyond the narrow boundaries of the little colony on the Isthmus, but destined to become world-famous figures, although two of the trio could neither read nor write and were of illegitimate birth, reared in the gutter, and one of whom had passed his youth as a swineherd.

A strangely incongruous trio they were. One, clothed in green and scarlet, was stocky, short, bull-necked and swarthy. His small black eyes were bold, shifty and cruel. His nose was as sharp as the beak of a hawk. His thin hard lips and receding chin were hidden beneath a thick black beard, and his black hair grew low above the shaggy brows. In every feature he bore the stamp of a cruel, arrogant, ill-tempered scoundrel; a Spaniard of the worst type —and a soldier. At his right was seated a much older man dressed in faded gray and blue. He was small, thin and angular. The hair that fringed his bald pate was almost white. A grizzled, ragged beard and mustache covered his chin and lips. His nose was long, crooked and reddened, and his protruding pale-gray eyes roved here, there and everywhere. He was, taken all in all, a rather kindly-looking, seemingly harmless and somewhat slow-witted old fellow, and might have been an out-at-elbows hidalgo, an impecunious merchant, a butler or almost anything other than the soldier and adventurer that he was.

The third member of the party was short, fat and pudgy. His hair was close-cropped, his face smooth-shaven, his cheeks pendulous. He had double chins and, even without his cowl and gown and his tonsured head, he would have been recognized as a priest. He was, in fact, the vicar of Panama, Padre Hernando de Luque, a scholar, a schoolmaster and a man of no little influence with the governor, Don Pedro Arias de Avila, better known as Pedrarias the Cruel. His associates were men of a very different stamp. The swarthy, soldierly fellow was a comparatively little-known adventurer, who had accompanied Ojeda on his ill-starred expedition to Colombia, who had been with Balboa on his march across the Isthmus to the discovery of the Pacific, and who had been in charge of one of Pedrarias' expeditions to Veraguas. Unable to read or write, he had risen to his rank of captain through his courage and skill as a soldier, and, as Captain Francisco Pizarro, he was well known to the inhabitants of Panama. In those days, and among the rough and ready adventurers who had swarmed to the New World, a man's past and antecedents were of no importance, and the fact that Pizarro was born a bastard and had been a swineherd did not detract from his reputation as an excellent soldier.

The third man was, like Pizarro, of obscure and doubtful origin and, like him, he was ignorant of reading and writing. But in character Diego de Almagro was far superior to the captain. Whereas Pizarro was surly, ill-tempered, cruel and unforgiving, Almagro, although as gallant a soldier as the other, was frank and liberal, honest and trusting, and though possessing a quick temper, he was easily appeased and was freely forgiving. But the two had long been fast friends, had shared hardships and good fortune together, and in Padre Hernando they had found a common friend who, being well-to-do and a generous genial soul, had oftentimes helped the two campaigners when they had been in need of financial aid. And it was largely a matter of finances that had brought the three together on this sweltering day in 1524.

From the time, more than ten years before, when Vasco Nuñez de Balboa had heard rumors of an opulent land to the south, vague tales of strange lands and strange races—whose commonest utensils were of gold and silver—had been drifting in to Panama. To be sure, Pascual de Andagoya had been sent forth on a voyage of exploration by the governor, and had returned little the wiser and none the richer. But he had heard even more definite tales of incredible riches farther south, and he had named the country "Peru," which was the nearest he could come to pronouncing the Indian word *Biru*, the name of the river that marked the southernmost limits of his voyage. Officially, all interest in the fabulous lands had ceased with the return of Andagoya; but there were romantic, adventurous souls who still had faith in the tales, for with the conquest of Mexico just completed, and the marvelous stories of the returning Spaniards being heard on every side, nothing seemed impossible nor improbable to the Dons. Prominent among those who believed implicitly in the tales of a vast civilization and treasures rivaling those of Mexico, somewhere "to the south," were Pizarro, Almagro and Padre Hernando.

To set out on such an adventure, as the search for this new El Dorado promised, was the cherished dream of the two soldiers, but expeditions, even in those days, were expensive undertakings, and neither Pizarro nor Almagro had any earthly possessions save their clothing, their armor, their trusty swords, and some plots of miserable land tilled by a handful of Indian slaves. Naturally, faced with this situation, they had turned to their old friend, the padre.

It was to discuss matters in detail and to come to some sort of arrangement that would enable the two to realize their ambitions, that the three men were in earnest conference. Already it had been argued and discussed from every angle. All details and plans had been agreed upon, and it remained only to record the agreement in writing. Slowly and carefully the vicar wrote with his quill pen upon the sheet of vellum spread upon the table before him, and, probably because he was a cleric and familiar with the phraseology of religious documents rather than with legal papers, the final result of his painstaking labors was a most remarkable and curious affair. Its very title savored of the Church, for it was headed "The Eucaristia" and it commenced by invoking the aid of the Holy Trinity and Our Lady the Blessed Virgin. Then, in quite legally complicated phraseology, it set forth at great length and in most verbose style the contract between the three parties to the instrument. Stated briefly, this was the arrangement made by the three, who had decided to undertake the exploration and conquest of the lands to the south. Pizarro and Almagro, being short of funds, agreed to give their time and services, while Padre Luque supplied the needful capital to the extent of twenty thousand gold pesos (about $100,-000). All treasures or other results of the proposed conquest would be divided equally among the three. It further provided that if the expedition should fail, Pizarro and Almagro were to repay the amount of the advance—though how they were to do so, more especially if the venture were barren of results, was not explained.

It may seem a bit strange that the vicar should have been in possession of so much ready cash. But, as a matter of fact, he was not advancing his own funds, but money provided by a wealthy citizen, the Alcalde of Darien, Gaspar de Espinosa, who, for some unknown reason, did not care to have his name appear in the document.

Having duly made their marks at the bottom of the sheet, and these having been witnessed, and the padre having signed his name with a flourish, the three bound themselves to abide by the terms of the contract by swearing on the Missal, on which they traced the sign of the cross, and, as a finishing touch, the Sacrament was administered, the wafer being broken into three equal parts.

Thus, as one historian remarks, "the three, in the name of the Prince of Peace, ratified the contract in which pillage and bloodshed were the objects."

Being thus provided with the means, the two militant members of the triumvirate rapidly completed their plans. Pizarro was to take charge of the actual campaign, Almagro was to have charge of the commissary arrangements, and Padre Hernando was to remain "at court" so to speak, and act as a go-between with the governor who was far from favorable to the expedition.

Two small ships were secured and fitted out and, with about one hundred men, Pizarro set sail in the larger of the two, after arranging that Almagro should follow in the other.

To detail the experiences of the little argosy on that first trip would be tedious, for it accomplished little or nothing, and its chief results were hardships, disaster and the loss of over one-fourth of the company. The vessels were beset by storms. Landings were made in unhealthy swampy localities, and provisions were exhausted. Almagro's vessel failed to meet them, and at last the ship was sent back to the Pearl Islands to secure supplies while Pizarro and his comrades remained on the coast. Famine, disease and hostile Indians took heavy toll of the Dons, and

when the vessel returned six weeks later, the survivors were scarcely recognizable. But with the new
supplies, and encouraged by the comparatively small
amount of gold they had filched from the natives,
they continued on. Finally, their vessel being in dire
need of repairs, they returned to Panama. But
Pizarro, ashamed to appear before the governor
after such a disastrous trip, remained at Chicama
and sent on what gold he had obtained.

In the meantime, Almagro had sailed south, but
had found no traces of his fellow adventurer. He
came, however, upon several large Indian villages
and, having driven off the owners and burned their
homes, secured considerable gold.

He paid dearly for his booty, nevertheless. In one
fight he was wounded in the eye, and, after suffering
agonies, finally lost the organ altogether. Deciding
Pizarro had returned, he, too, retraced his way to
Panama and rejoined his comrades. The governor,
however, was far more intent on learning why so
many lives had been lost than in furthering any
future expeditions. But Padre Hernando finally
won him over, although Pedrarias thought so little
of the venture that he signed away all his rights to
any treasure upon payment of a paltry ten thousand
dollars.

The next expedition was a trifle more successful
than the first. Pizarro found more villages and more
indications of a civilization further south; he had
direct news of the Incas, and he secured far more
gold than on his first trip.

On this trip, too, the Dons were amazed to come

upon a large canoe or *balsa* equipped with sails, for hitherto no American race had been found that was familiar with sails of any sort. Upon this raftlike craft were a number of Indians with gold and silver utensils and woven cotton and woolen cloth, which greatly astonished the Spaniards who, of course, appropriated the property of the Indians, and also took possession of several of the natives who belonged at Tumbes, Peru.

Also, Pizarro, guided by the captive Indians, reached Esmeraldas where he found a town of nearly three thousand inhabitants. Here the natives attacked in force, and the Spaniards were saved through a rather ludicrous incident. One of the soldiers fell from his horse, and the Indians, who had hitherto supposed that horse and rider were one creature, were so astonished at this sudden separation of the two component parts of the beast, that they turned tail and ran.

But, despite all the minor successes, the expedition was almost as disastrous as the first had been. Men died from sickness and the attacks of Indians, scores were ill and wounded and, as usual, food became perilously low and Almagro was forced to return to Panama for supplies. Moreover, the men had become discouraged and mutinous, and wrote numerous letters stating their case to the governor. Naturally, Almagro took possession of these, but one soldier—more crafty and farsighted than his fellows—concealed a note in a ball of cotton that was destined for a present to the governor's wife. As a result, the new executive, Pedro de los Rios, turned a deaf ear to pleas for further support, and, instead, dispatched a vessel with orders to go to Gallo Island and bring back Pizarro and his men.

Pizarro, despite his misfortunes and reverses, still remained undaunted, and upon the arrival of the governor's emissary he refused to be rescued. Drawing his sword, he marked a line upon the sand. "South of this," he cried, "lies toil, hunger, storm and death. On the other side lies pleasure and ease. South lies Peru with riches. North, Panama and poverty. For my part I choose the south."

As he spoke, he stepped across the line, to be instantly followed by the pilot, Ruiz, by Pedro de Candia, a Greek, and by eleven others. It was such acts as this—which even if a bit theatrical invariably appealed to the Spaniards—that were largely responsible for Pizarro's success and his remarkable ability to lead men on forlorn hopes and usually to ultimate victory. In fact, Captain Tafur, the governor's representative, was so greatly impressed by Pizarro's speech and the determination of the others, that, although he declared their acts to be open rebellion, he nevertheless supplied them with provisions. From Gallo, Pizarro transferred his base to the island of Gorgona, and here Almagro found him when, seven months later, he came sailing southward once more. No doubt the governor had been forced to admire the sublime faith and determination of Pizarro, for he had rescinded his former orders and had aided in fitting out the ship, his only stipulation being that Pizarro should return to Panama within six months, regardless of results.

Once more, the two hardy adventurers set sail for the south, and the golden lands of the Incas and, arriving at the present Bay of Guayaquil, anchored off Tumbes. Here the captive Indians proved of real value, for as their tribesmen swarmed about the ships they assured them that the Dons were friendly and—probably under pressure—dilated upon their kindness and virtues. Thus reassured, the Indians brought presents of fruits, vegetables and even a few llamas.

Among the natives was an Inca noble who was vastly interested in the vessels and the visitors. Pizarro, realizing he was a personage of importance, showed him over the ship, and invited him to dine with him. From this scion of royalty Pizarro heard of the Inca and his court, of the treasures of the palaces and temples at first hand. And, as usual, Pizarro bombastically announced that he represented the greatest king on earth, that he had come to assert the King of Spain's lawful supremacy over the country, and ended with a dissertation upon religion, and informed the Inca nobleman that he was worshiping false gods and was deluded by Satan. Whether the noble understood even a small part of Pizarro's discourse is problematical. But, at all events, he was far more courteous and polite than his host and, assuming to listen attentively, forebore from offering his opinions or from disputing Pizarro's assertions.

The following day Pizarro sent one of his officers, Alonso de Molina, ashore, accompanied by a negro slave from Panama, and with them a present of poultry and swine. When Molina returned, his story of his adventures made his comrades listen with amazement and wonder. The women, he declared, were beautiful beyond compare; he had seen a vast stone fortress, and he described most vividly his visit to the temple that, he asserted, was fairly ablaze with gold, silver and precious stones.

He also told, with great gusto, of the amazement he and the negro had created among the Indians. They were filled with wonder at his hair and beard, had thought the negro painted, had vainly tried to rub off the black coloring from his skin, and had fairly shouted with delight when the African grinned and showed his strong white teeth. When a cock had crowed, the astonished natives had inquired what it said, and, added Molina as a final touch, he himself had been promised a beautiful wife if he would remain ashore.

Possibly Pizarro doubted some of the more elaborate details of the fellow's yarn, or perhaps he wished to impress the inhabitants still more. At any rate he sent Candia, the Greek, ashore, dressed in full armor and carrying an arquebus. If the Indians had been astonished at Molina they were fairly dismayed at sight of the iron-clad Candia, and, after having overcome their first fears, they touched and examined the mail, thought it some sort of natural shell, like that of a lobster, and by signs asked the Greek what his gun was for. When, to demonstrate the weapon, Candia discharged it at a wooden target, the frightened Indians ran for cover. But his tale upon his return to the ship not only bore out that of

Molina but outdid it, and he related an incredible story of gardens filled with birds, flowers, fruit and even trees of solid gold and silver.

For once Pizarro showed diplomacy and controlled his desire to possess himself of the treasures at Tumbes. He realized that his tiny force could not cope with the horde of Indians and, moreover, he knew that the treasure would remain where it was until a more propitious occasion for seizing it should arise.

So, without molesting the natives or their property, he sailed southward, visited the ancient city of Chan Chan, cruised along the coast as far as the vast burial ground at Santa, and, finding his supplies getting low and thinking it time to report what he had found, he retraced his way towards Panama.

At Tumbes several of his men declared their intention of settling ashore among the Indians. Among them was Molina, who still longed for the bride he had been promised. This suited Pizarro, for, as was the usual custom, he could thus demand hostages as security for his countrymen. No objection was raised to this, and several Indians were taken aboard ship to be carried to Panama where they were to learn Spanish in order that they might serve as interpreters later on. Among these was one whom the Spaniards christened Felipillo and who, later, was destined to play a most important part in Pizarro's campaign, and whose eventual fate seems to have been one of those rare cases of just retribution that now and then crop up in the history of the Spanish Conquest.

When at last Pizarro and Almagro sailed into Panama Bay, great was the sensation that their arrival caused. The strange Indians from the almost mythical lands to the south; the gold and silver objects; the emeralds and precious stones; the woven fabrics, and most of all the llamas, excited the greatest wonder. But the surly governor refused to be impressed. He declared that a few pounds of gold, a few Indian captives and a few "Peruvian sheep" were a most inadequate return for the monetary expenses of the expedition, not to mention the loss of so many Spanish lives.

But Padre Luque and the others were convinced that, given proper facilities and support, the golden land of Peru would prove even more remunerative than had Mexico. Earnestly the matter was discussed by the three partners, and all agreed that the only course was to appeal directly to the Crown. But who was to be the emissary to cross to Spain and plead with the king? The vicar could not leave. Almagro, one-eyed and never an eloquent speaker, was unfitted for the delicate mission, and though Pizarro was an unlettered and rough soldier, it was finally agreed that he was the one and only man to make the journey.

So, in the spring of 1528, the former swineherd bade farewell to the Isthmus, and accompanied by a few of the Peruvian natives, with a store of fabrics, curios and golden and silver utensils, and with several live llamas aboard the vessel, he set sail for Spain.

CHAPTER XVII

THE SWINEHERD SETS FORTH ON CONQUEST

PIZARRO'S reception, when he again set foot in his native land, was not at all what he had expected. Unfortunately for him, one of his creditors in Panama, the Bachelor Enciso, was in Spain, and learning of Pizarro's arrival, he promptly had him arrested and placed in prison for debt.

As Pizarro cooled his heels in the dismal cell, and cogitated on the past, it must have seemed the irony of fate that, after fleeing from his home an unknown pauper, he should return with rank and fame, only to find himself in a debtors' prison. He was not, however, fated to remain long behind bars. Popular indignation at his treatment ran high, and, news of his incarceration reaching the ears of King Charles the Fifth, the monarch ordered Pizarro's instant release and sent word for him to come to the Court.

At that time the king was at Toledo about to embark for Italy; but he delayed his departure until Pizarro's arrival. He examined the articles from Peru with the greatest interest, appearing particularly impressed with the woven fabrics and the llamas. No doubt Pizarro fascinated the king with his tales of the new land he had discovered, and he probably vastly exaggerated in his accounts of the riches, the people and the results he had obtained.

At any rate, the indisputable evidence of the gold and emeralds was there; with his own eyes the king could see the captive Peruvians, the llamas and the innumerable specimens that proved the truth of Pizarro's story, and, satisfied that in the new-found land there was a source of wealth upon which the Crown could draw, he commended Pizarro to the Council of the Indies and departed on his way.

But councils, like most official bodies, are slow to act, and Pizarro, who was by no means too well provided with funds, saw his cash slipping away and himself no nearer to any definite arrangements. In fact he became quite desperate and, even at risk of losing all his chances, he demanded that some action must be taken at once or he would be in no condition to take advantage of any proposition made. Evidently the queen was far more businesslike than her royal spouse or the council, and, being in charge of affairs during the king's absence, she pushed matters so energetically that within a few days the contract with Pizarro was prepared and signed.

This document, known as the Capitulation, provided that Pizarro should have the sole right to discovery and conquest in New Castile, as the country south of Panama was called, for two hundred leagues south of Santiago (Chincha). He was to receive the title and ranks of Governor, Captain-General, *Adelantado* and *Alguacil*-Mayor for life— and was to receive a salary of 725,000 *Maravadis*. He also had the right to erect forts, to sign *encomiendas* of Indians, or in other words enslave them, and, in short, to act literally as a Viceroy. Almagro was declared Commander of Tumbes with a salary of 300,000 *Maravadis* and the rank of hidalgo, while Padre Luque was given the Bishopric of Tumbes and was made Protector of Indians—a most ludicrous title considering the attitude of the adventurers towards the natives. His salary was to be a paltry 1,000 ducats annually, and as in the case of the stipends granted the others, the sum was to be derived from treasure obtained in the conquest of the country.

Ruiz received the title of Grand Pilot of the Southern Ocean; Candia was honored by being promoted to Chief of Artillery, and the eleven members of Pizarro's expedition who had stepped across the line on the beach at Gallo were made hidalgos. Finally, Pizarro was enjoined to respect the rights of the natives and was ordered to carry priests on his expedition. But, very wisely, lawyers and attorneys were forbidden to accompany him, or to settle in Peru.

Pizarro on his part agreed to raise and equip two hundred and fifty men within six months, one-half of the company to be raised in the colonies, and to set sail for Peru from Panama within six months after his arrival there.

It will be noticed that the ex-swineherd made the most of opportunity and annexed all the high posts, although he had sworn to secure equal honors for his two partners and to secure the rank of *Alguacil*-Mayor for Ruiz. In all probability, the only thing that prevented him from grabbing the bishopric was the fact that he was a layman and not a priest.

But he made up for losing that honor by securing the Order of Santiago and permission to use armorial bearings. These consisted of the Royal Arms incorporated with the arms of the Pizarros, to which were added an Indian city with a vessel in the distance, and a llama. Finally, there was the legend which, as an example of arrogant conceit and unmitigated assumption, has few equals, for it read: "Under the auspices of Charles V, and by the industry, genius and resources of Pizarro, Peru was discovered and reduced to tranquillity."

Thus laden with high-sounding titles, and well provided with ready cash, Pizarro journeyed to his native town of Truxillo. He had left the city unnoticed and unmissed, a swineherd disowned by his own parents. But, as is always the case, money and fame work miracles, and he was received with all honors and acclaim due a hero, and the entire population took pride in welcoming him as a worthy son of Truxillo. Everywhere were friends and relatives pressing around to wish him felicitations and eager to have a share in his good fortune. Prominent among these were his four brothers, three of whom like himself were illegitimate. One of these was Francisco de Alcantara, the others Juan and Gonzalo Pizarro, while the fourth, Hernando Pizarro was, as one old chronicler puts it, "legitimate by birth as well as by character." All were proud as they were poor, and as eager to get some of the crumbs from Francisco's table.

Hernando, however, was the one who was most favored by the future conqueror, possibly because of his dominating character or perhaps because, in him, Francisco saw a kindred spirit, for Hernando was even more cruel than his half-brother. In appearance he was also more repellent than Francisco, a large man of great strength and with a character combining all of the worst and none of the best qualities of the Spanish race. He was cordially hated by all who came into contact with him, for he was jealous, impatient, arrogant and implacable in revenge, absolutely lacking in humanity or pity and utterly unscrupulous.

But despite the popularity with which Pizarro was received, and despite the efforts of the villainous Hernando, men seemed hard to get. It was all very well to listen wide-eyed to tales of a new land where gold could be had for the taking, but it was quite a different matter to risk life and comfort to go forth and try to secure the treasure. And, had it not been for the friendly coöperation of an old boyhood playmate and a distant relative by Pizarro's paternal line, Francisco could never have raised either the men or the money he had pledged. This friend in need was Hernando Cortes who had recently returned from his conquest of Mexico and who, ending his career as Pizarro commenced his, did all he could to further the new conqueror's interests.

Even with the help of Cortes, equipment and soldiers—or, rather, adventurers—were difficult to secure, and at the end of the allotted six months, Pizarro had not assembled all the men he had promised. He had, however, secured three small ships, and, learning that a deputation from the Council of the Indies was coming to inquire into conditions and ascertain if he had complied with his part of the Capitulation, Pizarro, fearing he would not be permitted to depart, slipped the cables on his ship and sailed out of Seville harbor for the Canaries. Hernando, it had been agreed, was to remain behind, face the music, and later, join Francisco at the islands. Hernando did his part nobly. He swore that the complement was complete but that the greater portion of the men had departed with his brother, and as the council could not prove this was *not* the case, they gave permission for him to sail. Without incident, the little flotilla arrived at Nombre de Dios where Pizarro was met by Almagro and Padre Luque who had journeyed across the Isthmus for that purpose.

But their joy at Pizarro's successful return and their whole-hearted welcomes were changed to bitterness, ill feeling and recriminations when they learned the details of the Capitulation.

"Is it thus," cried Almagro, "that you have dealt with the friend who has shared your trials, your hardships, your dangers and your risks, and regardless of your sworn promise to look after my interests as your own? How could you let me be publicly dishonored, and estimate my services as nothing compared to yours?"

In vain Pizarro tried to offer flimsy excuses. The queen, he declared, had refused to allow the higher posts to be divided among several individuals. That, she declared, would lead to dissensions and troubles.

But neither Padre Luque nor Almagro believed him, and estrangement began. And while Almagro quickly recovered from his first resentment, and generously forgave Pizarro for his double-dealing, Pizarro ever held ill feeling towards his partner, an attitude fostered and encouraged by his half-brother Hernando who, from the first, had taken an intense dislike to the one-eyed little soldier, whose virtues aroused the very worst in the despicable Hernando.

In fact, within a short time, every one complained of the latter's presence. "Wasn't it bad enough," they asked, "to be inflicted with one Pizarro without being forced to suffer from those of his family who came to fatten on the spoils?"

So high did the feelings run that Almagro even avowed his intention of sailing for Peru on his own account, and he actually went so far as to negotiate for ships. But Padre Luque, having received his coveted bishopric—not to mention being made Protector of the Indians—was quite satisfied, and finally managed to dissuade him and to reconcile, at least outwardly, the two men, when Pizarro agreed to relinquish the title of *Adelantado,* to apply to the king for a governorship for Almagro, and not to ask any favors for his brothers until Almagro was satisfied.

Very likely it was largely due to this dissension that few men could be induced to join the expedition, for with leaders jealous of each other and on a far from friendly footing, an expedition into a new and unconquered land was not too promising an undertaking. At all events, not more than one hundred and eighty men all told could be secured, and of these only twenty-seven were mounted, while the only available ships were three small coasting vessels.

Thus poorly equipped for the subjugation of a country of unknown size and resources, Pizarro decided to sail, leaving Almagro—as usual—to obtain additional recruits and follow after.

Before sailing, Pizarro invoked the aid of Heaven, had a Mass said for the success of his undertaking, and besought the aid of a merciful God to enable him to rob, murder and enslave.

Although he had set out for Tumbes, head-winds so delayed his ship that, after thirteen days, he decided to land at St. Matthew's Bay and march overland while the vessel sailed southward. It was a terrible march. There were deep swamps, broad rivers; dense jungles, burning deserts. The men muttered and complained, and many fell exhausted by the way, but when at last they saw an Indian village all thoughts save those of gold and loot fled from their minds. Rushing upon the town, they massacred the surprised and unresisting inhabitants, and helped themselves to the gold and emeralds of the murdered Indians. Pizarro himself secured an emerald the size of a pigeon's egg, and so numerous were the gems that many huge stones fell to the lot of the common soldiers. In fact, they were so large and so many that the Dons could not believe them genuine. At this psychological moment a priest—who certainly missed his vocation—the Fray Reginaldo de Pedraza, assured the soldiers that the way to test an emerald was to strike it with a hammer. The true gem, he declared, would resist the blow, whereas the imitation would be broken. Never doubting his sincerity, the men proceeded to put the stones to the "test by hammer," and feeling convinced they were merely glass, when they were shattered by the blows, they cast them aside. Apparently no one noticed that the worthy friar refrained from testing his own gems in this manner, and their suspicions were not even aroused when he was seen to pick up the discarded fragments left by the men, a harvest from which he reaped a tidy fortune when he returned to Panama.

Having stripped the village of everything of value, Pizarro had all the gold heaped in one pile and notified his men that then and thereafter any member of his forces who failed to turn in treasure would be instantly put to death. Then, having taken one-fifth of the accumulated loot as the "King's share," he divided the rest among the company, remarking piously as he did so that, "It pleased God we should fall in with this town of Coaque that the riches of the land might find credit with our people and that they should flock to it."

Taken all in all it was a rather good haul and, being the first, it went a long ways towards encouraging the soldiers. How much the loot was worth is impossible to say, but it must have been considerable, for Pizarro shipped gold to the value of over $100,000 back to Panama as proof of his success.

But gold cannot entirely offset suffering, as the men were soon to find. Hard as the march had been so far, that which followed the sack of Coaque was a thousand times harder. Under the blazing sun on the shadeless desert the men suffered tortures in their steel mail. Many fainted. Some died of sunstroke, and, to add to their miseries, a strange epidemic broke out and claimed many victims. Fortunately for them, the Indians they met gave no trouble. As a rule they fled when the Dons drew near, leaving all their possessions, including most welcome provisions, for the benefit of the Spaniards.

Eventually the little cavalcade reached a spot opposite Puna Island which Pizarro had decided to use as a base for his attack on Tumbes, for despite the hospitable way in which he had been received by the inhabitants of that town, and the friendship he had pledged them, he felt no compunctions about falling upon them, massacring them out of hand and stealing everything they owned. An excellent example of the way in which he carried out the provisions of the Capitulation concerning "respecting the rights of the natives."

Almost as soon as he arrived on the shores of the bay, the Caçique of Puna, accompanied by a number of his men, crossed in a *balsa* to meet him. The Tumbes interpreters warned Pizarro that the natives of Puna could not be trusted, that they were plotting to destroy the visitors in fact, but as the Tumbes and Puna people were hereditary enemies, little faith could be placed in their statements, and, paying no heed, Pizarro crossed to the island and was hospitably received. Then, having accepted their friendship and hospitality, he seized their chiefs—on the flimsy pretext of suspecting treachery —and without trial turned them over to the Tumbes men, who killed them instantly. Maddened by this atrocity, the Punas rose, but were driven off with severe losses by the Spaniards who—as usual— attributed their "glorious" victory over a few ill-armed, semisavage Indians to Divine intervention, and claimed St. Michael and his legions had appeared in the sky battling with Satan. However, even their saints had not made the Dons entirely immune in this engagement. Several had been killed, others wounded, and among these was Hernando Pizarro who received a spear thrust in the leg. And the Punas were not vanquished by any means. Few as they were, they resumed their attack after nightfall, and made it so hot for the Spaniards that when the ships arrived the next day Pizarro was glad indeed to leave the island and proceed towards Tumbes with a reënforcement of one hundred men and some horses under command of Hernando de Soto. But to their intense disappointment, the Spaniards found Tumbes deserted and most of the buildings in ruins, while not a particle of precious metal or a single gem remained in the town.

After some difficulty a scouting party succeeded in capturing some of the inhabitants, among whom was the local governor or *curaca*. According to him the town had been attacked and demolished by the Punas, but he could not give a very satisfactory account of the two Dons who had elected to remain there on Pizarro's previous visit. Whether, as some claimed, they fell in battle with the Punas, whether they were killed by the inhabitants of Tumbes as punishment for outraging the women, or whether they died of epidemic, could not be learned with certainty. But they were dead beyond any question, and Pizarro—for once showing common sense and a measure of decency—decided that the good will of the people was more important than revenge for a questionable wrong, and committed no atrocities.

Moreover, to do him justice, he gave strict orders that his men were to refrain from all acts of violence. And as the natives everywhere appeared friendly and showered the Dons with presents and hospitality, there was no excuse for disobeying these orders.

Wherever he went Pizarro bombastically announced that he came in the name of the "Vicar of God and the King of Spain" and informed the Indians that they were "vassals of his lord and master." As they made no resistance but listened respectfully, he took silence for consent, and had their allegiance to the Crown recorded by his notary.

Also, Pizarro decided that the locality was an excellent spot for a town, and San Miguel de Piura was founded on November 15, 1532. Houses were built, a municipal government was organized, and the men were given allotments of land. To do the work and till the soil, a *repartimiento* or gang of Indian slaves was given each Don, this being done with the full consent of the priests who declared that it would "serve the cause of religion and tend to the natives' spiritual welfare.'' Assuredly the old padres had a most extraordinary point of view.

Here, too, all the large accumulation of gold and silver so far obtained was melted down and cast into ingots, and Pizarro, who most urgently required gold with which to pay for his ships and appease his creditors in Panama, managed—by glowing tales of gold in store and by promises to repay them from his own shares—to induce the men to give up their portions, and sent the entire amount to Panama.

Throughout this district the Dons had been amazed to find the country not only tilled intensively, but by most advanced methods. Complicated irrigation systems led the waters of mountain streams for hundreds of miles to the arid coastal plain. There were sluiceways and reservoirs, and the natives—alone of all American races—used plows which, as there were no draught animals, were dragged by men. In fact, on every hand were abundant proofs that the Peruvians were a civilized race, that they had a thoroughly well-organized government, and that they were members of a vast empire far beyond the dreams of the Spaniards.

From the very first, Pizarro had heard tales of the ruler of this great kingdom, a ruler who, according to the people, was Divine and was known as the Inca, and who was accredited with being the ''Son of the Sun.'' He had also heard tales of the Inca capital called Cuzco, that lay hundreds of miles distant beyond the Andes, and of the incredible wealth in gold and gems that filled the Inca's palaces and temples. It was in fact his plan to march overland and sack the capital. But to attempt such a journey or to contemplate conquering such a vast country with so few men, even the self-sufficient, ever sanguine Pizarro realized would be an almost hopeless undertaking even with the help of the saints.

But fortune was destined to favor Pizarro. He learned of the civil war that was being waged between the two rivals for the Inca throne, and, remembering how Cortes had taken advantage of a similar condition in Mexico, he determined to follow his predecessor's example and use one faction to aid him in destroying the other, and then destroy his allies. Then, to his delight, he learned that, by a chain of circumstances that seemed little short of Fate, but which Pizarro attributed to Divine aid, the triumphant Inca, Atahualpa, was close at hand, resting with his victorious legions at Cajamarca, only twelve days' journey from Piura. Already the monarch seemed to be delivered into Pizarro's rapacious hands.

CHAPTER XVIII

THE CHILDREN OF THE SUN

THE Inca, Atahualpa, as I have said, had been victorious in the civil war and was now at Cajamarca. That much Pizarro learned and, also, something of the causes of the internal warfare that had resulted in Atahualpa's triumph and the overthrow of the other claimant of the throne, Huascar.

But in all probability his ideas on the subject were rather vague. As to that it mattered little to Pizarro who was right or who wrong, and the politics, the religion and the organization of the empire were of no importance to him. He had emblazoned on his newly acquired coat of arms that the country was "tranquilized" or, in other words, under the Spanish yoke; he had declared in the same legend that he had "conquered and subdued" it, and he meant to make his words good.

He was after fame and riches—though no doubt he was sincere in his desire to spread the Christian Faith—and neither decency, humanity, pity nor any other consideration counted in his one desire to conquer, rob and enslave.

In order for us to understand many of the events that followed after Pizarro's founding of Piura, it is necessary briefly to describe the Incan Empire and the conditions that existed when Pizarro arrived on the scene. The people ruled by the Inca, and who totaled at least twenty millions, were not of one homogeneous race, but were made up of countless tribes and sub-tribes confederated and organized to form a solidarity that stretched from northern Ecuador to central Chile, and from the Pacific coast to the tributaries of the Amazon, the largest single state under one ruler in the world at the time of the Conquest. That such a diversity of races—many of whom were enemies by tradition and heredity, and most of whom had been brought under Incan rule by conquest—could have been amalgamated to form a law-abiding, industrious, and intensely patriotic whole speaks volumes for the ability, the intelligence, the superiority and the power of the rulers or Incas.

Moreover, the empire was socialistic, practicing the most complete and successful socialism the world has ever known. Aside from the Incas—and this term included all of royal blood, the nobility and the priesthood—every individual had his or her life and actions regulated and controlled by inexorable laws. All men were forced to marry before their twenty-fourth birthday, the women before their eighteenth, and divorces could be enforced without the desire or consent of the parties when, for any reason, the authorities considered it advisable. Children were reared and trained for the sphere in life predetermined for them, and industries and arts were carefully proportioned and distributed so as to provide every want and need to the requirements of all, and to stimulate trade and commerce between towns and districts. Each man and woman was provided with a definite amount of land—or the necessities of the individual's occupation—and the results of all labor were divided into three parts; one for the Inca or government, one for the church, and the third part for the individual. But there were no other taxes, and once the individual had received his share it could not be touched or drawn upon by any one—not even by the Inca himself. Laws were most rigidly enforced, and though severe, were, on the whole, very just. Idleness was regarded as a crime, and so beneficial had been the results of this that the Spaniards declared that, throughout the entire empire, they never found a liar, a thief nor an idle person.

Broadly speaking, it was an agricultural community. Throughout the whole vast empire every available bit of ground was under cultivation. Hills and mountains were terraced and tilled to their very summits, and the rainless, sterile deserts were made to bear abundant crops by irrigation systems which brought water for hundreds of miles from the mountain streams. Nearly every crop of both the torrid and temperate zones of America was raised, for every variety of climate from the humid tropics of the coasts and Amazonian jungles to the frigid zones of the high Andes could be found. Prominent among the agricultural products were maize, cotton, potatoes, yams, bananas, plantains, peanuts, tobacco, beans and native fruits.

Aside from agriculture there were countless other industries that had been developed to a very high degree. In fact, the Incan Empire was a most remarkable example of a self-contained country able to provide every possible want of its multitudinous and diverse population from its own resources. Llamas, alpacas and guinea pigs had been domesticated and were all important. Llamas and alpacas—as well as the wild vicuñas—provided hair or wool used in weaving the marvelous Incan textiles—fabrics that never have been equaled by any machine-made cloth; and the llamas also served as beasts of burden and their flesh was used as food. Guinea pigs or cavies took the place of poultry or swine in other lands, and were extensively bred and reared for their flesh. Both woolen and cotton cloth were manufactured, the former being used in the highlands and colder parts of the country while cotton answered every purpose in the warm lowlands.

Metal-working in copper, gold and silver had been developed to a very high degree, and as the precious metals had no value as currency, but were used only because of their ductility and because they were symbolic of the sun and moon, their use was confined to the nobility and priests. As a result, during countless centuries, these metals had accumulated until the temples and palaces literally were filled with gold and silver objects, and the Incas possessed a greater store of gold than the world had ever known previous to the Conquest. In some sections of the country wood-working had been developed, in others stone-cutting and masonry had reached an almost incredible state of perfection, whereas, in other localities, the buildings were all of adobe or sun-dried brick. The ceramic arts had not been neglected, and the Incan pottery was of a very superior quality.

But it was in their public works and their engineering feats that the Incas showed their highest civilization. Throughout the land there were excellent highways connecting all important points, while from the extreme northern to the extreme southern limits of the empire stretched the "Inca's Road," in many ways the most remarkable thoroughfare in the history of the world. From Quito in Ecuador down to Chile, a distance of more than three thousand miles, this thirty-foot road crossed deserts, surmounted the mighty Andes, and spanned the deepest cañons and ravines as though they were nonexistent. By most perfectly computed grades, hairpin turns and zigzags it ascended for thousands of feet to the Andean crests. Immense suspension bridges of fiber or woolen ropes, supported by cables anchored to holes cut in the solid rock, stretched across abysses and roaring torrents. Deep ravines were filled, for hundreds of feet, with solid masonry to form causeways. Cliffs were pierced by tunnels. For hundreds of miles, retaining walls were built around steep mountain sides and on wind-swept deserts, and, throughout much of its length, the surface of the road was paved with asphalt. From this main highway, side roads led east and west, to the coast on one side and to the tropical *montaña* on the other. Connecting with the western branches, and following the shore line, there was a second arterial road extending nearly the entire length of the empire.

Throughout the extent of these roads rest houses or *tambos* were built at regular intervals of not more than twenty miles apart, and at longer distances—about forty miles apart—were "royal inns" which served as stopping places for the Inca when traveling about his domains. These stations served also as magazines or storehouses, and were invariably kept filled with provisions, arms, cloth and other articles to be used in case of war or famine or for the army when on the march. There were also mileposts at regular intervals that showed the distance to the nearest rest houses. At each of these *tambos* sentries were constantly on duty, and there was a complete system of signal lights or fires so that any message could be transmitted from *tambo* to *tambo* throughout the length of the road in an incredibly short time. When the people near Quito revolted, word of the outbreak reached Cuzco—over fifteen hundred miles distant—within four hours, and a message could be transmitted for the entire four thousand miles of the highway within eight hours. In addition to this, an immense corps of *chasquis* or runners was maintained. Each of these couriers covered only the short distance between his *tambo* and the next, and by this system of relays, messages, as well as light burdens, could be carried for immense distances with truly remarkable speed. Fish caught on the coast reached Cuzco, nearly five hundred miles distant, within thirty hours—more quickly than by the Mollendo-Cuzco railway to-day; fruit, grown on the Pacific slopes, was delivered at Cuzco within twenty-four hours, and fish caught in

Lake Titicaca in the morning were served to the Inca at Cuzco the same afternoon.

In their religion the Incas were—like nearly all American races — fundamentally sun-worshipers. But though they adored the sun, they did not regard that luminary as an actual god, but as the visual manifestation of a deity known as Inti who, they believed, could assume human form and visit the earth and who could suffer and die like mortals. His wife was the moon or Mama Quilla, and the planets, as well as the rainbow or Huaya Kauri and the thunder and lightning, were also revered as manifestations of deities of lesser degree. But back of all this, and the groundwork of all, was the supreme god known as Kamak or Kapak, the creator or Almighty, a rather vague, spiritual, invisible being. Indeed, in many respects, the Incan religion was very similar to our own. Like us, the Incas believed in their supreme god and, like us, they believed in his divine son who possessed human attributes and had made himself visible to man. But in addition to their true divinities the Incas had a hero-god or, as we might express it, a saint, known as Wirakocha, or the Creator of the Lake and King of the Condors. In many respects Wirakocha was strikingly like Quetzalcoatl of the Aztecs or Kukulcan of the Mayas, the Plumed Serpent of their mythologies. Like the Plumed Serpent, Wirakocha arrived mysteriously, taught the Incan races their arts, their civilization and their religion, and mysteriously vanished. Like the Plumed Serpent, he was supposed to have been a bearded white man, and, like the

Plumed Serpent, Wirakocha promised to return at some future time and foretold that the Incas would be conquered and overthrown by bearded white men from overseas.

Oddly enough, too, this prophecy stated that the fall of the empire would take place during the reign of the thirteenth Inca (Atahualpa) just as Quetzal-coatl prophesied to the Aztecs that their civilization would fall to bearded white strangers in the thirteenth age—as it did.

While the Incan and the Aztec religions were similar in some features, yet they were totally distinct. There was nothing cruel, abhorrent nor bloody about the worship of the Incas. Their gods were neither cruel, sanguinary nor repellent. No human sacrifices were demanded, although burnt offerings of fruits, vegetables and certain animals were made. On the whole it was a far more spiritual religion than that of other American races. The Incas believed in a Hell or Haek Pachak, a Satan or Supay and a Heaven or Hanak Pachak. There were few evil spirits, and no evil gods, in their mythology, and they believed in immortality and resurrection.

In addition to the numerous priests, who were always of royal or noble blood, there were seven orders of nuns, each order having certain duties and being dedicated to a certain deity or planet. Some of these were purely charitable organizations, others were industrial and were devoted to the Inca's household wants, while others, such as the Virgins of the Sun, were strictly religious orders. The nom-

inal head of the church was the high priest, but the
actual head was the Inca himself who was regarded
as the "Son of the Sun." This does not mean, as
many have assumed, that he was believed to be the
direct offspring of the planet. According to Incan
allegory, the first Inca was Manko Kapak, who, with
his sister-wife, Mama Ocllo, arrived from Lake Titicaca and announced they were Children of the Sun,
in other words that they were the offspring of Inti,
the sun-god. And as all the succeeding Incas were
the direct descendants of these two, all members of
the royal family were regarded as sacred and semidivine.

For this reason the Inca rulers held a far greater
power than would have been the case had they been
monarchs merely. But even in their rule the Incas
were by no means supreme. In many respects the
government was republican. In addition to the
Inca there was the Tribunal of Princes or Apu
Auquis composed of men of royal blood, and a cabi-
net of four wise men with its president or Apu Tukuy
Rikak, who acted as chairman and representative.
In Cuzco, the capital, these were appointed by the
Inca, but in other districts they were elected annually by the inhabitants, the nominees being men
who already had been in the service of the Inca. A
unanimous decision of the four was absolute, and
could be revoked or revised only by the Apu Auquis.
In addition to the central or federal government,
each district or colony had its mayor or governor
called Kuraka, and each village or town had its local
prefect or Suyuyok, as well as its board of aldermen

known as Auquis who acted as a sort of grand jury, court and governing body combined.

Aside from the local governors or Kurakas, and the local councilmen, all officials were of the nobility, and the higher nobles or princes of royal blood were distinguished by golden ear-coverings, while the Inca himself always wore, as an insignia of his exalted position, a woven fringed headband or *llautu*.

The origin of the nobles' golden ear-coverings, that caused the Spaniards to call the wearers *Orejones* or "gold ears" is rather interesting. A son of the Inca, Pacha Kutic, lost his ears during a battle and, to cover the mutilation, wore gold plates or "shells" over the scars. To commemorate his bravery, and in order that he might not be conspicuous, the other princes adopted the gold ear-coverings and they became recognized as an insignia of nobility, the princes who wore them forming a caste known as *Huancos* (literally golden-eared).

Although the monarch of a vast and tremendously rich empire and ruler of millions of subjects who were scarcely more than cogs in a wheel, yet, with few exceptions, the Incas were, in some ways, quite democratic and, aside from the strict enforcement of existing laws, they were not tyrannical. They always traveled about their dominions, visiting the various villages and towns and listening to any complaints or petitions of their people. And though despots in their way, and insisting on the most rigid adherence to court etiquette on the part of the courtiers and officials, no member of whom was allowed to enter the presence of the Inca unless barefoot and carrying a light burden upon his shoulders or back, yet, during their rounds of the country, the humblest of their subjects could have audience with them.

And while the Inca always maintained an immense, well-disciplined and well-drilled army, and did not hesitate to use these troops for wars of conquest, peaceful methods for adding to the kingdom were invariably exhausted before forcible measures were taken. Moreover, the subject tribes were permitted a considerable amount of freedom in their customs, laws, religion, etc., as long as they did not interfere or clash with Incan laws, and as long as they paid the requisite tribute to the Inca. In many respects, too, the Inca himself was beyond the law. Thus, polygamy was strictly prohibited among the inhabitants, but was permitted the Inca. This was, in a way, for reasons of State and inheritance. The first or legal wife of the Inca was usually his sister, and was invariably a near relative, and the offspring of these two were considered as the lineal "Children of the Sun" and hence eligible to rule as monarchs, whereas the offspring of the union of the Inca with his other wives were merely royal and, unless there was no other heir, could not occupy the Incan throne. And as a numerous progeny of royal blood was essential in order to fill the countless positions only eligible for nobles and princes, a plurality of wives was necessary for the Inca.

In astronomy and mathematics, the Incans were inferior in some ways to the Mayas and Aztecs, but in other ways they were superior. Their calendrical system was based on the lunar year of three hundred and sixty days, to which five days were annually added to bring it close to the solar year, while every fourth year, an extra day was added, like our own leap years. But unlike the Aztecs, who regarded the five extra days as unlucky, the Incans regarded them as a period for gayety and celebrations. They had no names and were, in fact, a time apart or, one might say, theoretically nonexistent, and formed an annual holiday on which no work was compulsory and which afforded an opportunity for the industrious people to enjoy themselves to the utmost.

As far as known the only Incan astronomical instruments were the *intihuanas* or sundials, consisting of stone cones erected on flat rocks so placed that the shadow of the gnomon would fall on niches dated as sun festivals, and devices known as *pachacta-unanchacs* for determining the times of the solstices. These consisted of stone pillars arranged in four groups with two columns to each group, two to the east and two to the west, and so placed on heights as to mark the extremes of sunrise and sunset.

By this simple means the Incans could determine the day of the solstice by observing when the sun never passed beyond the central pair of columns.

It is also surprising to note that despite their high civilization in many lines the Incans never developed a written or sculptured language, their only means of communicating and recording being groups of knotted strings or *quipos*. Originally, the *quipo* was derived from the human hand, the knots on the five strings or "fingers" representing the joints, the first "finger" denoting units to ten; the second finger, tens; the next, hundreds; and the last, thousands. But with time, innumerable strings were added, the arrangements of knots became complicated, and strings of various colors to indicate various ideas were devised. Specially trained men were employed to tie and to interpret the *quipos* which, arranged and classified, formed the government records and archives. For keeping accounts and recording business transactions, similar bundles of strings provided with beads were used. Those of the credit or "to have" side were known as *hankos* and were usually made of pearls or precious stones, while the debit strings or *charas* were of shells, seeds or beads. The *hanko* consisted of one hundred pearls or other objects distributed decimally upon a string, with a pendant string carrying nine pearls or units. The *chara* was similarly arranged. The Incans also used wooden trays, divided into compartments for keeping accounts. Ten pebbles or seeds were used as counters. These, placed in the ten compartment, for example, indicated one hundred, and by distributing them in the several compartments, and by taking one or more from the credit side of the tray and depositing them in the debit side, accounts of almost any size could be kept with accuracy.

Unquestionably, much of the Incan culture—the religion, the laws, the arts and the other attainments of the Incans—was borrowed from their prehistoric predecessors—the Tiahuanacans and pre-Incans,

whose remains and cyclopean buildings are probably
the most puzzling and most remarkable works of
man in America, if not in the entire world. But the
pre-Incans lived and vanished so long ago that even
the Incan traditions held nothing definite in regard
to them. Possibly the Incas themselves—who were
unquestionably of a superior race—were descendants of these pre-Incans, but whoever they were or
regardless of whence they came, we may feel sure
that the Incan tradition with its tale of Manko Kapak and his wife arriving from Lake Titicaca and
founding the empire, is purely allegorical. It is
highly preposterous to believe that such a vast empire, with such a highly advanced civilization, could
have been developed from raw material by a single
line of kings in three or four hundred years, which
would be a liberal allowance of time between the
reign of Manko Kapak and the arrival of Pizarro
during the reign of the thirteenth Inca.

But even if the Incan story of the origin of the
royal line was mythical, their history of Manko
Kapak's successors was clear, and, in all probability,
accurate, for the lineage and family of every Inca
and his wife who followed after Manko Kapak and
Mama Ocllo were well known and duly recorded.

Each Inca, upon his death, was preserved in mummified form and, wrapped in his robes and covered
with his insignia and decorations, was placed in the
Temple of the Sun at Cuzco. And beside each
mummy was placed a life-sized gold statue of the
deceased king, together with *Quipos* and records
of his deeds. It must not be supposed, however, that

these bodies of the Incas—nor any of the other so-called Peruvian mummies—were embalmed and prepared, as were the mummies of the Egyptians. Bodies buried in the dry, nitrate-impregnated sands of the Peruvian deserts, or placed in tombs in the thin dry atmosphere of the high Andes, do not decompose, but become dessicated and last forever. But the shriveled, dried skin, stretched over the bones, bears little resemblance to the being as he was in life. For that reason, perhaps, all Incan bodies were interred with the heads doubled forward and completely concealed in the cloth wrappings. An artificial head was then added to the bundle, and the face of this was often covered with a lifelike mask of wood, silver, copper, gold or pottery.

Judging from Incan history and records, the Incas appear to have been very much alike in their mentality, their attainments and their ambition to build up and increase their empire. But they differed as greatly in character and in appearance as ordinary mortals. Some were very peaceful and devoted their lives to improving the conditions of their country and their subjects. Some were patrons of the arts and encouraged industries and manufactures. Others were preëminently engineers and instituted marvelous public works, and some were ambitious conquerors who vastly increased the size of their empire and subjugated innumerable races and brought them under Incan domination. Such was particularly the case with the eleventh Inca, Huayna Kapak, who had died a short time before Pizarro's arrival on the shores of Peru. He had pushed the limits of the

Incan Empire far to the north and south and, as a crowning achievement of his career, he had conquered the Kingdom of Quito and had added Ecuador to his domains. The ruler of Ecuador had been taken prisoner, and his daughter had been taken as a wife by the Inca. From this union a son was born who was named Atahualpa, and who, from the first, was the favorite son of the Inca, whose first son Huascar, the child of the Inca's royal spouse, Mama Pahua, was the legitimate heir to the throne.

Before his death, the Inca, Huayna Kapak, ordered that Huascar should be given the throne at Cuzco while Atahualpa was made Inca of Quito, an arrangement which, though fair enough, was certain to arouse dissensions and jealousies, as the dying Inca might have foreseen. Each brother was jealous of the other's power and prestige, each felt that he should be in supreme control. Rapidly the breach widened, until the empire was in a state of civil war, which culminated with the victory of Atahualpa's forces with Huascar a prisoner of his half-brother.

It was at this juncture that the Spaniards arrived in Peru, and it was this chain of events which had resulted in the triumphant Atahualpa being at Cajamarca, instead of at Quito or Cuzco, and thus within easy reach of the unprincipled and scheming Pizarro.

CHAPTER XIX

THE BETRAYAL OF THE INCA

OF the civilization, the history, the religion or the traditions of the Incans, the Spaniards knew little and cared less. They had come to Peru to conquer and to steal. That the people, unfortunately for themselves, possessed gold, silver and precious stones was sufficient for the rapacious Dons who saw fortune favoring them in the disrupted condition of the empire and—as was invariably their habit—regarded it as a special dispensation of the Lord.

So, now that Pizarro had learned of the presence of Atahualpa in his vicinity, he lost no time in starting for Cajamarca. In all probability he had no very definite plans of action in view at that time, for until he knew more of the Inca's attitude, the Inca's forces and other details he could not well map out the precise course he was to follow. But there is no doubt that, from the first, he had some nefarious plot in mind and was ready to betray the Inca's confidence and friendship and to commit any atrocity as long as it resulted in his personal gain.

As the invaders marched inland, even they were astounded at the evidences of such high civilization as they met at every turn. Everywhere were neat villages surrounded with well-cultivated land; everywhere were the sluiceways and the network of irrigation ditches, and everywhere the Dons were received like honored guests and were shown every possible courtesy and hospitality. As they traveled along the great Inca's Road, they were given the use of the *tambos* and even of the Royal Inns, and they were loaded with presents of food, cloth, gold and silver ornaments and other objects.

But the farther they went the more they realized what a petty force they were to penetrate into a country teeming with millions, and, knowing their own devilish schemes and that they were only holding themselves in check because of prospects of greater opportunities beyond, they realized that, once their true object and their true natures became known, they would stand little chance among the multitudes of people they had come to rob and destroy. Even the dullest-witted of the soldiers felt that their company, of less than two hundred men, only sixty-seven of whom were mounted, and with but three arquebusiers and twenty crossbowmen, could not hope to survive if their actions brought on a battle, and the soldiers began to mutter and to grumble. Many were for turning back, and Pizarro, realizing this semi-mutinous state of affairs, determined upon a most remarkable and daring course. Halting his column, he harangued his men and informed them that any members of the company who wished to return to San Miguel were at liberty to do so. He took a tremendous chance, for he had no means of knowing how far the disaffection had

ATAHUALPA

spread, and he risked all in making his astounding proposal.

But he knew the character of his men and, moreover, he felt it would be far safer to proceed with a few thoroughly faithful and enthusiastic adventurers than with a force poisoned by the fears and dissensions of certain members of the company. But only nine men took advantage of his offer.

As he penetrated deeper and deeper into the mountains, Pizarro decided to send a scouting party in advance, and selected Hernando de Soto as leader of the party. Eight days later, De Soto returned, accompanied by an envoy from the Inca whom the Spaniards had met on the way. He welcomed Pizarro and his followers in the name of the Inca, gave them many presents, consisting of carved stone *pachas* or ceremonial drinking vessels, woolen cloth, golden trinkets and dried goose flesh, and assured Pizarro that the Inca would be pleased to have the Dons visit him. In return, Pizarro entertained the envoy, presented him with some glass beads, some cheap jewelry and a red cloth cap, and asked him to tell the Inca that he had come from a great king who, having heard of Atahualpa's victories, had sent the Spaniards to pay him their respects and to aid him against his enemies. Truly as stupendous a tissue of lies as ever issued from human lips.

The following day the Dons marched along a paved causeway where the great road was carried across a deep ravine and, in a fertile valley, came upon a small town where, as usual, they were received with every expression of friendship. But despite this, Pizarro made a prisoner of the Kuraka or local governor and questioned him as to the position of the Inca, the number of his troops, and the real attitude of Atahualpa towards the Dons.

Finding the Kuraka insisted that the Spaniards were regarded as friends and as the sons of Wirakocha, whose arrival had been foretold, and that he professed entire ignorance of the Inca's troops or plans, Pizarro ordered the unfortunate governor put to the torture. With his nails torn from his fingers, with his eyelids seared with red-hot irons, suffering every agony the devilish ingenuity of the Spaniards could devise, the Kuraka in his desperation declared that Atahualpa was setting a trap for the Dons, that his troops were assembled with the purpose of destroying them, and that the friendly attitude of the Indians was all a pose. In this wise did Pizarro "respect the rights of the natives."

As the Spaniards entered the deepest defiles of the Andes they crossed long suspension bridges spanning mountain torrents and terrible cañons, and they saw a number of strong fortifications, several hewn entirely from the living rock. Here they were met by a second emissary of Atahualpa who repeated the Inca's invitation and brought still more presents. While this envoy was in the Spaniard's camp, some of the Indians in Pizarro's service returned from a spying trip they had made to Cajamarca. Among them was the Tumbes youth, Felipillo. He complained bitterly that he had been mistreated by the Inca's people, that he had been re-

fused audience with Atahualpa, and declared that
the Inca's true intentions were hostile. The Incan
emissary smiled at this and replied that as Felipillo
had no credentials from Pizarro, and was of too
mean an origin to be received as an envoy of a great
king or his representative, it was quite natural that
Atahualpa should have doubted his authority and
should have refused to receive him. Moreover, he
informed Pizarro, the Inca was fasting and was engaged in a religious ceremony. Finally, he reminded
the Spaniard, as Atahualpa had just concluded a
long and extensive war and was returning with his
army, it was to be expected that he would be surrounded by large bodies of troops. All of this was
quite true and was obviously reasonable, and yet
Pizarro preferred to believe—or at least pretended
to believe—the story of Felipillo, who, being an
enemy of the Inca and a mischievous and depraved
individual anyway, could not be trusted in the least.

A few days later, the Spaniards crossed the last
ranges of the Andes and, rapidly descending the
eastern slopes, came to Cajamarca, the largest and
most beautiful town they had yet seen in Peru.
Everywhere were great stone residences, palaces and
temples. Prominent among them was the Temple
of the Sun and the convent of the Virgins of the
Sun, and, surrounded by the largest of the buildings, was the open central plaza with the paved
straight streets radiating from it. The Inca himself
was encamped a short distance from the town in the
midst of his army whose camps covered the hills and

valleys as far as eye could see, and whose numbers made the Spaniards' hearts sink.

As they entered the town, Pizarro and his men were received with cheers and acclaim; flowers and fruits were pressed upon them, the people prostrated themselves before the white men, and representatives of the Inca led Pizarro to the plaza and the surrounding buildings which had been vacated for their personal use. As soon as the Spaniards had disposed themselves in these commodious quarters Pizarro dispatched his brother, Hernando, with De Soto and a few others as his representatives to visit the Inca. Without dismounting, the mail-clad Dons approached the Inca, who was seated on a low stool surrounded by his nobles and who was dressed even more plainly than his attendants, his only distinguishing mark being the *llautu* about his head. Bowing, Hernando Pizarro informed Atahualpa that he had come as an ambassador from his brother, and proceeded with the usual bombast about the King of Spain and the Christian Faith, ending with an invitation for the Inca to visit Pizarro in the city. Without deigning to reply or even to glance up, the Inca listened, and one of his nobles assured Hernando that "all was well." Nettled at the superior attitude of the Inca, Hernando demanded that he should reply personally. With a condescending smile Atahualpa then spoke, informing the Spaniard that he was fasting as a thanksgiving for his victories, but that he would visit Pizarro the following day.

Always, hitherto, the Peruvians had shown great

amazement and even terror when they had first seen the armor-clad Dons on their horses. But the Inca evinced no sign of surprise nor even of curiosity, and De Soto, anxious to impress him, spurred his horse, putting the high-spirited animal through his paces and, dashing towards the Inca, reined in his steed so close to the monarch that foam from its mouth flecked the Inca's robes. But no sign of fright nor of surprise showed on Atahualpa's serene features. Several of the soldiers, however, drew back with cries of fright; a most unfortunate reaction for them, for that very night they were put to death for exhibiting cowardice.

That night the Spaniards drank *chicha* from golden *pachas* and dined royally on the best of viands supplied them by orders of the Inca. But as they drank and gorged themselves at the Inca's expense, and partook of the hospitality of the Indians, Pizarro and his captains were plotting and planning the most dastardly inhuman, the most brutally cruel, and the most uncalled for and inexcusable piece of treachery that blackens the pages of the Spanish Conquest. Remembering Cortes' exploits and his *coup* in securing the person of Montezuma, Pizarro determined to capture Atahualpa. But the swineherd was a man of a very different stamp from the Conqueror of Mexico. Cortes was cruel enough, God knows; he was unprincipled to a certain extent, and he was willing to sacrifice the lives and liberty of the Mexicans for the sake of gold and spreading the Christian Faith. But despite his faults, which were numerous enough and to spare, yet he pos-

sessed a certain sense of decency and honor which
was entirely lacking in Pizarro. He had, it is true,
made Montezuma a virtual prisoner, but the Aztec
monarch had given himself into Cortes' hands—
though under compulsion and threat, it is true—of
his own volition, and Cortes had not resorted to un-
derhand treachery or to out-and-out murder in order
to acquire his purpose. Pizarro, on the other hand,
was prepared to stoop to anything, and, as he was
by birth and nature the lowest of the low and had
no conception of honor or decency, he invariably
suspected every one else of the same vile schemes
and machinations as himself.

He had invited Atahualpa to visit and dine with
him. He knew that the Inca would arrive utterly un-
suspicious of danger and would be attended by his
nobles and courtiers and by a large cortege, and that,
coming on a peaceful mission and by invitation, they
would come unarmed. And he planned to use their
trust to destroy them and to seize the Inca. His
plans were carefully made. Sentinels were posted
on all the streets about the plaza, which was defended on three sides by the stone buildings. In
these were stationed the cavalry under his brother
Hernando, and the infantry under De Soto. Pedro
de Candia was in charge of a fortresslike building
commanding the plaza, where he mounted the three
small falconets or cannon, and Pizarro himself took
command of twenty picked men. The orders were
for all Spaniards to conceal themselves at their allotted posts as soon as the Inca was seen approaching, and to remain hidden and silent until Pizarro

waved a white cloth as a signal and then, at the sound of a gunshot, to rush forth, massacre the Indians without mercy, and seize the Inca.

With all these diabolical arrangements completed, Pizarro ordered the priests to celebrate Mass, and as the treacherous leader and his blood-lustful men knelt and followed the service, one might have thought them devout and repentent Christians about to defend the Faith against an attack by infidels, instead of the most despicable of villains on the eve of perpetrating an act that should have brought down the vengeance of God.

Presently the sentries reported the Inca approaching the city. Surrounded by his courtiers and generals, his nobles and the officials in their holiday attire of magnificent textiles and ablaze with gold and gems, Atahualpa was borne in his *juantu* or litter encrusted with gold and precious stones, and lined with feather mantles and robes of vicuña skins. Slowly the gorgeous cavalcade moved towards the city. But presently it halted, and to Pizarro's chagrin, a courier brought word that the Inca had decided to stop where he was and to visit the Dons the next day.

This did not please Pizarro in the least. He had prepared everything for murder and rapine, and he would not have his bloodthirsty plans upset. But he was a past master at deceit and dissembling, and he sent word that he was greatly disappointed (as he no doubt was in reality), that everything was already provided for the Inca's reception (which was strictly true) and that he had counted on Atahualpa dining with him that night.

Rather than disappoint his host, the Inca thereupon changed his plans, and leaving all his escort of soldiers behind, he entered the city accompanied only by his councilors, nobles, servants, wives, relations and courtiers, not one of whom was armed. Into the plaza the Incans filed until fully six thousand Indians had gathered there with their monarch in their midst.

Glancing about with a puzzled frown, Atahualpa asked where the Spaniards were, for not a Don was visible. At this moment a Dominican friar, Vincente de Valverde, stepped forward, a Bible in one hand and a crucifix in the other, and informed the Inca that he had been ordered to expound the True Faith. This he did at great length and with much verbosity, little of which the Inca could understand though he listened respectfully, until at length the padre ended by beseeching Atahualpa to renounce his own faith and to become a Christian. Also, he added, the Inca must acknowledge himself a vassal of the King of Spain. As the tricky and revengeful Felipillo served as interpreter, it is highly probable that he told the Inca many things which never came from the friar's lips, and it is certain that his statement that the Dons ''had three Gods and worshiped one, and that made four'' was not calculated to impress the Inca with the superiority of the Spaniards' religion.

Whether it was the tone adopted by the padre, whether it was some insult added by Felipillo, or whether it was the fact that he was received in this remarkable manner will never be known. But the Inca showed every indication of being insulted and indignant, and replied proudly that he would be no man's vassal or slave, and that he was a greater monarch than the King of Spain. "Your king may be great," he admitted, "and I am willing to be his brother and to welcome you and your fellows to my land. But your Pope, as you call him, must be crazy to give away countries he does not own. Neither will I change my faith. Your God was put to death by the men he created, but mine"—pointing to the sinking sun in the west—"still lives and looks down upon his children."

He then asked the priest by what authority he had talked to him in this way, and being told that the authority was the Bible, the Inca examined it and with a gesture of disdain threw it down. Picking up the book and crossing himself, the scandalized monk rushed to Pizarro and cried: "Why waste breath talking to this dog? Set on him at once; I absolve you."

That was enough. Pizarro had the approval of the Church for his acts to follow, and, waving his white scarf, he gave the signal for the most horrible and infamous deed of his whole career. As the gunshot rang out the concealed men rushed into the plaza, and with flashing swords, swinging axes and gleaming daggers hurled themselves upon the astonished, defenseless Indians. Clad in their mail, equipped with their terrible steel weapons, the Dons, even had the surprised Indians been armed, would have had every advantage. But with only their bare hands the

Incans were utterly at the mercy of their wholly mer-
ciless enemies and were cut down, butchered like
dumb brutes. Screaming, terrified, realizing too late
that they had been trapped, the poor Indians milled
and crowded, surging back and forth, striving only
to escape the slaughter. Struggling at the exits of
the plaza, they were cut down by scores, until the
narrow streets were piled high and choked with the
dead and dying. So terrible was their terror and
their mad efforts to evade the flashing, blood-stained
swords that one party actually burst through the
thick stone walls, and with their bare hands and the
pressure of their bodies, made a gap two hundred
yards in width through the masonry! But even
these did not escape. Those who reached the open
were chased by the cavalry and pierced by the lances
of the Dons.

But many made no attempt to flee. Gathering
about their revered and beloved Inca, princes and
nobles rallied to his defense, baring their own
breasts to the weapons of the Spaniards, seizing the
Dons' swords and spears, throwing themselves on
the pavement and grasping the Spaniards' legs,
until all had fallen. By this time only the Inca remained alive and the Spanish soldiers, maddened
by the sight and the smell of blood, crazed with a lust
to slaughter, drenched from head to foot with the
life-blood of their victims, turned towards the Inca
with the intent of murdering him and stripping him
of his golden decorations. But this was not part of
Pizarro's plans. Leaping to Atahualpa's side,
Pizarro shouted to his men, threatening instant

death to any man who harmed the Inca. But his men were almost beyond control, and before he could enforce his commands he received a wound in the arm from one of his soldiers. That trivial wound was the only casualty suffered by the invaders who, by treachery and unprovoked attack, had massacred over six thousand helpless, trusting, unarmed Indians within the space of half an hour!

And then, having butchered the thousands, having made the Inca their prisoner without a loss to themselves, the Spaniards knelt before their cross and gave thanks to God for their "glorious victory," crossed themselves devoutly as they spoke of the "miracle," and then fell to work stripping the bodies of their golden ornaments and even of their blood-stained garments.

CHAPTER XX

HOW THE SWINEHERD KEPT HIS WORD

THAT night, the Inca dined with Pizarro as planned, but we may be sure that he had little appetite. He was a prisoner; he had been shackled and chained; his royal insignia had been stripped from his forehead by a common soldier; he had seen thousands of his people—the flower of the land—mercilessly, brutally slaughtered; and he realized, too late, that the Spaniards he had trusted and welcomed were his worst enemies and the despoilers of his empire. And to crown his misery and his regrets, Pizarro, with an almost incredible piece of effrontery, assured Atahualpa of his friendship and good wishes, and begged the Inca to "confide" in him!

Possibly Pizarro's conscience may have pricked him—provided he had a conscience which is highly improbable—or it may have been that he was a bit worried as to how his demonstration of "respecting the Indians" would be received at Court. At all events, he tried his best to find some excuse for what he had done, and in Felipillo, the untrustworthy interpreter, he found an ally. Only too glad to even scores with the Inca, whose enmity he had incurred by having had a liaison with one of Atahualpa's wives, Felipillo assured Pizarro that the Inca had planned to lead the Spaniards into a trap and that he, Pizarro, had merely turned the tables on the Inca.

But had Pizarro possessed the brains or the reasoning powers of a ten-year-old child he would have realized the utter preposterousness of Felipillo's story. The Inca had not insisted upon Pizarro visiting him first, but had come with an unarmed escort to the Dons. Had he so desired he could have wiped the Spanish force from the face of the earth with his legions, or could have destroyed them as they passed through the mountains. Finally, there was the fact that the Incans believed implicitly in the semidivine origin of the visitors, that they were the long-expected descendants of Wirakocha, and that it would be madness to attempt to interfere with Destiny. In all probability Pizarro did not believe Felipillo's version, but as he had already committed himself to an act so inhuman, so dastardly that even many of his own men frowned upon it, and as he was even then plotting a still baser act, he considered it good policy to accept Felipillo's statements at their face value, and to circulate them among his men.

At any rate, he made the rascal's words his excuse for holding Atahualpa a prisoner and although, after a few days, the Inca was freed from his chains, he was closely guarded in his quarters. Meanwhile Pizarro had buried the victims of his massacre, and had sent his cavalry to the Inca's former camp to loot the palaces and temples and to drive off, cut down and make prisoners of the people who, amazed, overcome, and utterly disorganized by the seizure of their monarch, appeared helpless and at an entire loss. They made no resistance to the Spaniards who returned with thousands of prisoners, including the Inca's household and wives. These were permitted to attend the captive monarch, but the other prisoners were so numerous that they were a burden on the Dons. Hernando Pizarro thereupon suggested that they should be murdered to the last man, or at the very least, should have their hands chopped off so they could not bear arms in the future. This callously inhuman proposition was too much for Pizarro, and he ordered all the captives not needed for slaves to be released. The loot in gold, silver and gems was enormous, and vast stores of cloth, provisions and other commodities were also obtained, including thousands of llamas which served to provide the Dons with meat.

It was while the Spaniards were dividing this accumulation of loot that the Inca first realized their insatiable desire for gold. And with the realization came the idea of purchasing his own freedom. Turning to Pizarro, he declared that if gold was what the Spaniards desired he could give them more than they ever had dreamed of. If Pizarro would promise to release him upon his doing so, he would, he promised, cover the floor of the room wherein they stood with gold. The Dons gaped at this calm statement, for the room was over twenty feet in length by eighteen in width. Not, in the entire New World, they thought, was there enough gold to cover that area.

Despite all they had seen, despite the unquestionable amount of gold taken from Mexico by Cortes, they were incredulous, and Pizarro openly expressed his doubts of the Inca's words being serious. But the Inca misunderstood, and, thinking his offer had not been enough to satisfy the Spaniards, he declared that, in return for his freedom, he would fill the entire room with gold for as high as he could reach. As he spoke he raised himself on tiptoes and placed his outstretched fingers against the wall. Pizarro began to feel that even if the Inca could not fulfill his pledge he could at least command undreamed-of riches, and stepping forward, he drew a red mark upon the wall at the height indicated by Atahualpa. Then, as Pizarro hesitated, the Inca pointed to a smaller adjoining room and offered to fill it twice over with silver in addition. Pizarro hesitated no longer. Calling a notary, he had an agreement drawn up, signed, and duly attested; the document providing that, in return for the amount of gold and silver stipulated, the Inca Atahualpa was to be released unharmed and his freedom guaranteed thereafter. It was also agreed that the gold and silver to be supplied was not to be melted down or broken up, but that Atahualpa should have the advantage of the extra space occupied by bulky objects. For his part the Inca agreed to the others' terms, and also pledged himself to fulfill his promise within two months.

Ever since his capture Atahualpa had still remained a monarch, even though a prisoner. No noble who approached him failed to remove his sandals and to carry a burden on his shoulders, and the

people still regarded the Inca as their ruler and
were ready to obey his every command. And when,
the contract having been signed and witnessed, Atahualpa summoned some of his attendants and gave
orders for the temples and palaces to be stripped of
their treasures and brought to Cajamarca for his
ransom, no one demurred.

Couriers or *chasquis* hurried north, south, east
and west, carrying the orders of the Inca to every
part of the empire, to Quito and to Cuzco, to Pachacamac and to Pisco, to Cochabamba and Cocacabana.
Soon the gold and silver began to arrive, sometimes
a little at a time, sometimes in vast quantities, but
averaging from one hundred and fifty to three hundred thousand dollars' worth of treasure each day,
surely enough to satisfy the most avaricious of men.
But the Spaniards could never be satisfied. Pizarro
complained that the gold was arriving too slowly,
but Atahualpa begged him to remember that it must
be carried for great distances, and while a message
could be carried by *chasquis* to Cuzco in four or
five days, many weeks would be required for llama
trains of gold to come from Cuzco to Cajamarca.
But, he assured Pizarro, if the Spaniards doubted
his good faith or questioned his ability to supply
the amount of gold promised, he was willing that
Pizarro should send his own men to the capital in
order to verify his statements.

Had the Inca known exactly what was happening,
he would have doubted his ability to fulfill his part
of the agreement. Although he had won a great
victory over his half-brother, Huascar, and had

taken the latter prisoner, yet the country was still divided in its allegiance. About Cuzco, Huascar's adherents were in the majority, and no sooner had Atahualpa's messengers arrived with orders to strip the famed Temple of the Sun or Korikancha, than Huascar's friends, and especially the priests, rose in indignation at the command to desecrate the temple. But they were in a difficult position. If they disobeyed the Inca and he was ever released they would pay a severe penalty, they knew. And if they obeyed him and he was ransomed they would be aiding one who was regarded by them as an usurper, and thereby injuring Huascar's cause. Moreover, they had heard enough of the Dons to realize that it was gold the Spaniards sought, and, sooner or later, they felt sure, the Dons would reach Cuzco and would strip every vestige of gold and silver from the city and its holy edifices and shrines. They stood to lose their most sacred possessions no matter what course they followed, and they were in a dilemma until the high priest hit upon a very clever scheme. They would pretend to comply with Atahualpa's commands, would remove the largest and most valuable objects of gold and silver, and would send them towards Cajamarca. But they would be in charge of men faithful to the priests and to Huascar and, in a prearranged uninhabited district near Piscobamba, they would be secreted where neither Atahualpa nor the Dons could ever find them. Certain of the objects of precious metal would, however, be delivered to Atahualpa to allay suspicions, and enough would still be retained in the Temple of the

Sun to serve the purposes of ceremonials and worship. In doing this the priests felt they were quite safe, for Atahualpa had never visited Cuzco and knew nothing definite in regard to the contents of the temple, while if Huascar regained his freedom and returned to Cuzco, or if the Dons left the land and Cuzco was safe, the secreted treasures could always be secured and returned to their original places.

Moreover, so incredibly vast was the amount of gold, silver and precious stones at Cuzco that enough to satisfy Atahualpa could be spared without appreciably diminishing the amount in the temple. The building itself was completely covered with plates of beaten gold, and a gold band a yard in width encircled it like a gleaming metallic sash. Within, it was fairly ablaze with gold and gems. Above the high altar was an immense gold sun with silver rays tipped with huge jewels. Opposite this was an equally large image of the moon of solid silver, the rays being of gold tipped with topazes. Other gold and silver images represented the various planets, the rainbow and thunder and lightning, and standing beside their respective mummies, were the life-sized gold statues of the eleven deceased Incas. Everywhere, too, were vessels, vases, bowls and ceremonial objects of gold and silver. Everywhere were gold-embroidered draperies and articles encrusted with precious stones. *Quipos, hankos* and *charas* of golden threads strung with pearls, diamonds and other gems were hung upon the walls; the wooden beams of the ceiling were studded with gold stars, and even the door lintels and the cornices were of the same precious metal. Neither were these incalculable treasures confined to the interior of the temple. Within the garden that surrounded it were five great fountains of gold, and about these were trees, bushes, plants and flowers, as well as birds, quadrupeds, reptiles and even insects, marvelously wrought of gold and silver, decorated with jewels, and with the gardening tools made of solid silver.

In fact, so vast was the wealth of the temple and its garden that despite the fact that much of the treasure had been secreted near Piscobamba as planned by the priests, and much more had been delivered to Atahualpa, yet, the Spaniards, when they sacked the Temple in 1535, obtained loot valued in their official accounting with the Crown, at more than twelve million dollars! And this did not in-include the eleven golden statues of the Incas nor the original gold sun. The former had been concealed near Piscobamba and have never been recovered, and the latter had been buried in the Wilka Pampa or plaza of Cuzco and was not discovered until forty years later, when it was found, and sent by the Viceroy Toledo to King Philip II of Spain.

As the priests and friends of Huascar had arranged, so their plans were carried out. The eleven gold statues or *chuquihuancos* of the Incas, together with the most precious and sacred of the other contents of the temple, were hidden near Piscobamba, and the balance was duly delivered to Atahualpa at Cajamarca.

Huascar's adherents, however, had been unable

to resist acquainting Huascar with what was going
on. Knowing of his half-brother's bargain with
Pizarro, and feeling confident that he could secure
the concealed treasures for his own ransom, he sent
word to Pizarro that for every pound of gold Atahualpa could obtain he, Huascar, could double the
amount, adding that Atahualpa was ignorant of the
location of the treasures in Cuzco, never having been
there. This news must have made Pizarro rub his
hands and grin with delight. He had the two Incas
bidding against each other for their freedom, and he
had only to make a second bargain with Huascar in
order to secure all the gold in the empire without
effort on his part. Then, having drained their resources dry, he could murder both the Incas and take
full possession of the country. It was a scheme
worthy of his abominable mind, but being absolutely
lacking in common sense or in diplomacy, he made
the great mistake of informing Atahualpa of
Huascar's offer and of declaring that he intended to
bring Huascar to Cajamarca, and determining for
himself which of the two brothers was entitled to
the Incan throne.

Atahualpa, feeling confident of being ransomed,
was naturally greatly disturbed at this news. He
was astute and had acquired a very fair idea of the
treacherous characters of his captors, and he well
knew that once Pizarro had possessed himself of all
the treasure he could secure from Atahualpa he
would not hesitate to offer to reinstate Huascar in
return for what gold he could produce. His only
hope of freedom and life lay in Huascar being put

out of the way, and he might well have been forgiven
if, under the circumstances, he had ordered the death
of his half-brother. But there is no real evidence to
show that he did so. To be sure, Huascar was
drowned in the Andamarca River, and Pizarro
charged Atahualpa with his death. But the Inca
indignantly denied any part in it, exhibited every
symptom of regret and sorrow, and at first refused
to believe the news. Knowing Pizarro and his underhanded ways, it is far more probable that he had a
hand in Huascar's death or that, as Atahualpa
claimed, he was killed by some overzealous and
faithful subject of Atahualpa who had heard of
Huascar's offer to Pizarro and realized the dire
consequences that might follow if the Spaniards
secured possession of Huascar.

Regardless of who was responsible for the crime
or what brought it about, the fact remained that
Huascar was dead and, being dead, put an end to
Pizarro's dreams of obtaining riches from that
source. There is every reason to believe that Pizarro
never intended to keep faith with Atahualpa or to
release him when he had fulfilled his part of the
agreement. But he well knew that De Soto—who
was more friendly with Atahualpa than any other
Don, and some of the others who possessed a spark
of honor—would insist upon Atahualpa's release
once the entire ransom had been paid. And he well
knew that, once the Inca were free, the entire country
would be up in arms and that the conquest of Peru
would be hopeless—at least for the present. Moreover, Almagro, with a large force of men, had now

arrived and these men, brutally avaricious, and devoid of all decency, were demanding that the accumulated treasure be divided, the Inca murdered, and that the expedition should proceed. Their impatience was heightened by tales brought back from Cuzco by the men who had been sent there, and who brought with them two hundred cargoes of gold, mostly the thin plates that had covered the walls of the temple, and told of vast amounts of treasure which the priests had refused to deliver to them.

De Soto, however, stood up stoutly for Atahualpa, urging Pizarro to release the Inca even though the entire ransom had not been paid, while the Inca insisted that if they only waited until the expiration of his allotted two months, they would receive all he had promised. In all probability the full amount never would have arrived. Atahualpa had already provided the Spaniards with nearly fifteen million dollars' worth of precious metals—the greatest ransom ever paid by king or prince in the history of the world—and Pizarro even had had a paper drawn up, signed and attested, absolving the Inca from any further obligations in respect to supplying more treasure for his release. This, however, was done in order that he might convert the accumulation of gold into ingots for division and shipment, and with no idea of actually freeing the Inca. He was merely biding his time and trying to find some excuse for putting his captive to death without bringing down the protestations and vituperations of De Soto and the others, and, very possibly, the reprimands of the Crown. The death of Huascar gave him the excuse for which he had been waiting and cudgeling his brains, even if, as it is not improbable, he did not order Huascar's death in order to provide the excuse.

At any rate, he now had a flimsy pretext, and waiting only until De Soto could be gotten out of the way by sending him on a short expedition, Pizarro had formal charges drawn up accusing the Inca of squandering the public funds; of being an idolator, of adultery, of bigamy, of inciting his people to insurrection against the Spaniards, and finally of having usurped the crown and of ordering the death of Huascar.

Never was there a greater farce of a trial nor a greater travesty on law, justice, humanity and Christianity. The idea of invaders of a country trying that country's monarch for misuse of his own property, of accusing him of bigamy when polygamy for the Inca was legal; of calling the defense of their homes "insurrection" of the people, or even of daring to punish a free and independent emperor for crimes committed—if committed at all—in his own dominions, would be ludicrous were it not so tragic.

The fate of the Inca was sealed before the farcical trial commenced. Vainly he implored his inhuman tormentors to spare him, offering twice the ransom he had already paid. "What have I done," he cried, "that I should meet with this fate? And from your hands, too!" he exclaimed, addressing Pizarro. "You, who have met only hospitality and friendship from me and my people; to whom I have given all my treasures."

Not one of the stern-faced, pitiless Dons gave an ear to his pleas. Helpless, dependent for his defense upon the treacherous, prejudiced Filipillo; with his two worst and most treacherous enemies—Pizarro and Almagro, acting as judges, with the fanatical priests, who regarded him as an infidel and therefore beyond consideration, as advisers to the court, and lacking his one and only friend, De Soto, Atahualpa had no ghost of a chance. He was found guilty and sentenced to be burned to death in the great plaza at Cajamarca. But before the sentence could be carried out it was necessary to secure the approval of Padre Valverde who, with the memory of Atahualpa's rejection of his efforts still fresh in his mind, had no hesitation in declaring that, in his opinion, "the Inca deserved death anyhow."

To their credit be it said, there were a few among those heartless, bestial Dons who did not hesitate to protest against the unwarranted and high-handed methods of Pizarro and the others. But they were woefully in the minority and were soon silenced. Within a few hours the Inca was to die, and two hours after sunset on the 29th of August, 1533, Atahualpa, chained and ironed, was led towards the stake and its pile of faggots. Beside him strode the friar, Vincente de Valverde, who still had hopes of saving the Inca's soul, though quite willing to sacrifice and torture his body. As Atahualpa was being chained to the stake he promised the Inca that if he would embrace the Christian Faith his sentence would be commuted to the extent that he would be put to death by the garrote. As the

Inca firmly believed in the resurrection of the body, and that an incinerated body could never enjoy life in the hereafter, he grasped at this straw of comfort, and having been assured by Pizarro that Father Valverde spoke the truth, he consented to being baptized. No doubt the padre was greatly elated at thus hauling a soul from the very brink of Hell so to speak, and having baptized the Inca in the name of Juan de Atahualpa, he signified that the execution might proceed as far as he was concerned.

With stoical resignation and with a final appeal to Pizarro to care for his children, and with a last request that his remains be sent to Quito, Atahualpa submitted to his fate, and the last of the Incas was put to death like a common thief. The age-old prophecy had been borne out. The bearded white men had overrun the land, and the thirteenth Inca had met his death, betrayed by one of his own race.

CHAPTER XXI

IN THE CAPITAL OF THE INCAS

ONE would think that, having tortured and murdered the Inca in this cold-blooded fashion, the least the Spaniards could have done would have been to follow out Atahualpa's dying requests. But, disregarding his plea to be interred at Quito, the Dons buried the Inca in their cemetery at Cajamarca, after holding an elaborate funeral ceremony and donning mourning as if, by outward show, they might atone for their dastardly crime. During the services the relatives and family of the Inca crowded into the church, demanding their dead monarch should be buried with the ceremonies of his faith, while his wives insisted that they should be sacrificed in order that their spirits might accompany him. And when they were assured that Atahualpa had died a Christian—which is highly improbable—and they were driven from the church, several of them committed suicide.

Eventually, too, the Inca's body found a resting place in his beloved Quito, the Indians secretly disinterring it and carrying it to Ecuador. When or how it was done was never learned, and the fact that Atahualpa's remains had been removed from the Christian cemetery was only discovered when, in the hopes of finding gems or gold upon it, a ghoulish

Spaniard tried to rob the grave several years after the execution of the Inca.

A few days after Atahualpa's death, De Soto returned. Learning of Pizarro's despicable act, he expressed his indignation in no measured terms and roundly berated his superior, declaring that there had been no grounds for the accusations brought, that the Inca had been entirely friendly, and that he personally would have pledged his life on Atahualpa's innocence. Pizarro, who was dressed in deep mourning as if sorrowing for a dear friend, endeavored to exonerate himself by declaring that he had opposed the proceedings, but that Father Valverde and the others had forced matters. At this the padre and the others turned on Pizarro, upbraiding him for his part, and denouncing him as solely responsible. The dispute rose high, the lie was freely passed, and the participants would have come to blows and bloodshed had not De Soto and some of the cooler-headed men intervened. But denials and recriminations did not help Atahualpa, who had paid the penalty of being in Pizarro's way, and whose persecution and death form the blackest page in the history of Spanish America.

Moreover, Pizarro defeated his own ends by his vile deed. He had assumed that the Inca had exhausted all his resources, that there remained no treasure worth taking, and that he would lose nothing worth while by putting Atahualpa to death. But, as a matter of fact, the stupendous amount of gold that the Inca had accumulated for his ransom was only a drop in the bucket compared with what he

could have secured, and his offer, to furnish twice
as much gold in return for his life, was no idle
promise. During the very time that he was being
tried and condemned, treasure far exceeding all that
the Dons had secured was being hurried to Cajamarca for the ransom of the Inca. Somewhere on
the Inca's Road, hundreds of Indians and an almost
endless train of llamas were trudging across the
mountains from Chuquis, bearing with them seven
thousand loads of gold of seventy-five pounds each.
And somewhere else two hundred and fifty carriers
were making all haste towards Cajamarca, bending
under the burden of the ten-ton seven-hundred-foot
chain of solid gold that the Inca, Huayna Kapak, had
had made to commemorate the birth of Huascar.
Had Pizarro but waited a few weeks more, this
almost inconceivable treasure would have been in his
hands. But when news of the Dons' perfidy and the
Inca's death reached the bearers of the treasure the
entire amount, worth more than one hundred and
sixty million dollars, was so carefully concealed that,
to this day, it has never been found.

Throughout the country it was the same. Wherever there was gold or other treasures the natives
hastily concealed them, for the invaders had shown
their hand and their real object in overrunning the
land, and distrust and hostility took the place of
friendliness and hospitality. The expedition under
Hernando Pizarro, which had been sent to the holy
city of Pachacamac, found the far-famed Temple of
the Sun stripped of its holy vessels, its golden
images, its innumerable gem-encrusted objects which,

it had been reported, far exceeded those of Cuzco in value. For countless centuries the treasures of Pachacamac had been accumulating. Long before the first Inca, the forgotten races of Peru had worshiped their gods in this sacred city whose pyramidal mound, crowned with the massive temple, overlooked the vast Pacific. From every quarter of the Incan Empire, and from far beyond its boundaries, pilgrims had journeyed for hundreds of years to worship at the temple and countless thousands had been buried in the holy ground of the ancient city. From far and near, offerings of precious metals, of still more precious gems, of priceless objects of art, had been placed at the feet of the great wooden idol of the pre-Incas, and before the blazing golden sun-god in the later Incan temple.

But when Hernando Pizarro and his band of adventurers reached the ancient holy city they found the temple almost as bare as old Mother Hubbard's famous cupboard. The doors of the two temples were still studded with crystal, coral, turquoise and semiprecious stones; a few objects of gold and a few small emeralds were picked up from the floor where they had been dropped by the priests. The Spaniards, chagrined and furious, smashed the wooden images, erected a cross in their place, and were about to depart with almost empty hands, when they discovered that the wooden timbers of the temple were fastened together with gold nails. Ruthlessly they tore the timbers down, hacked them in pieces and burned them, and from the ashes raked the golden spikes to the value of more than half a million dollars.

But in comparison with what had been taken from the temple and hidden in the neighboring valley of Lurin, these thirty-two-thousand ounces of gold were a mere trifle.   Although later—by means of torture and mutilation—the hapless natives were forced to reveal the hiding places of some of the treasure, and gold to the value of more than half a million dollars was recovered by the Dons, yet the greater portion still remains as securely hidden as on that day when Hernando Pizarro burned the temple timbers for their golden nails.

Pizarro's act in destroying the Inca resulted in a state of chaos throughout the country.   With the death of Atahualpa, with no monarch to control the multitudes of diverse races and hold the empire together, it rapidly broke up into its original component parts.   Age-old intertribal feuds were renewed.   Provinces seceded.   Revolts and rebellions broke out, and each local chief, caçique and governor set up his own individual kingdom.   But in some respects all were united.   All realized the Spaniards were their arch-enemies.   All cordially hated and distrusted them, and all feared them.

Realizing too late that the people could only be pacified or controlled by a ruler of their own race, Pizarro determined to place a monarch on the Incan throne.   The true heir of the Incan line was Manco, the younger brother of Huascar, but for some reason —perhaps because of some pricking of conscience— he selected the younger brother of Atahualpa, a mere

youth named Toparca. With all the ancient ceremony of the Incas, Toparca was crowned in the
presence of the murderers of his brother; but he was
a mere pawn in the hands of the Dons, and not even
the Indians were hoodwinked by this hollow mockery
of enthroning an Inca to rule over them.

This farce accomplished, the Dons turned towards
Cuzco, and, accompanied by the young Toparca, they
marched towards the Incan capital five hundred
strong. But no friendly reception met them as they
traversed the great Incan highway. Everywhere were
black looks, lowering brows and sullen faces. Tambos had been striped of food and supplies. Food was
hard to secure, and many villages were deserted.
But not until the Spaniards reached the vicinity of
Xauja were they actually attacked. As usual, they
were triumphant, but they did not escape unscathed,
and to such a small company, the loss of a single
man or of a horse was most serious. Though hundreds of Indians were butchered for every Spaniard
killed, yet Pizarro and the others realized that such
dire reprisals did not help them any. With his
customary desire to let some one else bear the brunt
of dangers, and to safeguard himself, Pizarro sent
De Soto and a party of men in advance, and by so
doing came very near losing everything. De Soto
was attacked. After a desperate battle, during which
every Spaniard was wounded and a number killed,
the Dons were forced to withdraw, and for once the
Indians could claim a victory. Had they resumed
the attack that night there is little doubt that they
could have completely destroyed De Soto's com-

mand. But they made the mistake of waiting until the following day, and had barely started their onslaught when Almagro arrived with reënforcements and the Indians were driven off.

About this same time Toparca, the young Inca, died suddenly and mysteriously. The Spaniards, wishing to find a scapegoat, accused the captive chief, Challcuchima, of having caused the death, and also of inciting the Indians to revolt. In vain he denied the charges, pointing out that it was the Dons' own acts that had brought on hostilities, that he had no enmity towards Toparca, and that he had done all in his power to pacify his countrymen. A mock trial was held; he was found guilty and was condemned to be burnt alive. Here was another chance for the indefatigable Padre Valverde. As he had done in the case of Atahualpa, he trotted beside the condemned chief as he was led towards the stake, and as the faggots were piled about him the padre promised an easier death if he would embrace Christianity. But Challcuchima was made of sterner stuff than Atahualpa. He spurned Valverde's offer, and as his own people—forced to do so at the points of the Spaniards' swords—piled the inflammable wood around him and fed the roaring flames, the chief smiled, and gazing upwards at the sun, muttered a prayer to Inti and Kamak with his dying breath.

As the Spaniards neared Cuzco they were met by a company of nobles among whom was Huascar's brother, Manco. He was received with ceremony by Pizarro, who assured him that the Dons had come to Peru to see justice done and the rightful heir placed on the throne, and who, in this young scion of the royal family, saw another tool he could use to his own advantage. Accompanied by Manco, the Spaniards met with no resistance, and at length arrived at the Incan capital.

All they had heard of Cuzco had not prepared them for what they saw, for Cuzco was the largest and finest city in the New World, and could compare very favorably with most of the European capitals of the time. It was built in the symbolic form of a condor, the immense fortress of Sacsayhuaman forming the head; the Rodadero and Andenes representing the neck; the city proper, the body; and the Kori-Pata being the tail, while the outspread wings were represented by the surrounding hills. The city itself was surrounded by a massive wall of pre-Incan work composed of enormous beautifully cut and fitted stones, some of which weighed as much as thirty tons each. Magnificent houses, palaces, temples and government buildings were everywhere, and to give breathing places and to beautify the city there were numerous large plazas or pampas filled with flowers and trees. The streets, laid out at nearly right angles, were well paved though narrow. A river ran burbling through the town and was spanned at each street crossing by stone-flagged bridges, and everywhere, between the larger buildings were thousands of humble houses, the homes of the two hundred thousand inhabitants of the city.

To the Dons, who had hitherto seen nothing finer than Tumbes and Cajamarca, with their preponderance of low adobe edifices, Cuzco must have appeared most wonderful and imposing. Even to-day, after the lapse of four centuries, and despite the havoc and destruction of the Spaniards, the disastrous fire and the ruthless razing of many of the finest buildings, Cuzco is a marvelous city. One may still identify many of the ancient Incan buildings and works, and may get some idea of their glories in the days when Pizarro and his despoilers first saw them. On the street called Ahuacpita was the huge factory for the manufacture (by hand, of course), of cloth, ponchos, blankets, rugs, etc., for government use, for the army and the Incan Court. Near this was the imposing Temple of the Sun or Korikancha already described and now architecturally ruined by having been transformed into Santo Domingo Church. Where Santa Catalina Church now stands, the Dons saw the Aclla-Huassi, considered the finest palace in the city. At the present Portal de Panes was the imposing palace of Wilka-Chimpa or Inca-Roca, while the palace of Ychi-Urma, the residence of Maita-Kapak-Inca, is now the Portal de Harinas. This palace was later occupied by Gonzalo and Hernando Pizarro, while Francisco took possession of the palace of Ipa-Huako, which still stands and is now the residence of the Prefect of Cuzco. The palace of the Inca-Manko-Kapak, with its seventy-five-yard-long wall of marvelously cut stone, is still standing in practically the same condition as in the days of Pizarro, and, close to it, was the palace of the Inca-Sinchi-Roka, also with an enormous stone wall. At the present site of the Laguna Funda-

mental were the magnificent royal baths of Tiksi-
Kocha at the end of the splendid avenue, Kora-Kora
(now Calle del Triunfo) and on this same broad
paved avenue was the house of twelve corners built
by Inca-Pachac-Kutic. A few squares beyond this
was the immense palace of Yupanqui-Inca.

The largest of the plazas was known to the Incans
as the Kusi-Pampa, and is now the Plaza los Rego-
cijos, while the site of the great cathedral of Cuzco
was then occupied by the palace of the Inca-Wira-
Kocha. On the spot where the University of Cuzco
now stands was the house of Amarau-Kancha.
Finally, there was the famed Collque Machahuay, or,
as the Dons called it, *la sierpe de Plata,* a female
human figure from whose breasts issued streams of
clear mountain water, but which, on festival days,
was replaced by streams of chicha, of which all might
partake freely.

But the beauties, the architectural wonders, the
imposing palaces of Cuzco meant nothing to the
Spaniards. Thoughts of gold filled their minds to
the exclusion of all else, and rushing into the city,
they began plundering, looting and despoiling.
Nothing was sacred to them. The mummies of the
deceased Incas were hurled from their golden chairs,
were hacked to pieces and trampled under foot as
the Dons stripped the bodies of their golden ornaments. Homes and palaces were ransacked. Nobles
were attacked, robbed and brutally put to the sword
if they resisted. Men and women, unfortunate
enough to display jewelry, had hands and fingers
lopped off by the gold-mad soldiers who were too

impatient to withdraw the rings and bracelets from their owners' arms and fingers. And scores, hundreds of the citizens were put to the most horrible and excruciating tortures to force them to reveal the hiding places of their valuables.

Vast stores of gold, silver and gems were found. There were vessels and utensils of precious metal, gold statues and vases, dresses of gold beads, golden sandals and gem-encrusted ornaments, and among the loot were ten bars of solid silver, each twenty feet in length by a foot in width and three inches thick. Indeed, so vast was the treasure secured that, when it was gathered together for division, it was estimated at a value of more than twelve million dollars, and each common soldier received more than one hundred thousand dollars as his share of the booty. Yet by far the greater part of the city's treasures had already been removed and hidden by the inhabitants.

In their mad search for gold the Dons had come upon immense stores of maize and other provisions. But heedless of the future, thinking only of treasure, this had been recklessly thrown aside, destroyed or scattered. Far better had it been for them if they had seen in the golden grains of corn treasure of greater value than the gleaming gems and wrought metal, for in the near future many a hungry, famished Spaniard was deeply to regret that his pockets were filled with gold instead of maize.

Once the first wild rush for treasure had subsided and a modicum of order was restored, Pizarro proclaimed to the people that the young Manco was to be their future sovereign. This announcement was received with acclaim, for the people, even though they realized the Dons were the true rulers of the country, extracted some kernal of comfort from the fact that they would have a man of royal blood as their figurehead. With all the pomp and ceremony Manco was installed as Inca, for Pizarro was astute enough to realize that it was his best policy to maintain the illusion of the actuality of an Inca being enthroned. This accomplished, Pizarro at once established a municipal government of his own, patterned on the Spanish style, with two Alcaldes—his brother Juan and Gonzalo—and various other Spanish officials, thus completely taking all powers from the newly appointed Inca.

Without troubling even to ask permission, he took possession of the palaces and other buildings, distributed the property among his men, made Fray Valverde the Bishop of Cuzco, and proceeded to order the Incan buildings torn down and their materials used for erecting Christian churches. But the Incan, and more particularly the cyclopean pre-Incan masonry, was not so easy to destroy. Some few palaces were razed and the Cathedral, the University and some other Spanish edifices were built in their places. But most of the walls and edifices resisted every effort of the Dons. At last, deeming the results not worth the labor, the Spaniards abandoned all attempts to demolish the massive works, and contented themselves with erecting their own flimsy buildings upon the magnificent masonry of the natives. Even the marvelous Temple of the Sun, probably the most remarkable example of native architecture in the New World, was partly demollished and remodeled into the church of Santo Domingo, while the house of the Virgins of the Sun was converted to a Christian nunnery and the Incan nuns were turned over to the soldiery to be violated and ravaged.

It must not, however, be supposed that all the priests who accompanied Pizarro were of the same stern, fanatical, cruel type as the Friar Valverde. Many were gentle, kindly men who did everything in their power to mitigate the abuses and sufferings of the hapless Indians, and who protested loudly against the treatment accorded the Virgins of the Sun and other women by Pizarro and his men. Neither did all the Spaniards approve of the ruthless abuse of the Indians. De Soto was ever arguing in their behalf, and, time and time again, he and Pizarro were on the point of dueling, so high did the controversy run. But to Pizarro, to his brother Hernando, and to Almagro, the natives were beyond consideration or pity, scarcely more than beasts to be abused, enslaved and murdered out of hand if it served the Spaniards' purpose.

Cowed and conquered as they were, yet so unbearable was their position under the iron hand of Pizarro that the natives became threatening, and a large force of Atahualpa's followers gathered under his general, Quizquiz, prepared to attack the enemy. Hearing of this, Pizarro sent a small detachment of cavalry under Almagro, together with a large army of natives under Manco, to disperse Quizquiz's forces. A severe battle took place but the Indians, rather loath to fight against their fellows and the young Manco, were defeated and put to flight.

Soon after this, Pizarro had news that disturbed him far more than the reports of hostile Incans, for word was brought to him that a large force of Spaniards under Pedro de Alvarado had landed on the Peruvian coast. Here was an unexpected menace. His monopoly of Peru was threatened, for Pizarro well knew that Alvarado, who had served with Cortes and had conquered the Maya races of Guatemala, had not come to join his forces or to coöperate with him.

Treacherous, unprincipled and devoid of honor himself, Pizarro suspected all others of being the same sort, and he was not far off in this estimate when applied to Alvarado. A gentleman by birth, a Spaniard of the blond type with merry blue eyes and ever smiling face, Alvarado had earned the soubriquet of Toniah or the sun, among the Aztecs. But they had discovered to their sorrow that he was anything but sunny in nature, and that his pleasant features were merely a mask covering a cruel, vindictive and treacherous disposition. So, convinced, both by his suspicions and by his knowledge of Alvarado, that the latter's arrival on the scene boded him no good, Pizarro ordered Almagro to proceed with an adequate force against him.

Meanwhile, Alvarado, hearing that Pizarro's conquests had been confined to Peru, had decided that a magnificent opportunity was presented for the conquest of Quito (now Ecuador), and, instead of proceeding on the course he had set for the spice islands, he headed his fleet for the coast of South America. Marching inland, looting and killing as he went, he headed for the distant city of Quito. Greatly had he underestimated the difficulties to be met. Half-blinded by the dust and ashes from a volcano in eruption, frostbitten by the terrible cold of the high Andes, with many of his men frozen to death, and with all on the verge of starvation, he at last reached Riobamba, only to find that Pizarro's men from Piura had been before him, that everything of value had been already stripped from the country, and that his hardships and sacrifices had been for nothing.

Then Almagro and his forces arrived, and Alvarado, only too willing to abandon his enterprise, welcomed the one-eyed old campaigner with open arms, and declared his willingness to withdraw from the country upon the payment of half a million dollars, for which sum he offered to deliver all his twelve ships, his army and equipment to Pizarro. Almagro, realizing it was an excellent bargain, agreed, subject to Pizarro's approval, and together he and Alvarado returned to Pachacamac where Pizarro was staying at the time. The two conquerors met like old friends, embraced, and drank to each other's health and success. Then, after a round of festivities, Alvarado sailed away to resume his neglected governorship of Guatemala, carrying his half million with him.

This visit of Alvarado had convinced Pizarro that Cuzco was not suited as the capital of the country.

It was too far from the sea and ports where other soldiers of fortune might find foothold, and, in addition, was difficult of access and surrounded by Indians who were by no means friendly. Pachacamac was a far better and a very favorable site, but the neighboring Rimac Valley was even better. Here was a fertile valley, already intensively cultivated by the Indians, a large river to supply an abundance of water, a level plain whereon a large city could be built, and with an excellent harbor within a few miles. Deciding there could be no better spot, Pizarro founded his capital with pomp and ceremony. In honor of the day, January 6, 1535, the day of the Epiphany, he christened it La Ciudad de las Reyes (The City of the Kings). But it was a cumbersome name, and from the very first the new capital of Peru was known as Lima, the Spaniards' corruption of the Quichua "Rimac," and as Lima it is known to the world to-day.

CHAPTER XXII

A STROKE FOR FREEDOM

THE greatest achievement of Pizarro, one of his few commendable acts, was the building of Lima, the finest city on the Pacific coast of Latin America. Not only was it well planned and laid out, but the massive buildings erected by Pizarro and his men were so substantially built that they are still standing and in daily use, magnificent testimonials to what the Dons were capable of doing when they forsook their barbaric ways and turned their hands and minds to peaceful occupations.

But even in the building of Lima the Spaniards showed their cruel, pitiless characters. For hundreds of miles in every direction the Indians were seized, brought to Lima as slaves, and forced to labor under the eyes of their masters. Without rest, with barely enough food to keep life in their bodies, beaten and abused, these unfortunates died by thousands. But there were plenty more to be had for the taking, and the death of overworked slaves meant nothing to the Dons. One might say with little exaggeration that Lima's buildings were erected on the bodies of the Indians and were baptized with their blood.

Meanwhile, as the City of the Kings rose rapidly above the Rimac Valley, Hernando Pizarro was at the Court of Spain, whence he had been sent with reports of what had taken place, and with a vast amount of treasure. With him, too, was an emissary of Almagro, for the latter, although he pretended outwardly to hold no ill feelings towards Pizarro, was suspicious of him and had no faith whatever in his promises. Hernando was well received by the king, was made a Knight of Santiago, and was commissioned to enlist and equip a large force for Peru. Pizarro himself was made Marques de los Atavillos and had his territory extended seventy leagues farther south, while Almagro was rewarded by being given royal authority to explore and conquer the country for two hundred leagues south of Pizarro's sphere.

Not since the days of Columbus had any event aroused such interest and enthusiasm in Spain as this visit of Hernando Pizarro, and men of all ranks and stations flocked to him, anxious to go overseas to the marvelous land of gold. But few ever reached Peru. At Nombre de Dios they nearly succumbed for want of food, many died of disease, and many more turned back.

In Peru, too, important events were taking place. Almagro had been sent to take command of Cuzco with orders to explore and subdue the country to the south, and immediately upon his arrival the two Pizarros—Juan and Gonzalo—had resigned willingly. During their régime matters in the capital of the Incas had greatly improved. The brothers had treated the natives well, they had ruled wisely, and the Indians had become quiet and apparently resigned to their lot.

But with Almagro's arrival an unfortunate change took place. Feeling sure that Cuzco was south of the territory allotted to Pizarro, he felt independent of the latter, and in this assumption many of the Spaniards, especially the men and officers who had been with Alvarado, supported him. Neither Almagro nor these men had any respect for the natives, and helped themselves to the Indians' property and persons as they pleased. Manco was insulted, his favorite wives debauched by the Dons, and the sacred edifices of the Incans were used as stables for the Spaniards' horses. The conditions became almost as bad as when Pizarro and his men had first entered the city, and very soon the entire population was divided into two factions—one for the Pizarros, the other for Almagro.

So intense did the feeling run that open hostilities would have broken out had not Pizarro arrived on the scene. Hearing of trouble, and, like Almagro, believing Cuzco was south of his territory, he had hurried to Cuzco fearing that Almagro would possess himself of the city and declare himself in supreme control of the district.

He had already ordered his brothers reinstated, and he arrived in the nick of time to prevent a bloody civil war. But he greeted Almagro as cordially as if nothing had happened, and pretended to listen with unbiased mind to both sides of the controversy. Almagro attempted to place all the blame on Pizarro's brothers, but Pizarro's sympathies were plainly with them, although he made a pretense of reprimanding them at the time. Finally, the contending parties were reconciled, Pizarro and Almagro making out a new contract by which they agreed that neither one was to malign the other nor to communicate with the Spanish Crown without the other's knowledge, and that both were to share equally in all future operations. Heaven was invoked to punish the violator of the contract by eternal damnation, and at the conclusion of signing the paper a solemn Mass was celebrated.

Having thus smoothed over the difficulties, Pizarro suggested that Almagro should at once start on his delayed conquest of Chile. This he agreed to, and lost no time in making preparations. Two prominent Incas, Paullo Topa, a brother of Manco, and Villak Umu the high priest, were sent ahead to prepare the way among the natives, and following these, Captain Savedra with one hundred and fifty men started. Almagro had decided to remain to collect more troops, but fearing to be left alone with Pizarro and his brother, he left rather hastily with only a portion of his forces complete. Once Almagro was out of his way, Pizarro returned to Lima where he received word of the result of Hernando's mission to Spain; and shortly afterwards Hernando arrived in person with the remnants of the large force with which he had sailed from Spain.

But while the two Pizarros were congratulating each other on their newly acquired honors, and Francisco, now the Marquis, was devoting himself to founding cities and to building Lima, trouble of a serious sort was brewing at Cuzco. Heartily sick and tired of the Dons' rule, the Indians had decided to make a last attempt to throw off the Spaniards' yoke. They had carefully planned their revolt, and the true reason for Topa and Umu being sent ahead of Almagro's forces was to secure the coöperation of southern tribes in the impending uprising.

Manco was to lead the Incan armies in person, and when preparations were nearly complete he slipped from the city unnoticed. But even the Inca had enemies in Cuzco. At that time there were a thousand or more Cañarias in the city and these, being hereditary enemies of the Incan people, informed the Pizarros of Manco's escape. As a result, Juan Pizarro started at once in pursuit, and captured the Inca within a short distance from Cuzco. Heavily manacled, he was taken back and imprisoned, and the conspiracy was assumed by the Pizarro brothers to be at an end. But they had yet to learn the character of the Incans and their dogged tenacity, once they had set their hearts on anything. They were only awaiting their monarch's freedom to break out throughout the entire country.

At this time, Pizarro, who had decided to withhold Almagro's commissions, took the very worst course possible under the circumstances, and sent Hernando to take command at Cuzco. Although fully as cruel if not more cruel in some ways than Francisco, yet Hernando could regard the Indians as fellowmen, and he had become a very good friend of Manco. As a result, as soon as he reached that city, he released the captive Inca. Manco, apparently in

gratitude for this, revealed the hiding place of a
large amount of gold. Then, having aroused Hernando's cupidity, he told a tale of a life-sized gold
statue concealed in the mountains, and asked Hernando's permission to secure it. This consent was
willingly given, and, accompanied by two Spanish
soldiers, Manco left Cuzco.

When a week had slipped by and neither Manco
nor the soldiers had returned Hernando's suspicions
were aroused, and he sent his half-brother Juan to
bring the Inca back. On the way he met the two
soldiers who reported that although they had not
been harmed or hindered from returning, Manco
had joined his army, and that the entire country
swarmed with the Incan warriors. The Spanish
forces that were at once sent to the attack came into
contact with the Indians at the Yucay River. A
desperate battle ensued, and though the Spaniards
were victors, it was at a tremendous cost to themselves. They imagined that they had dispersed the
Indians, but to their amazement and chagrin the
next day dawned to show more Indians than ever.
For hours the battle raged, the Incans hurling down
rocks from the mountain heights, poured clouds of
arrows, javelins and stones from slings upon the
Spaniards, who barely held their own and were on
the point of retreating when they received messages
summoning them to Cuzco. Followed and harassed
by the triumphant Indians, they withdrew and, coming to Cuzco, they were dismayed to find the city
surrounded and besieged by fully two hundred
thousand Incans. No resistance was offered to the

Spaniards as they charged through the Indians' lines to the city gate, for the Incans were only too glad to have all the Dons within the town where the more mouths there were to feed the sooner the Dons would feel the terrors of famine.

Then began the deadliest and most prolonged struggle between the natives and Europeans in all the history of America. Ceaselessly the Indians poured a galling fire of missiles into the town, until, according to one chronicler who was an eyewitness, the arrows filled the plaza to a depth of more than a yard. But still worse was to follow. Blazing arrows were shot over the walls, and these, falling upon the dry thatched roofs, set fire to the buildings until the entire city was ablaze. Herded together in the open plazas, the Dons were helpless to extinguish the conflagration that raged for nearly a week and destroyed more than half the city, leaving only the largest stone buildings. Among the edifices that escaped was the Palace of Inca-Wira-Kocka (on the site of the present-day cathedral) and the Spaniards, ever looking for signs of Divine aid, declared that the Blessed Virgin was seen hovering over the building. Again and again the Dons made sorties, only to be driven back with heavy loss, and there was no rest day or night.

Then did the Spaniards bitterly regret the precious corn they had so recklessly destroyed in their mad search for gold when they had first entered the city. The magazines, always well stored with food in Incan days, were empty; much of the food in the houses and buildings had gone up in flames, and the gaunt, hungry Spaniards felt that their end was near. To add to their discomfiture, rumors were spread that every Spaniard in the country outside of Cuzco had been killed, and each day the ghastly heads of their fellow countrymen were thrown over the walls to bring terror to the besieged Dons. Moreover, the Indians were in possession of the fortress of Sacsayhuaman overlooking the city, and from this vantage point maintained a galling rain of arrows and stones upon the Spaniards. So desperate was their plight that at last Hernando decided to make a hazardous attempt to capture the fort, and detailed Ponce de Leon to take command of the attack. The fighting on both sides was terrific. The Incans, quick to imitate, had learned to use the Spaniards' own weapons. Many wielded swords, battle-axes, pikes and even crossbows; many wore armor taken from the bodies of the Spaniards who had fallen, and a few were mounted on the Dons' horses. Prominent among these was Manco, clad in a suit of mail and urging on his warriors. Here were Indians of a type the Spanish conquerors had never before met. Even the Aztecs had adhered to their own primitive weapons and had failed to use horses in their battles with Cortes, and De Leon, finding the foe as well drilled, as well equipped and as valiant as his own men, was finally forced to retreat, leaving a great number of his soldiers dead upon the field.

But the fort had to be taken, and Hernando, assisted by Juan and Gonzalo, undertook the second attempt. Profiting by De Leon's experience, they approached the fortress by a circuitous route, and managed to reach it and gain entrance through the outer walls undetected. But no sooner were they seen than the defenders fought with even greater stubbornness than ever. Defending each step of the way, inflicting terrible punishment upon the Spaniards, they retired to the higher battlements. During the attack Juan Pizarro was struck on the head with a stone, and was so badly injured that he died within a fortnight. Undismayed, Hernando and Gonzalo continued to urge their men on, until, after hours of desperate fighting, only the Incan general, a noble of high rank, remained to defend the fort. A giant in size and wielding an enormous copper-headed mace, he seemed to bear a charmed life and to be everywhere at once. Scaling ladders were raised, but each Spaniard who attempted to gain the parapet was instantly struck down by the valiant chieftain as the invader's head appeared above the walls. Even the Dons were forced to pause and admire the strength and bravery of this one defender of Sacsayhuaman, this sole survivor, who literally held the fort in the face of such terrific odds. Shouting to him that if he would surrender he would be given full quarter, the Dons made a concerted rush. For a moment the Incan general stood irresolute, gazing down upon the swarming, steel-clad Dons and upon the hundreds of bodies of his slain people. Then, hurling his mace from him, he gathered his poncho about his body, and shouting defiance, leaped from the lofty parapet to death upon the rocks below.

The taking of the fortress, though it mitigated the losses to the invaders from missiles, helped them very little. Hunger was a far deadlier weapon than arrows or stones, and though each Spaniard who succumbed left fewer to feed, they knew that death by starvation would be the fate of all unless help arrived soon. Months passed and there was no word from Lima. Five months slipped by and still no relief came. Were all the Spaniards in Peru dead? Were the famished, wounded, hopeless Dons in Cuzco the only white men remaining alive in the entire land?

Then, when their case seemed so utterly hopeless that the Spaniards contemplated rushing forth and dying at the hands of the Indians rather than succumb slowly from famine, they were amazed to see the Indians drawing off. Each day their numbers diminished, until only a few were left, and with their last strength the Spaniards made a final sortie. With scarcely any resistance the Indians retired, and the elated Spaniards returned with over two thousand llamas. There was no longer danger of starvation; the siege was over, and the Dons gave thanks to the Almighty for vouchsafing such a miracle and declared they had seen their patron saint, Santiago, driving the Incans away from the city.

It was no miracle that had saved them, however. The Indians themselves were getting short of provisions. They had been neglecting their fields, and as the season for planting drew near, Manco, realizing that unless crops were planted there would be famine the following year, withdrew all but a few

of his men, sent most of his army to their farms, and
with the pick of his forces, he retired to his fort at
Ollantaytambo.

Feeling confident that the Incas had been dispersed by Divine intervention, and anxious to revenge himself for his losses, Hernando led his men
to attack the Inca's stronghold. But no miracle
aided the Dons in the fierce battle that followed. The Spaniards were outgeneraled, surprised,
flanked, and with heavy losses were forced to retreat in disorder. For once the Indians had been
the victors. But it was their final triumph.

Meanwhile, though the reports brought to Cuzco
had been exaggerated, the Spaniards in other cities
and in the outlying country had been having a bad
time of it. Nearly all the settlers outside the cities
had been killed and their houses and property destroyed, and Lima itself had been attacked by thousands of natives. Pizarro, however, had managed
to disperse these, and, judging that Cuzco was in
trouble, he had sent strong bodies of men to that
city's relief. But of the five hundred sent not a Don
lived to get through the mountains. At last, convinced that he was powerless to cope with the situation, Pizarro sent messengers to Panama, Nicaragua
and Guatemala for help, and so desperate was his
state, that he even appealed to his old enemy, Alvarado, to come to his aid. But before there was time
for help to reach Peru from the northern colonies,
the siege of Cuzco had been lifted, the natives had
scattered far and wide, and for the time at least, the
insurrection was at an end.

CHAPTER XXIII

WHEN DON MEETS DON

WHILE Cuzco was being besieged, and the Spaniards in Peru were struggling desperately to maintain their foothold, and Lima was slowly growing into an imposing city, Almagro and his men were fighting for their lives against Nature. For a time they marched over the great Incan road, and going was easy; but as they turned their steps towards Bolivia, and entered the mountains, they lost their way—either accidentally or by being misled by their Indian guides—and their sufferings became intense. In the high altitudes, surrounded by everlasting snows and vast glaciers, the invaders were frostbitten, or afflicted with snow-blindness. Food was low and hunger added to their woes, while their horses, the most valuable of their possessions, found no herbage on which to feed and fell dead of starvation.

Terrible as were the sufferings of the Spaniards, they were nothing compared with those of their helpless Indian slaves. These unfortunates, chained or roped together by their necks, naked except for scanty loincloths, and bending under their burdens, succumbed by scores to the cold, the toil and the hunger. So desperate was their plight that whenever an Indian dropped, exhausted or dead, his companions fell upon the still warm body and, tearing it to bits, gorged themselves upon the raw and palpitating flesh, while the Spaniards devoured the raw meat of the horses that died.

Thus sustaining life by feasting upon the dead bodies of their comrades and their beasts, the company, sadly depleted in numbers, at last emerged from the mountains into the Valley of Coquimbo. Here were peaceful Indian villages, an abundance of grass and crops, warm sunshine and plenty of food to be had for the taking. But all the sufferings they had undergone had not softened the hearts of Almagro and his followers. He blazed his trail by burned and sacked villages, by the tortured and mutilated bodies of men, women and children, and as fast as his cargo-carrying slaves died by the wayside, he replenished his supply by capturing and enslaving the Indians he met.

Among the Indians whom Almagro had brought from Peru, was the Tumbes interpreter, Felipillo. Possibly this sly and vindictive youth wearied of being a spectator of the cruelties and oppressions practiced upon his people by the Dons, and plotted to incite the Indians to rebellion. Possibly he had word of the uprising in Peru and wished to do his part in helping the common cause. Or perhaps he was entirely innocent of any evil intentions towards the Spaniards. But at all events, Almagro suspected him of double-dealing—of which Felipillo had many a time proved himself quite capable—and of inciting the Indians to resist the Spaniards' advance. Once an Indian was suspected he was as good as dead, and there was no exception in the case of Felipillo. But even if the betrayer of the Incan Atahualpa richly deserved death there was no possible excuse for the horrible manner in which he was executed by Almagro's orders. Each leg and each arm was securely lashed by ropes to the saddle of four mounted soldiers, and at a signal from Almagro, the four horsemen spurred their steeds in opposite directions, rending the limbs from the Indian's body. Still alive, screaming horribly in his awful agony, Felipillo—or rather his limbless trunk and head— writhed upon the ground begging for his inhuman executioner to put a merciful end to his tortures. But Almagro watched him unmoved, gloating on the sufferings of his victim, until death ended the youth's groans. This was but one example of the extreme cruelty and inhumanity exhibited by the white-haired, one-eyed, old soldier whose benevolent appearance utterly belied his character.

On one occasion, three of the Spaniards were killed by the exasperated natives after the soldiers had sacked a village, had burned the houses, had outraged the women, had tossed children on the points of their lances, and had carried the men to slavery. In reprisal, and to castigate the Indians for revolting against their "lawful sovereign, the King of Spain," Almagro ordered thirty Indian chiefs, of villages whose inhabitants had had no part in the affair, to be burned alive. By such means did Almagro seek to "explore" and "subdue" his newly acquired territory. But Chile promised very little to its conqueror. While resting at Coquimbo, Almagro dispatched a force of men to explore the country farther south. Soon afterwards a detachment of men under Rodrigo de Orgoñez arrived from Peru, bringing with them the long-delayed Royal Warrant, which had been held by Pizarro as long as he had dared.

Meanwhile the men were grumbling and were becoming insistent upon returning to Peru. They had found no gold in the new land, and gold was all they cared for. So when the party returned from the south, and reported nothing of value, the Spaniards demanded that Almagro should abandon the expedition and retrace his steps to Cuzco. They argued that that city fell within the boundaries defined as Almagro's by the Crown, that nothing was to be gained by remaining in a goldless land, and finally clinched the matter by pointing out that only by such a course could their commander serve the interests of his son, Diego, his illegitimate child by an Incan woman. The one tender and human trait in Almagro's make-up was his love and devotion for this half-breed son, and at last, yielding to the pleas of his men and thoughts of Diego, he agreed to return to Peru.

Fearing to attempt the crossing of the Andes that had cost him so dearly, he decided to follow the road near the coast. But he was literally out of the frying pan into the fire. This route led across the trackless desert of Atacama, and the Spaniards and their slaves suffered as greatly from the heat, the thirst and the wind-blown dust of the vast waste

of sand as they had suffered from the cold, the snow
and the hunger of the Andean passes. At last, more
dead than alive, with fully half their original numbers missing, they arrived at Arequipa where, for
the first time, Almagro learned of the Incan rebellion
and heard that Cuzco was still besieged. Having
formerly been on fairly friendly terms with Manco,
he determined to try to use his influence to bring
about an end to hostilities, and sent an emissary to
the Inca, requesting a meeting and conference, for
he foresaw in an alliance with Manco, an opportunity of getting possession of Cuzco. The envoy was
well received by the Inca, who told of the abuses
suffered by the Indians and who agreed to confer
with Almagro at a spot near Yucay. Leaving most
of his force at Urcos, abut fifteen miles from Cuzco,
Almagro started for the meeting place.

In the meantime, Hernando Pizarro learned of
Almagro's forces encamped in the vicinity, and always having been an enemy of the one-eyed adventurer, he suspected Almagro was on no peaceful
mission. With a force of picked men he advanced
on Almagro's camp where he was told of the other's
visit to the Inca. Seeing this meeting of the two
parties of Dons, and suspecting Almagro's supposed conference was merely an excuse for gaining
access to Manco for the purpose of capturing or
killing him, the Peruvians fell upon Almagro's company with a force of ten or fifteen thousand warriors. In the sharp but brief battle that followed—
the engagement lasting barely an hour—the Span-

iards were victorious, although their losses were comparatively heavy and they were glad to retire to Urcos. Almagro's next step was to send a formal notice to Hernando Pizarro demanding that the latter should deliver the city to him, at the same time presenting a copy of the credentials he had received from the king to bear out his claims as governor of Cuzco.

Unwilling to come to open hostilities with Almagro's superior forces, and at the same time fearing to bring on trouble with Francisco Pizarro if they acceded to the former's demands, the brothers very diplomatically replied that, as neither party was positive whether or not Cuzco was within the territory of Almagro or Pizarro, it would be wisest to wait until competent pilots could be summoned to determine the exact position of the city. To this Almagro consented, and each party solemnly agreed not to molest the other. But Hernando's delay was merely to enable him to strengthen his defenses, and to send a messenger to Lima to summon aid. Learning of his duplicity, and that a large body of troops under command of Alvarado was on the way to Cuzco, Almagro decided—quite rightly, too—that the Pizarros had broken their promises and that he was justified in taking what means he could to possess himself of the city.

Without detection or molestation, he led his forces into Cuzco on a dark and tempestuous night (April 8, 1537), and taking possession of a church and the plaza, posted his men at points of vantage and sent a body of troops under Orgoñez to seize Hernando

Pizarro. The latter was at the time occupying the Maita-Pakak palace with his brother Gonzalo. This building was protected by immense, fortresslike doors and was guarded by a score of soldiers who fought stubbornly to protect their masters and to drive off Almagro's men. Provoked at their resistance, Orgoñez set fire to the thatched roof of the palace, and the inmates were forced to surrender or lose their lives in the flames.

Thus, without the loss of a man, Almagro was in full possession of the ancient city, and with the Pizarros in prison and with no opposition from the other officials or the inhabitants, he proceeded to reorganize the municipality.

It must be admitted that Almagro in this *coup* behaved himself most admirably. Neither he nor his men were guilty of excesses, the Indians were not molested, and he very fairly installed several of the Pizarros' men as officials of the city.

One of his first acts was to send a messenger to Alvarado, informing him of his occupation of Cuzco and demanding that Alvarado should obey his orders. Alvarado, however, had no such ideas on the subject. He had the envoys promptly clapped into irons, and sent word of Almagro's acts to Lima.

The peppery little old soldier was enraged at this and prepared at once to attack Alvarado and teach him a wholesome lesson; but he made the one great mistake of leaving the captive Pizarros alive. Several of his officers, especially Orgoñez, urged him to put an end to the two, remarking that, "The only

good Pizarro was a dead Pizarro,'' or words to
that effect. But Almagro, though he cordially hated
Hernando, still had some lingering feelings of
friendship for his former partner, Francisco, and
refused to follow the excellent advice to ''strike off
the heads'' of his prisoners. Merely placing them
under a heavy guard, he set out to attack Alvarado.
By a ruse, which was suggested to him by a traitor-
ous officer of Alvarado's forces, Almagro surrounded
his foes, and after a brief resistance, the former
surrendered.

Meanwhile, Francisco Pizarro had become
alarmed, and gathering all available men and supplies, including a force under Espinosa, the man
who had advanced the money for the triumvirate
when the three had first started on their careers of
conquest, he started for Cuzco. He had traveled
but a short distance when he heard of Alvarado's
surrender, and seized with panic and fearing the
victorious Almagro might even attack Lima, he
hastily returned to that city.

Pretending that he deeply regretted his old associate's resort to arms to settle a dispute between
friends, Francisco sent Espinosa as an envoy to
Almagro in an endeavor to negotiate a peaceful
settlement, although in reality the mission's object was to ascertain the extent of Almagro's resources and the attitude of the Cuzcans towards him.
Almagro, however, now that he was firmly established in the Incan capital, refused to listen to any
proposals, and declared his intention of marching

against Lima itself, which he now insisted also fell
within the territory allotted him by the king.

Possibly, in the end, Espinosa might have won
the one-eyed little warrior from his ambitious plans,
but his sudden and somewhat mysterious death
brought all negotiations to an end.

Almagro now prepared to lead his forces, which
had been more than doubled by the addition of Alvarado's soldiers, against Lima, and once more he was
urged to put an end to the Pizarro brothers. Better
by far would it have been for him had he done so.

Unknown to Almagro, the prisoners had acquired
a new friend and ally in one of his own officers.
This was Diego de Alvarado, half brother of Pedro,
the "sun" of Guatemala fame, who, soon after his
brother's departure from Peru following his ill-
starred effort to capture Quito, had joined Almagro
and had accompanied him on his expedition into
Chile.

An inveterate gambler, as were the Pizarros, the
young Alvarado had whiled away many a tedious
hour by gaming with the two prisoners under his
care, and as a result, he had become indebted to
Hernando to the extent of some four hundred thousand dollars. But when he offered to pay the sum,
Hernando grandiloquently refused to accept a *centavo*. As a result of this gesture, Diego Alvarado
became a stanch friend of the brothers, and it was
very largely owing to his advice that Almagro refused to execute his two prisoners.

"Very well," remarked Orgoñez, who from the

first had argued in favor of getting rid of them. "A Pizarro never forgets or forgives. Have you not had enough proof of this already? And what they have received at your hands is far too deep for any of the race to forgive. Take a care that, in the end, it is not *your* head instead of theirs that falls to the ax."

These words must have had some weight with Almagro, for when he again left Cuzco at the head of his army he carried Hernando, under close guard, with him, leaving Gonzalo in prison behind him.

But he had not proceeded very far before unwelcome and most disturbing news was brought to him. He had stopped at Chincha, where he planned to establish a town named after himself, and while there, a courier arrived from Cuzco with word that Gonzalo Pizarro, Alvarado and a number of prisoners had made good their escape by bribing their guards, and that they had succeeded in reaching Lima.

Evidently Almagro's age was beginning to tell on him, and his stern nature was being softened with advancing years, for instead of executing Hernando as a reprisal for his brother's escape, as he most assuredly would have done earlier in his career, he opened negotiations with Francisco Pizarro with a view to settling matters by peaceful methods.

Pizarro, always tricky, treacherous and subtle, consented to this, and both parties agreed to submit the dispute to an unprejudiced (?) arbiter. The man chosen was Fray Francisco de Bovadilla, a

priest of Lima in whom Almagro had great faith,
but who, living under Pizarro's rule and eye, could
scarcely have dared to jeopardize his living if not
his life by favoring Almagro.

When, this agreement having been reached, the
two leaders met at Mala for the conference and decision, Pizarro's attitude was hostile and overbearing. Old Almagro, cruel and unprincipled as he was,
was ever a rather sentimental fellow, and was willing to meet his old comrade more than halfway in
order to heal the breach between them. But it was
impossible to deal amicably with a man of Pizarro's
stamp, and the meeting developed into a heated dis-
cussion with recriminations on both sides, until Almagro, fearing treachery, left abruptly for his own
camp. Father Bovadilla then gave his decision, declaring that a vessel with a competent pilot and
navigator should be employed to determine the exact
latitude of the Santiago River, the point from which
all boundaries of Peruvian territory were calculated, and that, during the meantime, Almagro
should deliver Cuzco to Pizarro, should liberate
Hernando Pizarro—who was to leave for Spain
within six weeks—and that both parties to the controversy should retire to their respective territories
and abstain from further hostilities.

The decision was in fact exactly what might have
been expected. Pizarro was favored in every way,
and Almagro and his men were to seek what little
comfort they could in the wildernesses to the south.
No doubt, had they dreamed what riches in silver

lay hidden in the Bolivian hills, they would have been only too glad to have accepted the friar's decision, but at that time the fabulously rich mines of Potosi were still undiscovered. Bitterly did they denounce the padre; loudly they demanded the death of Hernando, and by so slender a thread did his life hang that Francisco determined to concede much to Almagro in order to save his brother—though he had no intentions of keeping his promises once Hernando was safe. So, pretending to be magnanimous, he offered to let Almagro remain in possession of Cuzco until definite instructions arrived from Spain, provided Hernando was set at liberty, pledging himself he would leave Peru. Orgoñez, when he heard of this offer, scoffed at it, and with a significant gesture of passing his finger across his throat, reminded Almagro of what he had already said regarding live Pizarros.

Almagro, however, always ready to be hoodwinked by his former partner, and never, by experience, having acquired a knowledge of his character, refused to listen to the suspicions of his officer. He at once visited Hernando, informed him he was free, and courteously remarked that he hoped all past differences might be forgotten and that only old friendship might remain. Hernando, replying that he could wish nothing better, swore on the Bible and by his "knightly honor" (something he did not possess) to abide by the terms of the treaty, and to leave for Spain within the stipulated six weeks. Then, having been wined and dined by Almagro and his officers, Hernando was escorted to his broth-

er's camp by Diego Almagro and the highest officers
of his father's army.

So well were they received by Francisco, and so
hospitably and lavishly entertained, that any lingering doubts they may have had were completely dis-
pelled.

But Almagro's men were scarcely out of earshot
when Pizarro called his men together, harangued
them at length, recapitulated all that Almagro had
done, and declared that the moment had arrived for
revenge. Possibly even his despicable mind shrank
from so outrageously violating his agreements and
the confidence reposed in him by Almagro, or possibly, like the latter, he was losing his nerve with
his advancing age. At any rate, he ended by stating
that he would not take command of the campaign
himself but would leave the matter and manner of
revenge to his brother Hernando, whom he absolved
of all obligations towards Almagro.

Hernando, to do him justice, refused to break his
pledges or to attack Almagro without warning, and
insisted that a messenger be sent to the latter, noti-
fying him that the agreements were at an end, and
warning him that unless he abandoned Cuzco and
withdrew his forces to Chile he must take the consequences.

Almagro, thunderstruck at this development, and
suffering from an incurable malady which rendered
him incapable of any great exertion, left everything
to Orgoñez who saw his dismal prophecies about to
be borne out.

His forebodings did not, however, prevent him from taking active steps to do what was in his power to avert the impending calamity. He quickly sent picked men to hold the various mountain passes about the valley where his forces were encamped, but only to find the enemy had moved even more rapidly and were in command of the hills. There was nothing to do but retire to Cuzco, and Almagro, now too feeble to bestride a horse, was carried upon a litter as the little army wound its way towards the distant Incan capital. Once at Cuzco, Almagro and his men felt themselves fairly secure, and the leader, weak and in agony from his malady, again proposed to try to smooth matters over with the treacherous Pizarros.

Orgoñez shook his head. "Had you taken my advice," he reminded Almagro, "this never would have happened. Now it is too late. Nothing remains but to surrender or fight. And," he added dolefully, "in either case we shall lose our heads."

"Better to die fighting than in prison," was the unanimous decision of the other officers, and preparations were made to attack Hernando's forces, which were now close to the city. Orgoñez's forces totaled less than five hundred, about one half being cavalry; he had few firearms and only six small cannon, while opposed to him, Hernando Pizarro commanded nearly one thousand men, almost all veterans, an entire corps of arquebusiers with firearms of the latest pattern, and a round dozen cannon of much larger caliber than those of Orgoñez.

The struggle that followed the meeting of the two forces was most desperate. This was no battle between mail-clad Dons and naked Indians, but between fellow Spaniards, comrades in arms; tough, seasoned campaigners, each side fighting for what it felt was its rights; each side urged on by the fury of long pent-up wrongs; every man fighting for his life. Deeds of personal valor were numerous and savored of the days of knight-errantry not long past. Orgoñez singled out Hernando Pizarro, and with set lance charged him and hurled him from his horse. Turning, he ran through another officer who had dashed to Hernando's aid and, casting aside his lance, he struck down a third with his heavy sword. As he rose in his stirrups shouting, "Victory," a shot from an arquebus or a small cannon smashed through the visor of his helmet, and grazing his forehead, momentarily stunned him. Before his brain cleared his horse was killed under him, and as he struggled to rise he was surrounded and overpowered. Still dazed from his wound, he glanced about and asked if no officer was present to whom he could surrender his sword.

A servant of Pizarro, a scoundrel named Fuentes, stepped forward and declared himself an officer. As Orgoñez handed him his sword the fellow whipped out his poniard and drove it through the prisoner's heart. Another of Pizarro's men thereupon lopped off Orgoñez's head, and raising it on a lance, shouted that the "traitor" was dead. The battle that had now raged for nearly two hours was practically over. With Orgoñez killed, Almagro's men became confused and fought uncertainly and with little cohesion.

Still the cavalry fought on, and Pedro de Lerma, in command of Almagro's horse, finding Hernando Pizarro still alive and fighting after being unhorsed by Orgoñez, set his lance and, in knightly fashion, called on Hernando to defend himself. Like avalanches of flesh and steel the two armored horses and two mail-clad Spaniards rushed together, while the soldiery momentarily ceased their hand-to-hand fighting to watch this duel between the two leaders. With a shock and a clash that sounded above the groans of the wounded and the screams of dying horses, the lances struck. Hernando's weapon pierced Lerma's thigh, lifting him bodily from his horse and throwing him to the earth, while Lerma's lance, glancing from Hernando's saddle, struck the latter in the groin, penetrated the armor and forced Pizarro's horse upon its haunches. Wounded and suffering agony, Hernando withdrew, while Lerma was left, wounded and forgotten, upon the field. Panic-stricken at thus seeing their only remaining leader defeated, Almagro's men fled in confusion to Cuzco with the victors in hot pursuit. No quarter was given and few of Almagro's men lived to reach the city.

Almagro, still upon a litter, had watched the battle from a distance, and realizing his cause was lost, had managed to mount a mule and had sought refuge in the fortress of Sacsayhuaman. Shouting in triumph, bearing the head of Orgoñez and other officers upon their lances and pikes, Pizarro's forces took possession of the city, and at Hernando's orders, poor old Almagro was seized, loaded with chains and thrown into the same prison where he had formerly confined the Pizarros.

Only a handful of Almagro's men remained alive and unharmed. Over two hundred men had fallen in the battle, not a large number as compared with modern warfare but a terrific loss in comparison with the total number engaged—and the greater portion of these belonged to Almagro's forces.

Still more were wounded, among whom was the gallant Pedro de Lerma who was brought into Cuzco suffering from seventeen wounds, all severe. By the express orders of Hernando Pizarro, who despite his faults could appreciate personal bravery and gallantry in another, De Lerma was given all possible aid, and Hernando personally expressed hopes for his recovery. As he lay upon his couch, helpless and weak from his wounds, he was visited by a soldier named Samaniego, whom De Lerma had once punished for disobedience. Recalling the incident to the sick man, Samaniego told him he had come for revenge and murdered him in cold blood.

But it must be admitted, in justice to the Dons of those days, that such dastardly acts did not meet with approval. The Spaniards might murder and torture helpless Indians, but there was a certain code of honor among even the roughest when it came to the treatment of their fellow countrymen. Fuentes was put to an ignominious death for his murder of Orgoñez, and Samaniego was hanged for killing De Lerma. Such examples of just retribution are among the few bright spots in the bloody history of the Conquest.

CHAPTER XXIV

RETRIBUTION

THOUGH the battle was over, though the forces of Pizarro had been victorious, and though Almagro was a manacled prisoner in the hands of his enemies, yet Cuzco was not won. Hernando had given free rein to his men to loot, pillage and despoil. As a result, the inhabitants, who might have resigned themselves to Pizarro's rule—for a change of masters was of little importance in those days and was an everyday matter—were filled with hatred and the deadliest rancor at the excesses committed by his men and by the personal injuries they suffered at his hands. Hernando, realizing that he was sitting on a smoldering volcano, sought to mitigate matters by sending expeditions into the surrounding country on searches for gold and other treasures. Thus relieved of the burden of nearly fifteen hundred irresponsible soldiers, the city quieted down and assumed its former aspect of tranquillity.

In the meantime, Hernando had sent Diego Almagro under a strong guard to Lima. Learning that Almagro himself was near death, and fearing that a merciful Almighty might remove the old man from his clutches and cheat him of revenge, he visited his prisoner and endeavored to cheer him up the better to prolong his agony. Assuring him that he only awaited his brother's arrival to free him, and adding that if Francisco did not arrive soon he would personally release him, he considerately asked Almagro what sort of conveyance would be best suited to his health and comfort when he left the prison. Then, declaring that the food supplied his prisoner was not suitable for a sick man, he ordered wines and delicacies sent to him from his own home.

Feeling sure that Hernando meant what he said, and as childishly trusting as ever, the old warrior improved greatly with the prospects of freedom in store, and he never dreamed that, all the time, his enemies were plotting his degradation and death. Charges of every possible sort had secretly been brought against him, and every one—no matter how lowly—was invited to bring and lodge any real or fancied complaints he might have against the prisoner. From the vast mass of accusations thus obtained—and many, indeed, secured by bribery, by promises of rewards and by threats—an imposing document of more than four thousand pages was prepared. According to this remarkable volume, Almagro had been guilty of everything from mutiny, larceny and deceit to insurrection, murder, blasphemy, defamation of the king, abuse of his men, cruelty, the death of Atahualpa, and in fact every crime in the Spanish calendar.

Naturally, under the circumstances, with no chance to defend himself, with no knowledge of the proceedings in fact, and being completely in the power of the vindictive Pizarros, Almagro's fate was already sealed. His trial was even more of a farce than that of the Inca with whose murder he was charged. He was of course found guilty, without knowing he was being tried, and was sentenced to be beheaded in the plaza of Cuzco.

The first intimation that he was being accused or tried came to Almagro when a priest brought word of his sentence. For a space he was too shocked to speak. He could not believe it possible, could not conceive that those whom he had trusted, who had promised him freedom, could have been so treacherous, so unjust, so cruel. He begged Hernando to grant him an interview, and the latter, delighted to gloat over the mental anguish of the man he had hated from the first, was only too willing to visit him in his cell. In vain, Almagro begged his enemy to spare him. He reminded his captor that he had but a short time to live, that he had spared Hernando and his brother when they had been in his power, and that the Pizarros had nothing to fear and nothing to gain by putting him to death.

Hernando jeered and scoffed at him. He was amazed, he declared, to find a brave cavalier demean himself and exhibit such unseemly cowardice. His fate, he assured him, was no worse than had befallen many another, including Atahualpa, and that as he was or was supposed to be a Christian his last hours could be more profitably devoted to prayers and confession than to pleading for a life already forfeited.

Finding it hopeless to appeal to his pitiless enemies, Almagro resigned himself to his fate, and calling a notary, gave instructions as to the settlement of his affairs. Under the terms of his Royal Warrant he named his son Diego as his successor, and appointed Diego de Alvarado as administrator of his estate. All his real and personal property he willed to the King of Spain, adding that vast amounts were still due which had been withheld by Pizarro who had never made a true accounting of his share. For once, poor old Almagro showed as keen a bit of diplomacy and cunning as Pizarro, for his will, leaving his property to the Crown, could not be concealed, altered or destroyed; it would be sure to bring his son to the attention of the Crown, and it was equally certain that the king would look most closely into the accounts and affairs of Pizarro when his suspicions of the latter were aroused by the cleverly inserted words of Almagro's last will and testament.

Had the poor deluded, bedridden old veteran known how news of his impending death had been received in Cuzco, his last hours might have been easier. He had been a great favorite with his men, and indignation ran high at the presumption of the Pizarros in sentencing him to death. Almost unanimously the people openly denounced Almagro's enemies; Hernando was loudly proclaimed a tyrant, and a number of officers—of both factions—visited him and demanded that he countermand the sentence. This he absolutely refused to do, but he finally consented to change the mode of death of Almagro who, instead of being degraded by being publicly executed, was to be put to death in prison.

Still, so strong and widespread was the feeling against him, that on the day of execution, Hernando placed the city under martial law, posted men with loaded weapons about the houses of Almagro's friends and partisans, and used every precaution to prevent a possible outbreak. Secretly the executioner, accompanied by a priest, entered the prison, where the betrayed and unfortunate Almagro was put to death by means of the garrote. Then, having complied with the letter of his promise, Hernando ordered the old soldier's corpse dragged to the plaza and beheaded as the final act of brutality and insult to the man who had—foolishly—spared his own life so many times. Thus perished the first of the trio who, a few years previously, had foregathered in Panama and had signed the "Eucaristia" and had sworn on the Cross and by the Holy Trinity to remain faithful to one another until the end.

While Almagro was being tried, convicted and executed, the Marquis Francisco Pizarro was in Lima waiting impatiently for news of his old comrade's death before starting for Cuzco. Villain that he was, he assured young Diego Almagro that no harm should befall his aged father, declared that the old friendship between himself and Almagro would be renewed, and thus calming the boy's fears, received him in his own home like a son. Similar assurances of Almagro's safety were given by Pizarro to Bishop Valverde, who had expostulated at Hernando's actions in trying and condemning the old man, and all the time, Francisco was secretly approving of his brother's actions and urging the immediate death of Almagro. Yet, when definite news of the execution was brought to him, he pretended to be greatly shocked and grieved—exactly as he had done when Atahualpa was murdered—and, as in that case, donned mourning. Never in the whole history of American conquest was there a more hypocritical character or a greater dissembler.

His subsequent actions, however, were not by any means in accord with his outward show of mourning. He entered Cuzco like a conquering hero, dressed in a magnificent costume and priceless mail presented to him by Cortes, and when Diego Alvarado appealed to him to ratify young Almagro's governorship of Chile, Pizarro replied that "his father had forfeited all rights by his rebellion," and added that he personally controlled "all territory on this side of Flanders."

He then confiscated the property and estates of all Almagro's officers and known friends, distributed them among his own men, and would not listen to the complaints of the natives who had been mistreated by his brothers. As rewards for Hernando's and Gonzalo's activities, he presented them with such vast tracts of lands and so many Indian slaves that even his own friends commented upon his acts, for among the lands thus granted were the richest mines of Potosi, whose wealth was just being realized. Having thus disposed—as he flattered himself—of his last enemies, and having firmly established his brothers in command of vast fortunes and great power, he returned to Lima.

Hernando now remembered his promise to go to

Spain, and having accumulated all the treasure he could lay hands on, he set sail, nearly a year after Almagro's death. Always careful of his own safety, he avoided Panama where he had heard plans had been made to detain him, and took the route across Mexico. Even then he was a bit suspicious of the welcome he might receive in Spain, and landed at the Azores where he could await word from friends at Court. These being reassuring he continued on his way, but met with a very cold reception, for Diego de Alvarado had reached Spain ahead of Hernando for the purpose of urging his claim in favor of the rights of his ward, Diego Almagro. Being a cavalier of high rank and aristocratic lineage, Alvarado had great influence at Court, and he made no bones of painting the Pizarros in their true colors, and of recounting the part they had played in the death of Almagro.

Once, as I have said, Alvarado had been most friendly with the Pizarros, and had been largely instrumental in saving the lives of Hernando and Gonzalo. But any kindly feelings he had had for the tribe had been utterly destroyed by their persecution and execution of his old leader. Hernando, however, possessed an argument that was far more convincing than Alvarado's frank statements and personal word. He had unstinted gold, and gold properly distributed worked miracles with the Spanish officials—as it always does. There were delays, excuses, and procrastinations until Alvarado, becoming impatient, challenged Hernando to a duel. But the latter had no desire to risk his precious

skin in this manner. Neither could he honorably refuse. He was in a bit of a dilemma, but he knew the
power of gold—none better—and within a few days
after the challenge Alvarado died suddenly from
poison. The coincidence was altogether too remarkable and too transparent to go unnoticed, and Hernando lost far more than he gained by getting Alvarado out of the way. There was no doubt that he
had been too high-handed in Peru, and the death of
Alvarado aroused popular indignation to such an
extent that the authorities dared not whitewash him
entirely as they had planned. Though he received
no formal sentence by the court, yet he was imprisoned in the fortress of Medina del Campo, where
he was left, forgotten and friendless, for twenty
years. He came forth at last, penniless, broken in
health and spirits; an aged, pitiable, bent and pal-
sied man. Even his worst enemies, even poor decapitated Almagro, could not have asked for greater
retributive justice than had been dealt out to him.

In Peru, matters were going from bad to worse.
The Crown's suspicions, aroused by the note in Almagro's will and by Alvarado's statements, led to
investigations as Almagro had foreseen, and the
authorities were convinced that steps must be taken
to bring order out of the chaos that prevailed.
Neither the Indians nor the Spaniards had any
rights that were respected. Pizarro had assumed
the attitude of an independent despot. His vaunted
patriotism and loyalty to his king had been cast
aside, and he was almost ready to openly declare
Peru an independent kingdom. Some one, the Crown

decided, must go to Peru quietly, secretly, without arousing Pizarro's suspicions; some one on whom the Court could depend for truth, loyalty and unbiased opinion. The man selected for this delicate mission was Vaca de Castro, a learned judge of law and a still greater judge of human nature. His instructions were explicit and secret. He was to present himself to Pizarro as a Royal Judge sent to Peru to confer with the marquis on the matter of adjusting grievances of the people, he was to acquaint himself with every feature and detail of conditions, and, in case of Pizarro's death, he was authorized to act as governor himself.

While all these events were transpiring in Spain, Peru was, as I have said, in a state of chaos, and Pizarro was not finding his governorship a bed of roses by any means. Taking advantage of the unstable state of the country and the civil war of the Dons, the natives had initiated a guerilla warfare of their own. Having learned by bitter experience that it was hopeless for them to attempt to cope with the Spaniards by open warfare and face-to-face battles, they had decided to inflict all possible damages by raids and ambuscades. Establishing himself with a large body of his warriors in the wildest and most inaccessible defiles of the Andes, Manco played havoc with outlying settlements, estates and travelers. Sweeping down from their fastness of Macchu-picchu in the mountains, the Indians would kill and destroy and vanish before their presence in the neighborhood was suspected. Even when troops were sent against the Indians they met with no success. Some were killed to a man without once sighting their wily foes. Others returned without finding a trace of the Indians, and others, decimated, were only too glad to escape and retreat to the nearest Spanish town.

Finding it hopeless to capture or kill the Inca by means of his armed forces, and realizing that if such a state of affairs continued the country would be laid waste, Pizarro determined to try his usual guile and treachery. In his own name, and in the name of the Bishop of Cuzco whom the Inca revered, he sent envoys to Manco asking for a meeting to discuss the subject of a treaty. Manco, trusting to the Bishop's protection, agreed, and indicated the Yucay Valley as the meeting place. Pizarro started for the appointed spot accompanied by a heavy guard, and as he approached Yucay he sent a negro slave with a rich present as a peace offering to Manco. Not realizing who or what he was, a party of the Indians waylaid the negro, killed him and took possession of the presents he carried. Without stopping to inquire into the matter or to ascertain whether or not the Indians had acted under Manco's orders or with his knowledge, Pizarro made terrible reprisal. Among his Indian prisoners was one of the Inca's wives, a very young and beautiful princess. Pizarro ordered her stripped, bound naked to a tree, and in the presence of his soldiers to be scourged with sticks and shot to death with arrows. Not a word, not a groan issued from the girl's lips as she endured the torture. Even the rough, pitiless troopers were moved by her sufferings and fortitude, and openly condemned the course of Pizarro in thus venting his vengeance and his temper upon a helpless woman.

Naturally, after this, all hopes of a peaceful solution of the Indian troubles were at an end. But in a way it led to good results. Pizarro decided that the only solution was to establish fortified towns throughout the country, and among those that sprang into existence through this necessity were some of the most important towns of Peru to-day, such as Huancayo, Ayacucho, Juamanga, Sicuani and even Arequipa.

Peru meanwhile was becoming richer and richer. The Potosi mines were being worked; the supply of precious metals seemed inexhaustible, and a steady stream of silver, and not a little gold, flowed from the incredibly rich mines as thousands of hapless Indian slaves toiled day and night and gave their lives that their brutal taskmasters might live in opulence and idleness.

With this prosperity and the rapid increase of immigrants and settlers, and the consequent growth and importance of Lima, Pizarro was fully occupied with the business of administering the country's government, and gave no heed—if for that matter he realized it—to a growing danger that menaced him. Almagro's friends had not forgotten their leader's death at Pizarro's hands, and though these "Men of Chile," as they were called, were scattered and were comparatively few in numbers they were united in spirit and only biding their time to even scores. Pizarro, however, regarded the partisans of his late enemy with the utmost contempt, and even allowed Diego Almagro—now grown to manhood— to remain in Lima. Whatever friendship or faith Diego might have had for Pizarro at first had been utterly destroyed by the marquis' deceitful promises and the part he had played in the death of the elder Almagro. His home became the headquarters for meetings of the Almagro faction.

Some rumors of this must have reached Pizarro's ears, and must have been believed, for he stripped the young Almagro of all his lands and property, declared his position in the government forfeited, and left him penniless.

Poverty, however, increased rather than diminished the determination of the "Men of Chile" to accomplish this revenge. Though it is said that twelve cavaliers who lodged together could muster only one coat among them, and wore this by turns, yet they remained true to their cause, and daily became more dangerous in proportion to their wants and sufferings. Then, when word was brought of the arrival of the judge, Vaca de Castro, the "Men of Chile" saw possible righting of their wrongs in store. But as months passed and no tidings came of his arrival, the Almagro faction became more and more open in their threatening attitude. Frequently they failed to take off their hats to Pizarro when they met on the street, and on one occasion Pizarro, his secretary and judge were found hanged in effigy on the public gallows. Still Pizarro, complacent in his power, feeling himself too great to be molested, arrogant beyond words, paid no attention to the smoldering hatred and longings for revenge that were ready to burst into flame at any moment.

And the flames burst forth on Sunday, the 26th of June, 1541. It was the hour of noon, the hour when Pizarro dined. Rushing through the unguarded open gate of Pizarro's palace, shouting, "Long live the King! Death to the Tyrant!" Almagro's friends, led by Juan de Herrada, dashed into the palace courtyard. Surrounded by a party of friends, Pizarro, aroused by the shouts and the screams of servants, one of whom had been struck down, hurried to arm himself, while his friends sought safety—or as they later claimed, weapons— in one of the corridors, and leaping over the railing into the courtyard took to their heels, leaving the marquis to look out for himself. Only one man remained in the room, the captain, Chaves, who, instead of closing the door, lost his head, and holding the door ajar, attempted to parley with the men intent on putting an end to Pizarro's career. Before two words had passed his lips he was run through with a rapier. Dashing into the deserted room, the men shouted, "Where is the Marquis? Death to Pizarro!"

Francisco's half-brother, Martinez de Alcantara, who was helping Pizarro to don his armor in an anteroom, sprang to the doorway with two pages and a cavalier who had remained, and threw themselves in front of the assassins. Two of the latter fell in the sharp struggle that followed, and Alcantara and the other defender were seriously wounded. Abandoning his futile efforts to buckle on his mail,

Pizarro, with sword in one hand and dagger in the other, rushed out to his brother's assistance. With all his old fire and impetuosity he leaped upon the invaders and two fell to his darting rapier. But the others were not dismayed. Shouting to his fellows to end the matter, Herrada lunged with his sword and caught Pizarro in the throat. As he reeled and sank to the floor the swords of the others pierced him in half a dozen places.

"Jesus!" he gasped, blood welling to his lips and choking off the words. Then, tracing the figure of a cross in his own blood upon the floor, he sank lifeless upon it.

Thus did death come to the second of the trio who set forth to conquer Peru—seemingly a just retribution and a proof of the old adage that "He who lives by the sword dies by the sword."

He died as he had lived, by treachery and violence. Few mourned him, none missed him, but throughout the country there was a general feeling of relief that the tyrant had come to the end of his career.

CHAPTER XXV

AN AMAZING MARCH

FEW chapters of the history of America are more thrilling, more filled with adventure and romance than the conquest of what is now Chile. And few of the men who had a part in the making of South American history were more daring, more picturesque, more ambitious or more cruel and unprincipled than Pedro de Valdivia, the conqueror of Chile.

Unlike most of the adventurers and conquerors who flocked overseas to the New World, Valdivia was a gentleman by birth, a scion of a titled family, and an educated and able man. He was born in 1500, either at Zalamea de la Serena or at Costuera —authorities differ—and at the age of twenty was a captain in the Spanish army, fighting under Charles the Fifth in Flanders and in Italy. He had already earned the reputation of being a courageous and valiant soldier possessing great military knowledge, and was specially honored for the part he played in the battles of Milan and Pavia. Contemporaneous writers agree that he was of commanding presence, tall, erect, heavily built, and of almost gigantic strength. He was affable, merry, and was noted for his gallantry and his fondness for the ladies. But he had quite another side to his character.

330

As events proved, he was cruel, dishonest, underhanded in his methods, and, at heart, was a coward. But despite his faults, which were legion, we cannot but admire the physical courage he displayed, the reckless bravery he exhibited at times, his perseverance and his ambitions.

For a man of his stamp, Europe held few attractions, as, like many another scion of ancient aristocracy, he was as poor as the proverbial church mouse and, in order to attire himself in the silks and satins and the magnificent armor he affected, he was rapidly getting deeper and deeper in debt. Even his marriage to the Doña Marina Ortiz de Gaete did not help matters, and, fascinated by the tales of conquest and easily won riches that drifted back from the New World, Valdivia slipped away to America.

He arrived in Venezuela in 1535. But the tales he had heard regarding the riches of the country were not borne out, the country failed to appeal to him, there was no fighting to speak of to arouse his martial spirit and, hearing of the conquest of Peru and the incredible wealth of the Incas, he crossed the Isthmus of Darien and sailed for Lima.

The bloody civil strife between the Pizarros and Almagro was then at its height, and the dashing captain at once placed his services and his sword at the disposal of the marquis, Francisco Pizarro, who appointed Valdivia his Field Marshal. He acquitted himself with such valor and resource that, in reward for his services, Pizarro granted him a vast area of land, several thousand Indian slaves, an incredibly rich silver mine, and a large sum in money.

Thus, at a single blow, as it were, the impecunious Captain Pedro Valdivia had been transformed to the Field Marshal Pedro de Valdivia, one of the wealthiest of colonial Dons. But Valdivia's appetite for glory and fortune was insatiable.

He dreamed of becoming the wealthiest man in the New World, and his ambition was to become a viceroy, or at least a governor. He could scarcely hope for either such wealth or power in Peru, but there were plenty of new lands to be conquered, plenty of treasure to be had for the taking elsewhere, and there were tales of rich lands, of amazing countries and of wealthy Indians "somewhere to the south and west."

Poor old Almagro, whose decapitated body had been laid at rest in Lima, had already trekked into this mysterious unknown land and had returned little the wiser and much the poorer for his pains. But the fact that Almagro had accomplished little, that he had not considered Chile worth its conquest, did not influence Valdivia. He had become firmly convinced that his destiny, his fame and his fortune lay to the south, and he appealed to Pizarro for official authority to conquer Chile in the name of the King of Spain. In vain Pizarro endeavored to dissuade him, arguing that he should be satisfied with the riches and honors he already possessed, and pointing out that Almagro's expedition had been a total failure, in so far as any results were concerned. But finding Valdivia determined, he finally consented, presented him with the desired official authority, together with the title of Lieutenant Gover-

nor of Chile, the only condition being that the new
colony should be subject to the Viceroy of Peru for
all time.

Armed with the official sanction of the representative of the king, and in name, if not in fact, a governor, Valdivia set about preparing for his conquest.
But he soon found that his enterprise was far from
a simple or easy matter. His entire fortune proved
insufficient for securing the men and equipment he
needed. There were horses to be bought, vast quantities of supplies and merchandise to be secured, armor and weapons to be purchased, powder and ball,
horseshoes and trappings, blacksmiths' forges, fur-
niture and a thousand and one articles to be obtained. Enough food supplies to feed his expedition
for months had to be carried on the journey; live
sheep, oxen and goats, swine and fowl; barley and
wheat, maize and rice, fodder for the livestock, and
to transport this immense amount of cargo, hundreds
of llamas and still more hundreds of Indian slaves
were required.

Long before Valdivia had accumulated the barest
necessities for his proposed conquest, his funds were
exhausted and he was forced to borrow money at a
usurious rate of interest. Even then the largest sum
he could secure was a miserable nine thousand
pesos, not one-half the amount he required. It began
to look as if he would be forced to abandon his enterprise, a ruined, disgraced man, when a Spanish merchant, Francisco Martinez, came to his aid. Martinez was not actuated by a philanthropic motive by
any means. He was a keen and canny business man,

albeit a bit of a gambler, and in Valdivia's expedi‑
tion and conquest he saw possible profits. So he
proposed to supply the future governor of Chile
with whatever he required in the way of arms,
horses, negro slaves and other necessities, provided
Valdivia would sign a contract guaranteeing Mar‑
tinez one-half of all the profits derived from his
conquest, as well as fifty per cent of all future busi‑
ness conducted in the new territory, and exempting
Martinez from taking a personal hand in the enter‑
prise.

They were hard terms, but Valdivia could do no
better and signed the contract. But even now that
he possessed all the equipment for conquering Chile
he was not much better off, for he had no army to
equip. Few men could be found who had any desire
to try their fortunes or misfortunes in the desert
lands to the south. They had heard the tales related
by those who had accompanied Almagro, and these
were neither alluring nor encouraging.

The best of the Spaniards had settled down in
Peru and Bolivia and were living comfortably and
piling up fortunes. The more adventurous and dar‑
ing had drifted to other lands and conquests, and
only the riffraff, the ignorant, thieving, out-at-elbows
common soldiery could be induced to join Valdivia's
expedition. Even these were scarce in and about
Cuzco, and realizing that his livestock and his slaves
were merely eating their heads off and running up
expenses while he remained in the capital, Valdivia
decided to trust to picking up fellow adventurers *en
route.*

So in January, 1540, with his slaves and horses, his llamas and flocks and herds and with his embryonic army, consisting of a secretary, a field marshal, a notary, several priests and seven soldiers he set out from Cuzco and headed for Tarapaca. At Tarapaca he was to be joined by twenty men enlisted by Alvar Gomez. Gomez, however, had died, the men were not forthcoming, and Valdivia's enterprise suffered a severe blow. At Tarija (Bolivia), however, he secured thirty-six men under Rodrigo de Araya, and a few more under Bartolome Flores. But even Valdivia realized the futility of attempting the conquest of Chile with such an inadequate force.

The addition of seventy men under the captains Juan Bohon and Francisco de Villagran, and one hundred and ten volunteers, helped matters greatly and, having joined Captain Francisco de Aguirre with twenty-five men at San Pedro de Atacama, Valdivia and his little army started into the desert.

In the meantime, other troubles had been brewing. The King of Spain had issued a Royal Warrant to Pedro Sancho de la Hoz, authorizing him to explore and conquer "lands to the south of Peru" by way of sea. De la Hoz, who had been one of the leading figures in the conquest of Peru, had retired to Spain with an enormous fortune in loot stolen from the Incas, but, in a few years, he had completely dissipated this in luxurious living and reckless expenditure, and again turned his eyes towards the New World to recoup his fortunes. Naturally Pizarro could not ignore the king's authority exhibited by De la Hoz, and neither could he countermand his own authorization granted to Valdivia. Both men, moreover, were old friends and fellow soldiers of the marquis, and he suggested that De la Hoz and Valdivia, together with Martinez, should form a triumvirate and share in the conquest and riches of the new lands to the south, imposing upon De la Hoz the condition that he would supply two vessels and should arrive upon the coast of Chile within four months, carrying with him fifty horses, two hundred sheep and a number of other supplies for Valdivia.

This he agreed to, but being wholly without funds he found himself in a pretty fix. In his extremity he borrowed from merchants, representing himself as the real "Conqueror of Chile," with the result that when the facts became known he was prosecuted for fraud and was cast into prison.

By the time he was released it was too late to follow his original plans—even had he had the wherewithal to do so, and he hatched out the scheme of following Valdivia, assassinating the latter, and placing himself in command of the expedition. To aid him in this nefarious enterprise he enlisted the services of the hidalgo, Antonio de Ulloa, and three obscure thugs, and the five set out on Valdivia's trail. Knowing nothing of this, but having heard that De la Hoz had not fulfilled his obligations, Valdivia wrote to Pizarro from Atacama, stating that he considered all agreements with De la Hoz null and void, though why, in view of his later actions and his character, he took the time or trouble to bother about such a trifling formality, is a mystery.

To-day the overland journey from Cuzco in Peru

to Santiago in Chile, via the Atacama desert, is one that few living men would care to undertake, even with every modern and up-to-date facility and convenience. Think then what it meant in 1540. Imagine if you can the hardships, the privations and dangers of such a trip as Valdivia undertook. Try to visualize his "army" of barely two hundred and fifty men, accompanied by slaves and cattle, setting off across that trackless waste of sand, with the objective point an indefinite semimythical spot "somewhere to the south and west"; knowing nothing of what lay before them, entering a hostile land, cutting themselves off from all contact, all communication with the rest of the world for months, perhaps years, to come. Clad in garments adapted to the penetrating cold of the high Andean regions, wearing cumbersome armor, carrying all supplies, equipment, even water, upon the backs, shoulders and heads of Indian slaves, Valdivia and his little company left the known trails of the Bolivian mountains behind and plunged into the desert. Columbus, setting sail from Spain in search of a theoretical land beyond the seas, did nothing more courageous and heroic. Indeed, in many respects his venture was less perilous, and it certainly promised less of suffering and hardship. Like Columbus, too, Valdivia was setting out to cross a sea—albeit a sea of sand—in search of a new land, the only knowledge of which had come from Indians and from the little that Almagro had learned on his ill-starred expedition over a totally different route.

It was an undertaking calling for the utmost en-

durance, the stoutest hearts, the strongest bodies
and limbs, and on which privations, sufferings, hardships, hunger and thirst, sickness and attacks by hostile Indians were inevitable.

And yet, along with that cavalcade of adventurers,
went a woman! A strange paradoxical, truly wonderful woman, the Doña Inez Suarez, the daughter
of a proud aristocratic family of Old Spain, and the
mistress of Valdivia.

Doña Inez had about as many faults for a woman
as Don Pedro had for a man Aside from all ques-
tions of morality—which after all varies in different
lands and at different times and is often a question
of self-determination or conscience—Doña Inez was
as cruel, as heartless, and as brave, as her lover.
Neither can any one deny that her love must have
been one of the greatest passions in history, for all-
powerful and all-consuming indeed must be the love
of a woman for a man when that love will cause her
to endure the sufferings and privations and the dangers that Doña Inez met and endured without whim-
per, complaint or regret. Indeed, of all that
company of stout men-at-arms and tough old campaigners, Doña Inez was ever the most cheerful, the
most optimistic member, and by her words and acts
and her example, she encouraged her lagging, haggard comrades.

At heart she was a true woman. There was nothing uncouth, rough nor even masculine in her appearance or her character. Instead, she was essen-
tially feminine—a slight, beautiful creature with
delicate features, and who, if need arose, could be

as tender and pitying, as sympathetic as an angel. All the rough soldiers of the little army fairly worshiped her, as well they might. Through sickness and injuries she nursed them back to health; she dressed their wounds, and she made their broth and prepared their delicacies with her own hands when they were lying helpless and weak. With equal charity and kindliness she ministered to hidalgo or man-at-arms, to friar or servant, and even the padres, who frowned officially upon her liaison with Valdivia, were forced to admire and approve of her, ex-cathedra, even declaring later that, had it not been for her, no member of the expedition ever would have won to the journey's end.

On one occasion, her watchfulness, her ready tact and her bravery saved Valdivia's life (more's the pity!). This was when De la Hoz and his cutthroat companions caught up with Valdivia's party and, under cover of night, the would-be assassin crept to Don Pedro's tent, a bared dagger in his hand, prepared to murder Valdivia in his sleep. But Doña Inez was awake. She surprised the scoundrel, and facing him boldly, demanded what he wanted there, berated him roundly and, summoning the guards, handed the traitor over to them.

But on the following day, when Don Pedro pronounced the death sentence upon his former partner, Doña Inez begged for clemency, enlisted the priests in the scoundrel's behalf, and induced Valdivia to commute the sentence to two months in irons.

No doubt, before De la Hoz had endured the tortures of heavy manacles on that fearful march for

less than half the allotted period, he cursed Señorita
Suarez for her interference, and wished fervently
that he *had* been executed.

It must have made his sufferings even worse to
see his former accomplice, Ulloa, taken into Valdivia's service and given a responsible post. The
other three members of the murderous quintet had
been turned adrift, without food or water, to find
their way back to Peru as best they might or to perish in the desert—a punishment in some ways even
worse than that accorded to the ringleader.

As a matter of fact, De la Hoz was far more of a
nuisance than he was worth, and before the expiration of the sentence, Valdivia was heartily sick of
being hampered by his manacled compatriot. So,
when De la Hoz fell on his knees and vowed eternal
loyalty to Don Pedro, and offered to relinquish all
claims to any honors or riches to be found in Chile,
Valdivia magnanimously—so it seemed—agreed to
release him. Accordingly, a voluminous document
was drawn up by the scribes, was signed by both
parties to it, and was duly attested and witnessed
by the priests. In this it was stated that De la Hoz,
of his own free will, and without threat, compulsion
or duress, transferred all his rights and claims to
Valdivia. Of course, under the circumstances, no
such instrument was necessary. With De la Hoz a
red-handed felon and at the mercy of Don Pedro,
the latter had things all his own way. Moreover,
De la Hoz had already forfeited any claims he had
by violating his original agreement. But Valdivia
was nothing if not meticulous in matters of business,

and everything he did was done with all the legal requirements. Unfortunately for himself he appears to have judged others by his own standards. But De la Hoz cared not a jot for either a spoken or written promise and, as will be seen later, his one idea was to rid himself of the galling irons and to be a free man once more.

Doña Inez on another occasion won the day when, the water being exhausted and the expedition faced with death by thirst, she ordered the men to dig in a certain spot. To their amazement they found abundant water a few feet beneath the surface of the desert. Naturally this raised Señorita Suarez tremendously in the estimation of the superstitious Spaniards and still more superstitious Indian cargobearers, for to them the discovery of water just under the dry and burning sand was nothing less than a miracle.

To be sure, one padre, who seems to have been blessed with more intelligence than his fellows, remarked, when recording the event, that "no doubt the lady used her eyes to advantage and, noticing slight moisture or some small vegetable growth in the sand, chose wisely the spot wherein to dig that water might be found."

But as he very sensibly kept his conclusions to himself, and as such a simple explanation apparently did not occur to any one else, Doña Inez was thereafter regarded with reverence akin to worship.

But if she could be kind to her own comrades and could weep with pity for their sufferings, still she could be a fiend incarnate when occasion arose, and could gloat over the agonies of tortured, mutilated Indians with the callousness of Satan himself. And there was nothing weak nor feminine about her when it came to fighting. She could wield sword, dagger, ax, pike or arquebus as well as the next, and among her other soldierly attainments, Doña Inez could outswear any hardened old campaigner of the lot.

Of that terrible march across the desert into central Chile, one might write pages filled with horrors, sufferings and death. The poor Indians, chained or roped together, burdened with heavy boxes and bales, poorly fed, lashed, beaten, flogged and abused; with their flesh cut and galled by their bonds, covered with open sores and ulcers, wholly unaccustomed to the lowlands, the heavier atmosphere and the climate, sickened and died by scores. No pity, no consideration was shown them by their inhuman masters. If they stumbled or fell or fainted from sickness, exhaustion or injuries, they were beaten, kicked, tortured, seared with red-hot irons until they staggered on beneath their burdens. Only when death came to end their sufferings were they freed, and even then their bestial masters did not take the trouble to unloosen their bonds. When an Indian fell lifeless—or obviously too exhausted to proceed —his head was lopped off with sword or ax to release the rope or chain about his neck, and his corpse was left to the buzzards. And with each Indian who succumbed, a greater burden, greater hardships, fell to the lot of the survivors.

The Dons, too, had their share of suffering and privations. Many had dwelt for so long in the high altitudes of Peru and Bolivia that they tired rapidly on the desert. Others were weakened by dissipation and diseases and were in no condition to undergo any hardships, others contracted fevers and died. The trail of the expedition was marked by the corpses of men, by the carcasses of beasts of burden, and by the flocks of carrion-hawks and repulsive vultures that circled overhead with watchful, hungry eyes.

But in the end Valdivia and most of his fellow adventurers, together with Doña Inez, won out. They left the deserts behind at last and came to the Mapucho Valley with its green fields, its Indian farms, its broad silver river and its two pyramidal hills rising above the level plain. To the haggard, weary-eyed invaders the spot seemed a veritable Paradise, and here Don Pedro decided to establish his capital, the first Spanish city in Chile.

Fortunately for him and his followers, the Mapuche Indians, who dwelt where Santiago now stands, were ignorant of the Spaniards' ways and aims, and welcomed them with every hospitality. Even when Valdivia, in glittering mail, and Doña Inez in gorgeous velvets and silk, stood beneath the fluttering standard of Spain, surrounded by the bearded, armor-clad soldiers, and the leader pompously announced in flowery Castilian that he took possession of the Mapuches' lands in the name of God and his Most Catholic Majesty the King of Spain, and called upon the wondering and greatly impressed Indians to acknowledge allegiance—or in other words serfdom—and the cowled and shaven

friars chanted *Te Deums* and planted a crucifix
upon the plain, the poor Mapuches hadn't the least
idea what it was all about. Unable of course to understand a word of Spanish, the Indians did not
dream that the newcomers were robbing them of
lands and liberty, but rather, in all probability, they
deemed the show some sort of tribal ceremonial of
the strangers, something akin to their own dances.
And so, as they raised no protest and made no resistance, but maintained a reserved and dignified silence, Valdivia and his rascally crowd accepted
silence as consent, declared the Indians had acknowledged the sovereignty of Spain, and thereby paved
the way for any future murders or cruelties they
might see fit to inflict, without offending the Church,
the Law or their own elastic consciences.

Having thus "conquered" the country and secured the "allegiance" of its rightful owners without hostilities, Valdivia, at the head of his army,
rode, like the King of France in the nursery rhyme,
up the nearer of the two high hills, the better to have
a view of his new domain. Reaching the summit,
with Doña Inez by his side, the conqueror christened
the mount "Santa Lucia," and gazed with vast delight upon the valley spread at his feet.

It is evident that Don Pedro believed thoroughly
in preparedness, for, with admirable forethought, he
had brought along a competent engineer and architect. Moreover, procrastination was not one of Don
Pedro's faults. He believed in "doing it now," and
accordingly he at once ordered his engineer to draw

up plans for a city to be laid out upon the plain. Pointing with his sword, he indicated the principal features of his imaginary town—the central plaza, the main streets, the palace and cathedrals, the squares or blocks and other details.

Although the city grew according to the plans thus detailed by Valdivia from the summit of Santa Lucia, and from the hilltop presents much the same appearance to-day as Don Pedro saw it in his imagination, it did not rise upon the plain as rapidly nor as easily as the conqueror had so confidently expected. Hardly had work commenced when troubles with the Indians began to brew. As was always the case, whether the natives were friendly or hostile, the Dons regarded them as no better than brutes and as created solely for the benefit of the Spaniards. So, despite the fact that the Mapuches had treated Valdivia and his men in the most friendly fashion and had made no objection to their occupying the land and starting their town, Valdivia and his comrades forced them to labor like slaves, robbed them of whatever they possessed in the way of gold and supplies, helped themselves to their wives and daughters, and treated them abominably.

Even the most timid and peace-loving of aborigines would have smarted under the oppressions and cruelties of the invaders, and the Mapuches, instead of being a servile, timid race, were renowned for their independent spirit, their pride and their fighting abilities. No one could have blamed them if they had massacred every European in the valley. But with most commendable self-control they endured and suffered, until, unable to endure longer, they showed open resentment.

Thereupon Don Pedro had the chiefs or caçiques seized and tried for treason, claiming that they had given allegiance to the King of Spain, sentenced several to death, and held the others prisoners. By threats and tortures he attempted to force these captives into ordering their tribesmen to bring treasure for ransom. But the Mapuches were of different stuff from any of the Indians the Dons had hitherto met in South America. Pizarro and his followers had conquered the Incans of Peru without great difficulty; they had overcome the more redoubtable Aymarás of Bolivia; and the few tribes they had met in their wanderings about the coast, in the Andean foothills and on the Atacama desert, had proved timid, docile folk, who—even if they fired a few futile arrows at the invaders—took hastily to cover or fled precipitately when attacked by the mail-clad soldiers. Moreover, Valdivia and his men had been greatly misled by the attitude of the Mapuches when they had first reached the Mapuches' country.

Just as Cortes had underestimated the temper and the warlike characters of the Aztecs, owing to their friendly attitude when first the Spaniards entered the Mexican capital, so Valdivia vastly underestimated the character of the Mapuches because they had not shown open hostility at the first. Now, however, he was to discover that there are Indians *and* Indians, and that, in dealing with the Mapuches, he was dealing, not with subservient, peaceful Qui-

chuas who had been kept under the tyrannical rule
of the Incas until all sense of liberty and personal
independence had been lost, but with the most valiant, warlike, independent tribe in all South America.

Atahualpa had been frightened and threatened
into filling the coffers of Spain to overflowing with
gold, silver and precious stones in the vain hope
of securing his freedom, and many a lesser Incan had
been held a captive and forced to produce fortunes
in gems and precious metals as a price for liberty,
which usually meant death. Even Montezuma and
the other Mexican rulers had striven to ward off
their doom and the doom of their people by attempting to satisfy the Spaniards' insatiable lust for gold.
But the Mapuche caçiques laughed in the Dons'
faces, and their tribesmen, instead of bringing treasure to ransom their chiefs, brought bows and arrows, slings and spears, and fell upon the Spaniards
like fiends incarnate.

Indeed matters soon began to look as though Valdivia's dream city might remain forever a dream,
and as though Don Pedro, Doña Inez, and the little
army might leave their bones in the embryo town.
Desperately as they fought, the Spaniards seemed to
make no effect upon the hordes of thoroughly enraged Mapuches who swarmed about the little fort,
and, despite the inferiority of their savage weapons
and the carnage wrought by the firearms and crossbows of the Spaniards, took heavy toll of the invaders, seemingly utterly oblivious of their own
losses. Not a Spaniard but felt that it was merely
a question of time until they were wiped out, and they

devoted themselves to selling their lives as dearly as they might.

It was at this point, when the settlement seemed doomed to capture, and the Spaniards saw defeat and death staring them in the face, that Doña Inez—who had fought as savagely and as lustily as any soldier —made a suggestion to Don Pedro.

This was that some of the captive caçiques should be murdered and their heads displayed to the attacking Indians, with a threat to kill the remaining chiefs if the Mapuches did not withdraw. It was not by any means an original idea, for it had been employed by many another Don, notably by Cortes, Alvarado and Pizarro; but it appealed to Valdivia as an excellent plan which, even if it did no good, could do no harm. So, accompanied by his ladylove, he hurried to the prison where the seven caçiques were heavily ironed and confined in stocks. Whether it was because Don Pedro's microscopic streak of humanity and fair play asserted itself, or whether for some other reason history does not record, when it came to the point, he hesitated to slice off the head of the first helpless captive. But Doña Inez had no scruples. Sneering at her lover's squeamishness, she raised her heavy sword with both hands, and with a terrific blow, decapitated the caçique as neatly as any professional executioner could have done. Then, grasping the gruesome trophy by its long hair, she hurried with it to the parapet of the lttle fort.

Not to be outdone by a woman, Valdivia hastily cut off the head of another chief and hurried after the Doña. Presently the two gory heads were raised high, and word was shouted to the Mapuches that a similar fate awaited the remaining five caçiques if the fighting was continued.

But, once again, the Dons had misjudged their enemies. The sight of the caçiques' heads only made the Indians the more savage and determined, and with blood-curdling cries of defiance they redoubled the attack. Hastily Doña Inez and Don Pedro lopped the heads from the other captives and raised them above the fort. But even this made no impression, and while, eventually, the Indians temporarily drew off, still the embryo city was in ashes; crops, stores, equipment, everything of value, had been destroyed or seized by the Mapuches, and more than half the Spanish force had been killed.

Despite this, the invaders, with their customary egotism, considered themselves the victors and, with their characteristic if curious commingling of religion and superstition, firmly believed they had been favored by Divine intervention, though why they should have thought that the Almighty should have encouraged and countenanced their crimes and cruelties, is a mystery. With perfect seriousness they officially recorded that the patron saint of the settlement, Santiago, had appeared in person at the height of the battle and had taken command of the Dons' forces, his miraculous apparition having proved far more efficacious than the Spaniards' powder and ball.

But there was cold comfort in claiming a victory, even if, by a saintly presence, they *had* saved their lives and their fort, when all appeared to be doomed to perish by starvation in the near future. And as Santiago failed to come to their succor, and as no manna fell from the skies, matters began to look very black indeed.

In this dire emergency true heroes appeared in the persons of Captain Alonso de Monroy and private Pedro de Miranda, men whose leonine courage all must admire, but of whom the world knows nothing. These two men volunteered to attempt to slip through the lines of the Indians, cross the desert and bring aid to the besieged and stricken settlement. It was an almost hopeless undertaking, an undertaking almost unequaled in all the annals of the conquest for sheer bravery and in unselfish willingness to sacrifice their lives for the sake of their comrades. Not only would they be forced to penetrate the hordes of ever-watchful, alert Mapuches, but in addition they would have to cross the waterless, trackless desert, the wildest hills and mountains, that had proved almost too much for Valdivia's army with all its resources and equipment. Yet, no sooner had they offered to make the attempt, than four other soldiers stepped forward and volunteered to accompany them. It was such deeds as this that cause us almost to forget the cruelties and inhumanities of the Spanish conquerors. And it is such deeds as this that prove that, whatever else they may have been, the old Dons scarcely knew the meaning of the word fear.

CHAPTER XXVI

IN DESPERATE STRAITS

NEVER was there a more incongruously equipped cavalcade than that of Monroy and his five courageous comrades. Though they were setting forth to almost certain death, with the slender hope of saving the lives of their besieged and starving countrymen, though their clothes were in rags, their armor dented, rusty and battered, and their faces gaunt and drawn with hunger, yet the hilts of their swords and daggers were of gold, they rode upon saddles with golden stirrups and accouterments, and gold bits were in the mouths of the horses that actually were shod with gold. This lavish display of the precious metal was not, however, for ornamental purposes nor because Monroy and his fellows were inordinately wealthy, but was the result of two very different causes. The horses were shod with gold for the simple reason that it was the only metal the Spaniards possessed, and the golden accouterments and sword hilts were part of a clever plan of Valdivia. Since he and his followers had been in Chile they had been accumulating gold, partly stolen from the Indians, but largely washed— by the labors of Indian slaves—from the placers of the country. Realizing that no plea nor argument would carry so much weight with his fellow country-

men as the sight of gold, he relied more upon tales
of the new El Dorado than upon sympathy or humanity to bring help in his extremity. But he also
realized that, in a country like Peru, where gold was
so plentiful that even the commonest utensils were
made of it, the inconsiderable quantity of raw gold
that he could boast would attract little attention.

So, as a grand gesture and to prove to the Peruvians how little value was placed upon gold in Chile,
Don Pedro hit upon the plan of converting his store
of precious metal into saddle trimmings and sword
hilts, while the necessity of using gold for horseshoes
would—the necessity being unknown—add a finishing touch to the whole.

So, in rags and tatters, their sole provisions a few
pounds of parched corn, Monroy and his companions mounted on their gold-shod steeds, slipped out
of Santiago under cover of the night, accompanied
by the blessings, the prayers and the farewells of
their half-famished and wholly hopeless fellows.

Fortunately for them the Mapuches had temporarily withdrawn, and without molestation they
passed through the valley and headed for the distant Atacama desert. Several times they were beset by small parties of Indians, but without casual-
ties, until they entered the district of the caçique
Andequin. Here they were attacked by a large
force of the Indians, and though the latter were at
last repulsed, four of the Spaniards had been killed
and only Captain Monroy and private Miranda, both
badly wounded, survived.

Among the subjects of this caçique was a renegade

Spaniard, Francisco Gasco, who had deserted from Almagro's party several years previously. Learning that Monroy and Miranda still lived, this renegade led a small party of Indians under cover of darkness to the spot where the two wounded Spaniards, utterly exhausted, were sleeping oblivious of danger, for, as a rule, the Indians never attacked at night.

Taking them prisoners, Gasco and his savage allies brought the two men and their one remaining horse in triumph before the caçique. Gasco, however, must have had a spark of decency remaining in his breast, for despite the nefarious part he had played, he begged the chief to spare the lives of the prisoners, and, in this plea he was seconded by an Indian woman whose heart, apparently, had been moved by pity for their miserable state. For a time the caçique hesitated, and the lives of Monroy and Miranda were hanging by a thread, when the former noticed a flute that had been looted from some Spaniard killed in a former foray. Seizing the instrument, he commenced to play upon it. Never was the truth of the old adage that "music hath charms to soothe the savage breast" more amply proved. Fascinated by the music, the Indians ceased clamoring for the blood of the two captives, and treated them with every kindness and consideration.

For three months the two dwelt in Andequin's village as court musicians, so to speak, and rapidly recovered from their wounds and regained their health and strength. But always they were haunted by thoughts of their starving, harassed comrades in

Santiago who depended upon them for succor, and day and night they were planning some means of escape and of continuing on their mission.

At last the opportunity arrived. The Indians were holding a feast and dance, and, waiting until the savages were befuddled with drink, Monroy crept up behind the renegade, Gasco, gagged and bound him, and seizing the renegade's dagger, killed the caçique with a single blow. Then, springing onto the horse behind Miranda, who had secured the beast, and dragging Gasco at the end of a tether behind them, the two spurred their mount through the mob of surprised and half-drunken Indians. A few arrows were discharged at the fugitives, but, poorly aimed by the tipsy and excited savages, they did no damage other than to slightly wound the renegade, with the result that he increased his efforts to keep pace with the overloaded horse.

In a short time the shouting, disorganized Indians were left far behind, and the fugitives slowed down to an easier gait. Though they had made good their escape and had their prisoner to guide them through the country where they were totally lost, yet their position was literally that of being out of the frying pan into the fire.

Their only weapon was the dagger used to such good effect upon the caçique, their armor had been left behind at the Indian village, and they were without food or provisions in a hostile wild land. Fortune, however, favored them. A short time after escaping, they met an Indian driving a llama laden with sacks of corn. The poor fellow immediately took to his heels upon the approach of the Spaniards, leaving his beast and its burden behind. Slaughtering the llama, the three dined royally and, transferring the maize and the remaining meat upon their horse, they proceeded on their way.

To relate all their adventures thereafter would be tedious and would occupy many pages. All the dangers, the privations and the sufferings endured by Valdivia and his companions on their march were as nothing in comparison to those the three men faced. But eventually, more dead than alive, they reached the village of San Pedro de Atacama on the Peruvian frontier. From that time, De Gasco vanishes from the picture. Whether he was permitted to escape and eventually rejoined his Indian friends, whether he was pardoned on account of the services—forced though they were—that he had rendered Monroy and Miranda, or whether he was summarily disposed of are matters of conjecture, for no historian mentions his ultimate fate.

As for Monroy and Miranda, when at last they had won through, it appeared as if all their sufferings and self-sacrifices had been in vain. Pizarro had been assassinated by Almagro's son in revenge for his father's death. The assassin had declared himself ruler of Peru, and the country was in the throes of revolution between the factions of Almagro and Vaca de Castro. At the time of their arrival, Almagro's forces were in control, and being an enemy of Valdivia, neither he nor his followers would lend an ear to the pleas of Monroy. Discouraged and weary they turned as a last resort towards Porco where Valdivia had friends, and after a terrible trip across the snow-clad Andes, they reached the out-of-the-way mining town. Here they met with better success, and two of Valdivia's friends, a Portuguese priest, Francisco Yañez, and a Don Cristobal Martin de Escobar, raised nearly fifty thousand dollars each which they agreed to turn over to Valdivia's emissaries for the purpose of securing food, equipment and a vessel to be sent to Don Pedro's relief. It is gratifying to know that, later, these two true friends of Valdivia were recompensed by being made respectively the curate of Santiago and the mayor of that city.

While at Porco, Monroy learned that the revolution had been ended with the battle of Chupas, and that Vaca de Castro was in power, and he at once applied to the new ruler for aid. The condition of Peru was such, however, that De Castro could spare neither funds nor men, and declared he would rather see the conquest of Chile abandoned than to strain his resources in encouraging it. Nevertheless, he consented to give Monroy authority to enlist men and to secure boats and equipment. This was easier said than done, however. Chile had won a bad name and few men could be found who were willing to trust their fortunes in the new land. But at the end of six months he and De Escobar had succeeded in gathering some seventy men, and it was agreed that while De Escobar sailed southward in a small vessel, Monroy was to proceed overland.

At Arequipa, another of Valdivia's old friends, Martinez Vegaso, came to the aid of Monroy and

agreed to supply a vessel, the *Santiaguillo,* as well
as a cargo of supplies, arms, food and wine amounting to a value of more than sixty thousand dollars.
Truly Vegaso was a friend in need, and his generosity is the more remarkable inasmuch as he made
his contribution with no strings tied to it, but informed Monroy that Valdivia could repay him
"when he felt able" or "not at all," a unique agreement in an age when rapacity, usury and gain were
the chief factors governing all transactions. Moreover, there was every chance that neither ship, cargo
nor men would ever reach their destination. The
coast of Chile was unknown, there were no charts
of the local seas in existence and—as is still the case
—the Pacific was treacherous, and head winds and
rough weather were the rule rather than the exception. One scarcely knows which to admire the most
for their courage: the adventurous Monroy who led
his little column of men across the deserts and
through hostile Indian country or the intrepid
master of the *Santiaguillo,* Captain Diego Garcia de
Villalon, who, navigating his vessel by landmarks
on shore and literally feeling his way, sailed southward as far as the present Bay of Talcahuano before
he discovered his error, and, putting about, eventually dropped anchor at the present site of Valparaiso, two years after Monroy and his party had
left Santiago for Peru.

Meanwhile Captain Monroy was marching overland, and much to his surprise, found a great change
had come over the Indians whom he met. Everywhere they seemed peaceful. And when the

Spaniards reached the spot where Monroy and Miranda had been held prisoners and had bought their lives by playing on the flute, the Indians, to show their friendliness, presented him with the gold stirrups and horse trappings they had taken from his party two years before. No doubt the presence of such a considerable body of well-armed and mounted Spaniards had much to do with the Indians' change of heart, but whatever the reason, it made little difference to Monroy and his followers as long as they were not molested. In fact the only casualty that was suffered on the entire journey was the loss of good Cristobal de Escobar's nose, which was frostbitten while crossing the Andes. But the loss of his nose appears to have had no ill effects upon the old man, for he animated and encouraged the others and led the way through the most difficult places.

It is difficult to do adequate justice to the scenes that greeted Monroy and his company when at last they arrived at Santiago, for he and his comrades had long since been given up as dead and when, almost coincidentally with their arrival, word was brought that the *Santiaguillo* was anchored off the port, the Spaniards went almost mad with joy and thanksgiving.

But there was a fly in Valdivia's ointment. The grasping old merchant, Francisco Martinez, who, with Sancho de la Hoz and Ulloa, had formed a syndicate and a partnership with Valdivia and had advanced some nine thousand *pesos* towards the expenses of the conquest, arrived on the ship. Tears

came into Martinez' eyes when he learned of
De la Hoz's acts and the subsequent cancellation of
the contract with Valdivia, but worse was yet to
come. Don Pedro informed him that, instead of
repaying any of the sum he had advanced, he intended to collect a share of the actual expenditures
involved, which he calculated would amount to some
twenty-five thousand *pesos*. Seeing utter ruin staring him in the face, the usurious old merchant was
glad to sign a relinquishment of all claims in return
for a payment of five thousand *pesos*. To his dismay, however, Valdivia informed him that he could
not spare that amount in cash, and in lieu thereof,
gave him a grant of land together with a company
of Indian slaves. As there seemed nothing else to be
done, Martinez swallowed his disappointment, and,
making the best of a bad bargain, settled down and
devoted himself to cultivating his new domain, with
the result that he eventually became one of the
wealthiest and most respected citizens of Santiago.

Naturally Monroy, who had gone forth so bravely
to find succor for the besieged and starving handful
of men, was vastly amazed to find them not only
alive and well but apparently prospering when he
returned. But although the Spaniards had survived
and had vastly improved conditions, they had had
hard sledding of it. The Indians, to be sure, had
never resumed their first attack *en masse,* and although they had made many forays and had set upon
small bodies of the Dons from time to time, they had
been held in check and even forced to evacuate the
immediate vicinity of the settlement.

Had it not been for the Peruvian Indian slaves, not a member of the company would have survived more than a few months after Monroy's departure. These abused, beaten, maltreated slaves had—for some mysterious reason—remained loyal to their brutal masters throughout. They had never joined the Chilean members of their race against the Spaniards, but instead, had kept constant vigil against surprises by the enemy, had proved of invaluable service as scouts and, most important of all, had tilled the ground close to the fort and, from a few pounds of wheat and corn left from the burning of the city, had raised bountiful crops. To be sure, during that first season while waiting for their harvest, the daily ration of the Dons had been but fifty grains of maize each, eked out by wild roots and the flesh of their starving dogs.

Neither had Don Pedro had an easy time of it. At one time he had decided that it was hopeless to attempt to remain in Chile and had—at the cost of infinite labor—managed to construct a boat at Valparaiso in which he hoped to transport his countrymen back to Peru. But an attack of hostile Indians had resulted in the death of several Spaniards and the retreat of the others. The survivors cursed and raged impotently as they saw the Indians set fire to the vessel and watched their only hope of salvation go up in flames.

De la Hoz also had had a part in the misfortunes of the little colony. His intriguing, warped mind had hatched a plot even in the midst of the privations, and together with a few chosen friends he had planned to kill Valdivia and set himself up as governor. Fortunately for Don Pedro, the plot was discovered in time and De la Hoz, with his usual success, managed to plead so eloquently for his life, and so earnestly disclaimed any part in the plot, that Valdivia pardoned him. One would suppose that, after his former experiences with this rascal, Valdivia would have had him put to death then and there. But Don Pedro realized that he could ill spare even one able-bodied man, and De la Hoz, regardless of his shortcomings, had more than once proved himself a valiant soldier when it came to fighting.

Once the colonists had escaped starvation and had succeeded in raising crops they had no further worries on that score, and, as they gained strength and confidence, they made numerous assaults on the Indians until the entire valley was fairly safe.

Hence, when Monroy arrived, the embryonic town had been not only rebuilt but enlarged, the people were well fed, and though half naked for want of clothes, they were relatively wealthy, for the placers of Malga-Malga had yielded abundantly of their precious gold, washed from the sand by the captive Indian slaves.

Nevertheless, the additional men with their horses and the rich cargo of necessities and even luxuries were most grateful, and the people lost no time in changing their half-savage mode of dress and life for an existence of comparative comfort and luxury. Almost any man, in Valdivia's place, would have lavished every honor and reward within his power upon Monroy. But not so Valdivia. When the devoted captain asked him to ratify the title of Lieutenant Governor of Chile, bestowed upon him by Vaca de Castro, Don Pedro arrogantly refused, and the only recompense that Monroy received was a grant of land that cost Valdivia nothing.

The conqueror, now that he had received reënforcements and supplies, once more resumed his interrupted plans to possess himself of all of Chile, and during the months succeeding, he pushed Spanish dominion to considerable distances north and south, among other things founding the city of La Serena near the present site of Coquimbo.

Had Valdivia and the others confined themselves to cultivation of the Mapucho Valley and to peaceful occupations, Santiago no doubt would have grown rapidly and the settlement would have become prosperous and stable. But, as was always the case, gold was an irresistible lure to the Dons, and Valdivia devoted most of his time and the best of his men and resources to seeking new spots where gold might be obtained. And he was far from unsuccessful in his quest. Within three years he had accumulated more than three hundred thousand dollars' worth of gold and, deeming this too large a sum to be kept safely in such a remote spot as Santiago, and, moreover, wishing to secure additional armament and supplies, he decided to ship most of his fortune to Peru. That he should have selected Captain Monroy as one of the men to take charge of the bullion is not surprising, but that he should have selected such a man as the infamous Ulloa as another of the trio is nothing short of amazing. Not only that, but for greater safety he decided to have half the treasure carried overland by Monroy while the remaining half was to be taken by ship in charge of Ulloa, and for some mysterious reason he gave Ulloa a most complimentary letter recommending him to the Viceroy of Peru and other influential personages. Naturally, and as any one with an ounce of sense might have foreseen, that was the last that Don Pedro ever saw of Ulloa or his gold.

It was about this time, too, that Valdivia exhibited a streak of humanity, an infrequent occurrence with him. The Indians, forced to labor incessantly in the mines, half starved, beaten and maltreated, were rapidly dying off, and Valdivia foresaw a shortage of labor in the near future if such conditions continued. Hence he issued a proclamation prohibiting the working of Indian slaves on Sundays and Holy Days, under penalty of a fine of twenty *pesos* for each offense. Regardless of the sentiments that actuated Valdivia in promulgating this law, it proved most welcome to the poor slaves—but only temporarily. The avaricious Dons quickly realized that an Indian could wash out more than twenty *pesos* of gold in one day and that, by keeping their slaves at their tasks without respite, they could still pay their fines and make a good profit. It was not until the fine was raised to twenty *pesos* of gold that the law had any beneficial effect.

There is no question that Valdivia possessed great personal magnetism and a most plausible and convincing tongue, that he was a born leader, and an excellent soldier, that he could undergo tremendous hardships and face seemingly insurmountable obstacles with sublime optimism. He was also intensely patriotic. But while his people obeyed him, and depended upon him as their leader and their savior in time of need, still he never was a favorite. He was selfish, avaricious, overbearing, and at heart was a coward—although he managed to conceal this weakness under a cloak of bravado. But no one had dreamed that he was such a scoundrel as events were soon to prove.

CHAPTER XXVII

THE END OF VALDIVIA

DOUBTLESS this was a far from happy period for Valdivia, and it must be admitted that he faced a very difficult task. He was constantly meeting with reverses, he was well aware of conspiracies and plots directed against his life and his authority, he was far from popular, and no word had been received from those to whom he had entrusted all his wealth, together with his letters and reports to the viceroy and the king.

Had he known the actual state of affairs, he would have been far more troubled than he was. Peru was again in the throes of civil war and Gonzalo Pizarro was in control of the greater portion of the country. Poor Monroy had died of fever a few days after he had arrived at Callao, and the treasure he had carried had been appropriated by the enemies of Valdivia. Ulloa, on the other hand, was alive and active, and was making use of Valdivia's gold to secure men and equipment with which to start on an expedition against Valdivia, his object being to kill Don Pedro and install his old friend and fellow plotter, De la Hoz, as governor of Chile. Fortunately for Valdivia, however, Ulloa's schemes fell through, for Gonzalo Pizarro, who was well aware of his plans and was furthering them, was meeting with reverses and ordered Ulloa to forego his contemplated trip into Chile, and to place himself and his men in the service of the revolutionists. Of course Valdivia knew nothing of all this, and it was not until the return of the faithful Juan Pastene, the third member of the trio who had set out with Don Pedro's treasure, that the latter learned how matters stood.

Unquestionably it was very unwelcome news and a great shock to him, but that was no excuse for the nefarious scheme that he evolved and which showed beyond any question the utterly worthless character of the Conqueror of Chile. His plan was nothing less than to secure all his own gold and that of the colonists, load it aboard Pastene's ship, and by false pretexts and at the opportune moment sail away leaving his fellows to shift for themselves.

He planned matters very craftily and cleverly. He announced that the vessel would soon sail for Peru, and that any members of the colony who were old, infirm or for any reason wished to return to that country or to Spain, could secure passage. Also, he declared he would send a number of his men to aid the national forces in the civil war still continuing in Peru and, appealing to his fellows' patriotism, he vowed that as he was sending most of his own gold to aid the government it would be a worthy deed for his companions to loan the government a portion of their wealth also. In this manner he induced a number of the colonists to agree to sail, and never dreaming of his duplicity, they entrusted him with their gold to the value of more than seventy thousand gold *pesos,* or roughly about three hundred thousand dollars.

Then, with all their possessions aboard his ship, the crafty Don Pedro invited his hoodwinked comrades to attend a farewell banquet or *despedido* on the eve of the ship's departure. At the height of the festivities Valdivia slipped away, embarked in a small boat, and with a few trusted men, was rowed to the waiting ship. Very possibly he might have made good his escape without detection had it not been for his cruelty and inhumanity.

Aboard the vessel was Pedro de Gamboa, the architect and engineer who had served as superintendent of public works for Valdivia and who had aided him in planning the city of Santiago. In a recent battle with the Indians, poor old Gamboa had lost an eye, and he had been taken aboard ship to rest and to recover from his wound. Finding him there, Valdivia ordered him taken ashore and left to shift for himself. In vain, Gamboa fell on his knees and implored Don Pedro to permit him to remain aboard ship and to return to Spain. Valdivia was adamant, and, deaf to the pitiful pleas of his old friend and aid, he had Gamboa seized, tossed into the boat and taken ashore. By this time Valdivia had been missed, and as the boat carrying Gamboa reached the beach, and the wounded man shouted the news to his fellows, and the deceived men realized Valdivia's treachery, they cursed, raved, hurled vile epithets at Valdivia, and attempted to seize the boat. Beating them with their oars, striking them with their swords, the crew drove off the desperate,

deserted men whose entire earthly possessions—
even including their clothes and weapons—were
aboard ship, and pulled away.

Impotently, helplessly, the men on shore watched
the sails spread, the anchor weighed and the little
vessel bear out to sea carrying with it Valdivia and
their gold.

Many of Valdivia's friends and defenders would
have us believe that Don Pedro was actuated by a
sense of patriotic duty in thus decamping with the
property of the colonists. In fact, he so announced,
after he was safely out at sea, and declared to his
secretary, Juan de Cardenas, that he was "determined to secure the treasure so it could be used in
the service of the King and to aid Pedro de La
Gasca and to suppress the revolt of Gonzalo Pizarro," and that, after the conclusion of the war, he
would "repay every *peso* from his own funds."

But his high-sounding words were not in accord
with his actions, for had he really desired to aid the
national cause he could have done much more by
bringing his men along with their gold. Moreover,
as far as known, not a *peso* of the fortune he carried
away was ever expended for the use of the government.

Before his departure, Valdivia had delegated
Francisco de Villagran to be his successor as Governor of Chile, a man even more ruthless, cruel and
arrogant than Don Pedro himself. However, it was
no doubt quite necessary to rule with an iron hand,
and that Don Francisco could do to perfection, as
was soon proved when our old friend, De la Hoz,

again resumed his former habits of hatching out intrigues and conspiracies. But this time the fellow was not dealing with Don Pedro, as he discovered to his sorrow. His plot was discovered, and he and his fellow conspirator, Juan Romero, were promptly seized by order of Villagran. Without even the pretense of a trial he was sentenced to death; a gigantic negro slave decapitated him with a single blow of a heavy sword, and bearing the severed head on a pike, and dragging the body by the bloody neck, the negro paraded the streets of the little town. Romero was also executed, being hanged in the plaza, thus having the rather doubtful honor of being the first Spaniard hanged in Chile.

Throughout Villagran's tenure of office, he was beset by plots, intrigues and riots, and his harsh and swift reprisals seemed only to make matters worse. In fact, he was so much more tyrannical and oppressive than Valdivia had ever been that the colonists welcomed the latter with open arms when he at last returned to Chile after having taken an active part in the battles that resulted in the final victory for Pedro de la Gasca in Peru. In view of his services —although nothing was said of any gold not donated to the cause—the viceroy was willing to aid Don Pedro to the best of his ability. But reports of Valdivia's acts had reached his ears and, having little trust in the man, he employed several spies to watch him. As a result, Don Pedro was arrested and sent back to Lima. But he managed to clear himself, by telling a glib tale in which he claimed his old enemy Ulloa had libeled him, and the vice-

roy, no doubt realizing that he could make use of
Don Pedro's services at some future time, and that
he was no worse than the others, dismissed most
of the fifty-seven charges brought against him, but,
before releasing him, he imposed certain penalties.
Among these was the repayment of the seventy thousand gold *pesos* he had stolen from his fellows, a
pledge not to revenge himself upon those who had
brought the charges, the promise not to show favor-
itism in the allotment of lands or slaves, and finally
that Valdivia was to terminate his liaison with Inez
Suarez.

As the viceroy had set no hard and fast date for
the consummation of these promises on the part of
Valdivia, Don Pedro took his time in complying with
them. When or how the stolen gold was refunded is
rather doubtful, but it was not until five years later
that he parted with Doña Inez, and then for the very
excellent reason that she most properly and reli-
giously married Don Rodrigo de Quiroga, an octoge-
narian hidalgo of wealth and station. Apparently
Don Pedro was not greatly disturbed by the loss of
this woman who had repeatedly saved his life, and
had combined the services of Red Cross nurse, sur-
geon, cook, soldier, secret-service agent, advisor and
sweetheart, all in one, for he soon found a successor
to Doña Inez in the person of her niece, Juana
Jimenez, who eventually followed her aunt's example
and left Valdivia to marry Don Gabriel Cifuentes.

But to return to Don Pedro after he had been
absolved by La Gasca, who, crafty as Valdivia, had
unloaded upon Don Pedro some two hundred vaga-

bonds and deserters from the army. To quote his own words he was "glad indeed to clean Peru of such bad weeds, for as long as they remained there was no assurance that silver from the mines would ever reach Lima." "But," he added to his confidant, "what is too bad for Peru is good enough for Chile."

After a two-months' voyage in a leaky ship, and with little to eat but "an abundance of water" as Valdivia remarked in a letter to the viceroy, Don Pedro and his two hundred scalawags arrived in Valparaiso, bringing with them the sad news that La Serena had been burned by the Indians, and that only two of its inhabitants had escaped alive.

One of Valdivia's first acts upon his arrival at Santiago was to display his almost incredible cruelty. La Serena had been attacked and burned by the savage Copiapo Indians, and to "teach them a lesson" and to "castigate them," as he declared, Valdivia dispatched Francisco de Aguirre and a force of troops with orders to capture all the Indians he could find and, after binding them, to place them, one hundred at a time, in straw huts and burn them alive. But even this incredible holocaust of defenseless and peaceful Indians who had had no part in the attack on La Serena was to be exceeded in cruelty by Valdivia's later treatment of the natives.

Although Santiago was well on its way towards becoming a real city, and although Valdivia had done much and was now firmly established as Governor of Chile, he still longed for more worlds to conquer. He had heard great tales of the wealth of the country to the south, and of the still unconquered Indians in that section, and he was keen on adding more lands, more slaves and more gold to his laurels. So impatient was he that, despite a badly injured foot, received through the fall of his horse during a review, preventing him from riding or walking, he determined to set out on his new conquest seated in a chair carried on the shoulders of Indian slaves.

Although the country traversed by this expedition held no such terrors and hardships as the deserts of the north, yet it called upon all the resources, courage and endurance of the Dons. At every step there were hostile Indians to be met. Wide rivers had to be crossed, and it required many weary months for the Spaniards to cover the distance that is traversed to-day in a few hours by railway. Here and there settlements were established, and, ultimately the city of Concepcion was founded on the shores of Talcahuano Bay at the spot where Penco now stands.

Hitherto the Mapuches had given way before the Spanish advance, and the Dons, perhaps amazed at their own victories and trying to explain the matter to their own satisfaction, again declared that miracles had occurred and that they had been aided by Heaven. Possibly, too, it eased their consciences to be able to convince themselves that they had the Lord on their side, and hence must have been in the right. But there seems to have been an unfortunate dearth of trained observers, for no two persons, who claimed to have witnessed the alleged miraculous happenings, agree as to details. At the battle of Concepcion in 1550, it was duly affirmed and re-

corded by some that the Virgin Mary appeared at
the head of the Spanish forces, and that the Indians,
realizing their enemies were protected by supernatural allies, retreated in dismay. But others just
as seriously declared and recorded a very different
miracle. According to their version, a volcano burst
into violent eruption; a torrent—carrying immense
trees on its flood—swept down upon the Indians;
enormous eagles circled overhead, weird monsters
appeared, and the clouds rolled apart to disclose a
vision of the Spaniards triumphantly driving the
Indians before them. Such a combination of terrify-
ing events might well have dismayed the stoutest and
most unimaginative of men, much less superstitious
savages, but it does seem as if Providence was rub-
bing it in and might have been satisfied with any
one of the astounding events.

However, the Dons, in this particular instance,
may not have been as imaginative as we might think.
In many respects this marvelous series of apparent
miracles is much more credible than bodily reincar-
nations of saints. The whole thing savors very
strongly of a volcanic eruption and its natural
accompaniments. The swollen river, frightened
condors seeking safety from the smoke and fumes
of the volcano, and mountain beasts—perhaps
jaguars and pumas—fleeing from destruction, would
account for all but the heavenly vision, and any excited, superstitiously religious Don would have seen,
in the rolling, turgid steam and smoke, rent by
lightning and illuminated by the glare of molten
lava, the forms of struggling men and the flames

and smoke of battle. Moreover, the Mapuches, fully realizing the perils of such a cataclysm, would naturally and sensibly have cleared out as fast as they could go, fearing the forces of Nature far more than the forces of the Dons, and utterly failing to recognize anything supernatural about it.

And the Spaniards were as much given to exaggerating their own deeds as the visions of their divine allies. Valdivia did not hesitate to report in his official letters that in a single battle his men killed fifteen hundred or two thousand Indians without the loss of a Spaniard, and it was a regular thing for him to put the losses of the enemy at from one to three thousand times that of the Spaniards. But when it came to atrocities, even Valdivia could not exaggerate. In fact, in all probability, he went to the other extreme, for his cruelties were not approved by the viceroy or the Crown, and were so inhuman that even his own men often protested.

In one battle the Spaniards secured some four hundred prisoners and, in order that their people might see the results of "rebellion" against the King of Spain, as Valdivia put it, he had the hands and noses lopped from the captives. One can scarcely conceive of the horrible effect of these handless, noseless, agonized Indians, as, helpless, covered with blood and maddened by pain, they reeled about, waving their bloody stumps, screaming maledictions at their inhuman torturers, and at length falling weak and dying from loss of blood.

But if Valdivia had thought to intimidate the Mapuches by such acts he was greatly mistaken in the character of these natives of southern Chile. Even the northern tribes, who had been more or less under Incan dominion and were comparatively docile, had proved to the Dons that they were brave, hard fighters and almost impossible to subdue. But the Mapuches of southern Chile had never been conquered by the Incas. They did not know the meaning of fear, they were ready to defend their lands and their liberty to the last drop of their blood, and they possessed military tactics and organization far superior to their neighbors farther north.

Despite all the Spaniards could do, despite miracles and cruelties, the Indians remained as undismayed, as unconquered and as implacably hostile as ever. But they were an intelligent lot, far more intelligent than any Indians Valdivia's men had hitherto met, and they realized that they were playing a losing game, that, at each victory of the Dons, they suffered great losses, and that the Spaniards were steadily advancing and establishing their settlements. If they were to resist the Dons successfully, if they were to retain their independence, their liberty and the lands of their forefathers, they must, they knew, adopt Spanish methods. They must be as well organized and drilled as their enemies, and must have a leader who was familiar with Spanish ways and plans, and who knew the weakness as well as the strength of the enemy. In short, what they needed and awaited and "made medicine" for, was a Mapuche Messiah. And presently, as though in answer to their primitive prayers, he appeared in the person of a young Indian named Lautaro.

Lautaro was, in fact, an escaped prisoner of the Dons and had been a combined interpreter and body-servant for Valdivia. He had learned Castilian, had intently observed all the Spaniards' ways, and had made excellent use of his time during his enforced stay among the Dons. He had discovered the weak points in their organization, he knew their plans and their methods, and he had learned everything of value regarding their powers and their resources.

And now he called upon his people to rise, to unite, and, under his leadership, to drive the hated white men from the land.

Better by far had it been for Valdivia if he had included Lautaro among the unfortunates whose hands and noses had been chopped off. Under the leadership of Lautaro the Mapuches were no longer driven off, decimated and defeated. In every battle they were triumphant. No miracles occurred to save the Spaniards when Lautaro led his warriors to battle, and terror and dread took the place of confidence and contempt in the hearts of the Dons.

Then came the opportunity Lautaro had been expecting, the trap into which he led Valdivia and his men. By thousands the Mapuches swept down upon the Spaniards, and though many fell, though their slings, their lances and their arrows were far inferior to the weapons of their enemies, they were victorious and the Dons were utterly annihilated. Of all the Spaniards only two men remained alive— Pedro de Valdivia and a friar, the Padre Pozo, both captives of the triumphant Indians.

In view of all he had done and the inhumanities he

had practiced on the Indians, Valdivia might reasonably have expected to be tortured with all the devilish ingenuity of which Indians are capable, and the Mapuches could have given lessons in the art of refined tortures to our own Apaches. In fact several Spanish historians—who no doubt felt that nothing less was reasonable to expect—recorded that Don Pedro was tortured for three days before he died, one of these historians even going so far as to describe how Valdivia's arms were cut off and, after being cooked, were devoured by the Mapuches while the tortured captive watched the cannibalistic feast. But as the Mapuches have never been accused of being cannibals, and as it was only natural for Valdivia's countrymen to paint the worst possible picture of the Indians' treatment of their prisoner, it is far more probable that the reports of the few Indian slaves who survived are the more reliable.

According to their stories, Lautaro's people proved far more humane victors than the Spaniards. To be sure, Valdivia was treated far from gently and was subjected to every abuse, insult and indignity. He was stripped of weapons, armor and every stitch of clothing—with the exception of his steel casque which the Indians for some reason could not remove—and, trussed up with rawhide thongs and beaten with rawhide whips, he was led naked, like a captive wild animal, before the Mapuche chief.

Valdivia the conqueror; Valdivia the Governor of Chile, had ever been haughty, swaggering, unflinching and apparently brave. But Valdivia the conquered: Valdivia humbled, naked, bound, beaten, surrounded by hordes of Indians whose friends and relatives he had oppressed, tortured and slain, was a very different man. Like a whipped cur he whimpered and cringed. Wild-eyed, shaking and trembling, with tears streaming down his cheeks, he begged piteously for his life. There was no honor, no satisfaction in torturing such a craven, and the caçique, realizing what a coward his captive was at heart, put a merciful if ignominious end to Don Pedro's career by having him clubbed over the head as though he had been an ox.

CHAPTER XXVIII

THE AFTERMATH OF THE CONQUEST

THE Conquest of Spanish America was practically completed. From northern Mexico to southern Chile the Spaniards ruled the land, held the Indians slaves, had established settlements, ports and towns, and garnered the golden fruits of their ruthless conquests. To be sure, there were yet vast tracts of territory still unexplored and unsettled by Europeans, there were millions of Indians still free, independent and unsubdued. But there were no more advanced civilizations to destroy, no more great cities to demolish, no more vast accumulations of treasure to steal, no more organized governments and trained armies to fight, no more empires to conquer. What territories remained were wild, jungle-covered, untamed—a wilderness rich beyond dreams in natural wealth and resources, but holding little promise of gold or gems all ready for the taking, and hence of no great interest to the conquerors. To penetrate these, to battle with roving Indian bands, to establish tiny settlements here and there was not, properly speaking, conquest, even though it required as much determination, as much bravery, as many sufferings and hardships as any conquest the Spaniards had undertaken.

The heroic men who battled savages and nature

and added these vast areas to Spain's dominions seldom found fame as conquerors. A few rose to
prominence, blazed in the firmament of glory for a
time, and fell to earth like shattered meteors; and
fewer still left names like Quesada, the hero of
Colombia's invasion, that have gone down in history
and will forever be famed in the annals of the New
World.

Magellan circumnavigated South America, discovered the straits that bear his name, entered the
Pacific, and, to his unbounded amazement, reached
the Indies where he met his fellow countrymen who
had sailed eastward. But though he discovered new
lands and seas, though his voyage was the most
remarkable feat of navigation since the days of Columbus, though he told tales of gigantic Patagonians,
weird monsters and beings that stretched the credulity of his credulous times, yet he found no gold nor
other riches worth mentioning.

Romantic, imaginative Sir Walter Raleigh also
had his fling. Fired by the tales of El Dorado, the
gilded king and his golden city of Manoa, the British
cavalier sailed overseas in search of the mythical city
and its monarch. He discovered the Guianas, explored the coasts, ascended the Orinoco—after attacking and defeating the Spaniards in Trinidad as
a side issue—but he failed to find either El Dorado or
Manoa. His imagination made up for what he lacked
in success, however. His stories of Amazons, of
claw-handed men, of Indians whose heads were in
their chests, of lands where every rock was filled with
gold and where nuggets the size of hens' eggs were

to be picked up on the shores, outdid anything that had been related of the New World. But the only gold he brought back to Merry England was fools' gold—worthless pyrites—and good Queen Bess, who was sadly deficient in a sense of humor and imagination or in sentiment for old times' sake, repaid Sir Walter for his troubles and his tales by having his head severed from his body.

We cannot class even Coronado, De Soto or Ponce de Leon as real conquerors. Coronado's expedition from Mexico, in search of the fabled Seven Cities of Cibola, was a marvelous feat, as romantic as Raleigh's quest and with as little foundation, and the story of Coronado's adventures, hardships, battles and discoveries reads like a fictional romance. But the only conquests he made on his long overland march, that led him and his men across our southwest and as far as Missouri—or perhaps farther, were the conquests of a few Indian tribes and some of the Pueblos. He made no real conquest of the territory, he did not establish settlements within it, and he left no lasting effects or influence upon the land or the natives.

The discoverer of the Mississippi was a stout-hearted old Don, a valiant soldier who served well under Pizarro, and who was far more notable for his humanity, his honor, his sympathy with the Indians and his disapproval of Pizarro's methods than for his explorations and discoveries, important as they were. Of all the Spaniards who had a part in the conquest, perhaps De Soto was the best. His bravery was equal to that of any of the conquerors;

he was neither treacherous, untrustworthy nor un-principled, and while he doubtless committed many an atrocity, yet he acted under the orders of his superiors and was not by nature cruel nor inhumane. In fact, he more than once came near to open hos-tilities with the Pizarros, as I have already men-tioned, and he was ever a warm friend and a cham-pion of the betrayed and murdered Atahualpa.

But by himself, De Soto was no conqueror, and neither was the seeker for the Fountain of Youth, though Ponce de Leon may be said to have con-quered Porto Rico if the settlement of that little island and the massacre of its peaceful natives may be dignified with the name of conquest. Like Raleigh and Coronado, De Leon was a romantic, imaginative soul—the living counterpart of a story-book hero, an ardent lover, a poet at heart, a knight-errant in character, who found life and love and the beauties of this world far too attractive to be left without regret, and who feared the effects of old age far more than he feared Indians' arrows or the heat of battle.

Also, we might mention Captain John Smith, who had the makings of a conqueror, but who arrived a bit too late on the American stage. Rover, adventurer, pirate, soldier-of-fortune, the "Ingles Smeet," as he was called by the Latins, had led a most romantic life long before he rose to fame in connection with Virginia and Pocahontas. In fact, these were no more than passing episodes in his ex-citing career. A fugitive from England, he turned soldier of fortune in Flanders, rose to prominence, rank and affluence, and decided to see the world. Shipwrecked, he was picked up by a passing vessel, was thrown overboard as a Jonah, joined a pirate crew, and, tiring of the sea, again took up the sword and buckler and joined in the wars of Christians against the infidels in the Orient. If we are to believe even one quarter of his own memoirs, he was the most valiant and important knight in the long campaign. His cleverness and ingenuity resulted in numerous victories, he outwitted and outgeneraled the Saracens and, when time hung heavy on his hands, he challenged the Turkish chiefs and Bashaws to meet him single-handed on the tilting field, with the opposing armies—and many fair ladies as well—for an audience.

He seems to have borne a charmed life, for, each time, he overthrew his opponent with his trusty lance, and springing from his steed, sliced off the head of his prostrate foe and tossed the grisly trophy to the furious Turks. But his luck turned at last. He was taken prisoner, was sold as a slave, escaped and wandered in disguise over a large portion of Arabia, Bulgaria and Russia. He was a keen observer, a fluent writer, and he left a vivid account of his observations and the habits of the wild, strange tribes he met on his wanderings.

Eventually reaching home in safety—as poor as he had started, but rich in experience—he turned his attentions to America. Although we always associate his name with the Virginian colony, yet the settlement of the Dominion State was but one of his American ventures. He had a hand in the settlement of the

Bermudas, and he was probably the most important figure in the settlement of the British West Indies. He was particularly interested in St. Kitts and Barbados, and his descriptions of the difficulties, the disappointments and the hardships which he and his fellows went through on the islands are both illuminating and fascinating. Especially was he interested in the hurricanes—the "monstrosse stormes" as he calls them, which annually and periodically destroyed the settlements as fast as they were established and which, in his day, were evidently of more frequent occurrence than at the present time.

The worthy captain was no conqueror, however. No doubt, had there been more nations left in the New World to conquer, Captain John would have been there, for adventure was the very breath of life to him and where it was to be found—whether on land or sea—he was always in the thick of it. Moreover, he was as good a sailor as he was a soldier, and he could wield the pen as well as the sword. Though we seldom hear of him as an author, yet he wrote a number of books, among the most noteworthy of which were his *True Travels, Adventures and Observations of Captain John Smith in Europe, Asia, Africa and America, from Anno Domini 1593 to 1629; His Accidents and Sea Fights in the Straits; His Service and Stratagems of War in Hungaria, Transylvania, Wallachia and Moldavia against the Turks and Tartars; His Descriptions of the Tartars, Their Strange Manners, Customs, Religions, Diets, Buildings, Wines, Wars, Feasts Ceremonies and Living; How He Slew the Bashaw and Escaped from the Turks and Tartars; Together with a General History of Virginia, the Summer Isles, New England and Their Proceedings Since 1624 to this present 1629,* and his *Sea Grammar for Young Seamen or Their Pathway to Experience.*

Surely any man who could produce such titles and works was entitled to being deemed a conqueror, even if only a conqueror of words. Yet it is a bit fascinating to speculate on the results had Captain John lived a few years earlier and had he taken a part in the conquest of Mexico or Peru; to picture what would have happened had the British, instead of the Spaniards, conquered the Aztecs and the Incas. But even though they had no hand in the conquest itself, they did in its aftermath, and, indirectly, they reaped as great and more lasting benefits from the conquests than did the conquerors themselves.

But that is another story, and the real tale of the conquerors ends with the death of Valdivia by the war club of a Mapuche Indian.

BIBLIOGRAPHY

ALVAREZ DE ABREU, A. J.—*Victima real legal* (Madrid, 1769).

Cartas de Indias, publicada por primera vez el ministerio de fomento (Madrid, 1877).

Cartas del Fray Alonzo Martinez, escrito por ordenes del Capitan Francisco Pizarro, Gobernador (Cuzco, n. d.).

Cartas de Mancio Sierra (Cuzco, 1589).

Cuentas Yncaicos, por el Ynca Domingo Checo, escrito por el Virrey Don Francisco de Toledo (Lima, 1572).

CASTILLO, Bernal Diaz del.—*The True History of the Conquest of New Spain,* translated by Alfred P. Maudsley.

CERVANTES DE SALAZAR, Francisco.—*Cronica de Nueva España escrita por Cronista del la Ciudad de Mexico* (Madrid, 1914).

CIECA DE LEON, Pedro.—*Parte primera de la cronica del Peru* (Seville, 1553).

CIECA, F. Lopez de Gomara.—*Historia de Peru y conquista de Yucatan* (Venice, 1560-99).

CORTES, HERNANDO.—*Historia de Nueva España* (Mexico, 1770).

Costumes of America (Paris, 1780).

DIAZ DEL CASTELLIO, B.—*Historia verdadera de la conquista de la Nueva España* (Madrid, 1632).

DIEGO LOPEZ DE COGOLLUDO.—*Historia de Yucatan* (Merida, 1867).

FANCOURT, Chas. St. John.—*The History of Yucatan from Its Discovery to the Close of the Seventeenth Century* (London, 1854).

FERNANDEZ DE NAVARETTE.—*Coleccion de los viages y descubrimientos que hicieron por mar los Españoles* (Madrid, 1829).

FREJES, Fr. Francisco.—*Historia breve de la conquista de los estados independentes del imperio Mexicano* (Guadelajara, 1878).

GARCILASSO DE LA VEGA.—*Histoire des Yncas, rois du Perou* (Amsterdam, 1737).

GORDON, Thomas F.—*The History of Ancient Mexico* (Philadelphia, 1832).

HAKLUYT, Richard.—*The Principal Navigations, Voyages, etc., of the English Nation* (London, 1927).

HELPS, Arthur.—*The Spanish Conquest in America* (London, 1855).

Historia de las Indias (Madrid, 1875-76).

Historia de la Familia Cortes (Publicado por Don Martin Cortes, Seville, 1657).

HODGE, F. W.—*The Six Cities of Cibola 1581-1680* (Santa Fe, 1926).

LAS CASAS, B. de.—*Relation des voyages et des decouvertes que Les Espagno les ont fait dans les Indes accidentales* (Amsterdam, 1698).

LAS CASAS, Fr. Bartolome.—*Collecion de trayados 1552-1553* (Buenos Aires, 1924).

LEDON, Luis Castillo.—*La fundacion de la Ciudad de Mexico, 1325-1925* (Mexico, 1925).

MAUDSLEY.—*The True History of New Spain* (Hakluyt Society, London, 1908).

OVIDEO Y VALDES, GONZALO, Fernandez de.—*L Historia General de las Indias* (Seville, 1535).

PEDRAHITA, Fern. L.—*Historia general de la conquista del Nuevo Reyno de Grenada* (Hamburg, 1688).

PRESCOTT, Wm. H.—*The Conquest of Peru.*
The Conquest of Mexico.

ROCHA, D. A.—*Carta al Excmo. Señor Don Baltasar de la Cueva* (Lima, 1675).

ROJAS, JUAN.—*Historia de Chile* (Santiago, 1889).

SAHAGUN, Fray Bern. de O.S.F.—*Historia general de las cosas de Nueva España* (Mexico, 1829).

SALAZAR Y OLARTE, J. de.—*Historia de la conquista de Mexico* (Cordoba, 1743).

SMITH, Capt. John.—*History of Adventures etc.* (London, 1754).

SOLIS, A. de.—*Istoria della conquista del Messico* (Venice, 1733).

SOTOMAYOR, Damaso.—*La conquista de Mexico efectuada por Hernan Cortes segun el codice jeroglifico Troano-Americano, Edicion especial* (Mexico, 1897).

SUSTO, Juan Antonio.—*Panama en el archivo general de Indias* (Panama, 1927).

ULLOA, A. de y Jorge Juan.—*Relaccion historica del viaje a la America Meridional* (Madrid, 1748).

Histoire des Yncas du Perou (Amsterdam, 1752).

(I)